W9-BPN-759

My
Life With
Elvis

Also by Clifford L. Linedecker
Psychic Spy
The Man Who Became a Woman

My Life With Elvis

BECKY YANCEY WITH CLIFF LINEDECKER

ST. MARTIN'S PRESS
NEW YORK

Library of Congress Cataloging in Publication Data

Yancey, Becky.
   My life with Elvis.

1. Presley, Elvis Aron.   2. Rock musicians—United States—Biography.
I. Linedecker, Cliff, joint author.   II. Title.
ML420.P96Y3   784'.092'4 [B]   77-10377

ISBN 0-312-55834-1

For All Elvis Fans

Contents

My Life With Elvis

Several individuals deserve credit for assistance during preparation of this book. The authors wish to thank:

Mrs. Lilly Kingsley, Null Adams and Harold and Harriet Mansfield for helping in the collection of photographs.

Kathy Morgan for typing.

Special thanks go to Jerry, Jerry, Jr., and Junko for their forbearance, understanding and support during the past year.

Introduction

Introduction

"Elvis Presley
1935—1977"

Elvis's epitaph might almost as appropriately read 1954-1977 because it was between those years that he earned a reputation as the most popular and famous entertainer the world has ever known.

In slightly more than two decades, as he was firmly establishing rock-and-roll as a radical and popular new musical form, Elvis became the bestselling recording artist of all time, eclipsing the number of records sold by Frank Sinatra and the Beatles combined. Prior to his death on August 16, 1977, at 42 years of age, he had 45 gold records, each of which had sold more than one million copies. No artist had ever sold one million copies of one record before Elvis, and he is credited by some within the industry with singlehandedly reviving a record business that was sagging dangerously in the days before stereo. He was named by *The Sunday Times* of London as one of the people who helped shape the century.

It was Elvis, the white boy who sang Black, who shook, rattled and rolled his way into headlines during the staid fifties, and staggered comfortable middle American parents with a shocking new musical style aimed at their children.

There were other pioneers of the disturbing union of Black and White Music called rock-and-roll, of course. Jerry Lee Lewis, Bill Haley and the Comets, Chuck Berry and others were also thumping and bumping and carrying the message to the kids of America that at last here was a music with fast uptempo numbers like "All Shook Up" and "Hound Dog" that they could shake to. And the new music was performed by artists near their own age.

But if Elvis wasn't the only early rocker, he was at the forefront. It was Elvis whose bloodpounding blend of White country music and rockabilly and Black soul and rhythm and blues was given most of the credit for the vigorous new musical genre. And it was Elvis and his erotic visual flair who made raw sex synonymous with rock music.

Some say that was not only the beginning of rock-and-roll, but that it was also the beginning of the so-called youth rebellion. After all didn't Elvis wear a greasy looking ponpadour that had a thick forelock of hair spilling over his forehead, and sideburns, when most other American boys his age were walking out of barbershops every two weeks with neatly trimmed butches and crew-cuts?

Even more disturbing were his blatantly sexual body

movements on stage. The sensually exciting gyrations of his pelvis, the quivering legs, the squirming and the caressing of the microphone as if it were some insurance man's daughter. This was not for parents of the fifties. But it was for their children. Especially their daughters.

The effect on female fans was electrifying. The effect on parents, clergymen, and self-appointed overseers of public morals was alarming. Elvis was condemned by clergy, music critics, and parents as an evil pied-piper of song intent on leading the young down a carnal path of forbidden pleasure.

High schools announced bans on Elvis haircuts and tight-fitting pants. Convicts wrote editorials in prison newspapers condemning Elvis and his music. A Christmas album he recorded was banned by some radio stations. Elvis was denounced for singing "White Christmas" with a rock beat. A judge in Cleveland linked Elvis and television, identifying them as twin evils while warning that the tube carried a steady fare of crime, violence and sex into the home. Elvis, with his suggestive gyrations, the judge warned, was a symbol of what was wrong with television. Elvis's hip wriggling was censored from the screens when he made a television appearance on The Ed Sullivan Show and was photographed only from the waist up.

Today after years of The Rolling Stones, Alice Cooper, Kiss, and David Bowe, Elvis the Pelvis's hip-swivelling seems about as carnal as Oreos and milk. But in the 1950's it was considered disturbingly erotic.

It also helped make Elvis exciting enough so that fans became fanatically devoted to him. Hundreds of thousands of Elvis fans have bought every record he made and every book, magazine, and newspaper which carried stories about him, with a fervor unmatched by fans of any other celebrity.

Elvis received marriage proposals—and other proposals—nearly every day in the mail. Unknown numbers of grandmothers, mothers and teenagers readily would have left their homes, husbands or boyfriends for Graceland immediately if Elvis had but snapped a finger. Psychiatrists theorized in print and amateur psychologists echoed in public and private that Elvis maintained his appeal as he and many of his fans moved into middle age because they had grown up together. Many of the fans saw him as a reflection of their own vanished youth and their adoration of him was an attempt to recapture their younger days.

From the beginning to the end of his career there were young men, and some not so young, who dressed like Elvis, wore their hair like Elvis, and did their best to mimic his voice and movements. If they were good enough, lucky enough, or ambitious enough, they did their imitations in nightclubs. No celebrity's fans were more devoted.

Imagine then, one of his fans being offered a job working inside Graceland for Elvis. That's what happened to Becky Yancey.

Becky was a pretty fourteen-year-old brunette from Memphis when she first met Elvis in 1954. It was at the beginning of his career and he was singing from the back of a flatbed truck at the opening of a shopping center. Seven years later she became his secretary.

During her nearly thirteen years at Graceland, from March 1962 to July 1974, Becky cemented a friendship and became a sometime confidante of Elvis. She would listen attentively during the times he would walk into the office to chat, informally perching with one leg dangling over the side of her desk. He might chat about his favorite actress, his latest hobby, or the meaning of life. Seldom about music. In the early years he would sometimes leaf through pictures from pretty female fans kept in Becky's desk.

Becky remembers when Priscilla came to Graceland from Germany to live and to complete high school. She was there when Elvis and Priscilla were married, and when their daughter Lisa was born. And she was there through the breakup of the marriage.

Becky became a personal friend of members of the so-called Memphis Mafia, Elvis's bodyguards and buddies who lived at or near the mansion with their wives and girlfriends. She came to know Elvis's father, Vernon; his wife, Dee; and after the breakup of their marriage, Vernon's live-in girlfriend, Sandy. She is a friend of Elvis's other relatives who live at Graceland and who worked for him.

If important information about Elvis's career is noticeably missing from the story it is not accidental. His career has been covered in dozens of other books and in magazine and newspaper articles. The story has been told many times of the young $35-a-week truck driver from Mississippi who became the biggest selling recording artist the world has ever known and a multimillionaire before he was 25.

Books have been written about the 33 movies Elvis has made, about his music and his revolutionary singing style, about the poverty of his early life and about his rise to stardom.

No one has ever written a book from the inside of the extended Presley family group at Graceland about the admirable personal qualities and the human imperfections of Elvis the man, and about the people he loved.

No one outside the family at Graceland and a handful of other intimates really knew Elvis Presley. Colonel Tom Parker, the brilliant manager who took a boy who was unable to read music, and built him into a culture hero for 25 percent of the action didn't often allow his world-famous charge to sit down and talk with the press.

While Elvis was doing for American females what Marilyn Monroe did for males, his manager was also helping him build his mystique as he built up his bank account.

Part of that mystique was achieved by always leaving Elvis's fans wanting a little bit more. There were probably fewer than a half-dozen press interviews with him from the time Parker began guiding his rise to superstardom to the time of Elvis's death. His family, girlfriends, employees and others close to him helped protect the mystery he built up while living a unique, secluded and ultimately unhappy existence behind his famous Music Gate at Graceland, his Memphis estate.

Although Becky first spoke to Elvis in 1954, it was not until 1960 and 1961, after his two-year tour with the U.S. Army, that she became a regular guest in his home. If Elvis remembered the 14-year-old he had kidded at a shopping center in suburban Memphis about her "Marilyn Monroe" sweater he never mentioned it. Becky was just entering her twenties when she became one of the crowd of handsome young people who gathered nightly at Elvis's stately antebellum mansion or for movie and amusement park parties.

Their easy friendship did not end when she became an employee. Elvis socialized with many of his employees, and in the Presley household the line between employee and personal friend was often vague. While maintaining her relationship with Elvis and those close to him, Becky was also making friends with many of his fans who telephoned or wrote from such varied locales as England, Belgium, Haiti, South Africa, Memphis and Indiana.

A few months before she left Elvis to devote full time to her family as mother and homemaker she began to develop a friendship with Lou Wright. Mrs. Wright was then an Indiana housewife from Boonville near the southern tip of the state, and was also a wellknown psychic who read for Charlie Hodge, one of Elvis's closest companions. Through Charlie she began reading for Elvis, and as their friendship developed, for Becky.

As a writer specializing in parapsychology and the unknown, I had worked closely with Mrs. Wright on many stories. Our mutual friendship with Mrs. Wright led to collaboration by Becky and me on a book about Elvis.

Elvis had always projected an image to me of a nice guy who somehow managed to retain some of the better human qualities despite the brutally destructive pressures of show business and superstardom. I admired him for his devotion to his parents and for his attitude and willingness to enter the Army when he was drafted, even though many people believed at the time that it would cause irreparable damage to his career. Not least of all, I respected him for his talent.

It wasn't until I had begun to research newspaper files, read magazine articles and books, speak with people who knew Elvis, and had made my first trip to Memphis to meet with Becky and her husband Jerry, however, that I realized what a uniquely phenomenal figure and complex individual that Memphis's most famous citizen was.

Trite as it sounds, I realized finally that Elvis Presley was truly a legend in his time. No entertainer alive or dead, not Frank Sinatra, nor Tom Jones, nor the late Rudolph Valentino nor Marilyn Monroe nor all the Beatles and Rolling Stones lumped together generated and maintained over a period of two decades the epic appeal of Elvis.

Elvis fans, I learned, were unquestionably the most numerous, fanatic and devoted in the world. That fact was dramatically illustrated when a national tabloid printed a story about Elvis which gave the erroneous impression that he was a Gemini with a May or June birthday. Elvis was born on January 8, 1935 in Tupelo, Mississippi, and thus was a Capricorn. This was pointed out in an angry torrent of letters-to-the-editor. Many were abusive. Some were threatening.

The message was clear. Elvis was a Capricorn and anyone who did not know his birthday or his astrological sign was about the same kind of American who wouldn't know that Independence Day was observed every year on the Fourth Of July.

I was awed with the unparallelled fan appeal generated by Elvis. And I was impressed with the man that Elvis was.

Becky and I have attempted here to capture some of the very special essence that was and always will be Elvis. I hope that after reading her story you can agree that we succeeded.

Clifford Linedecker

Chapter One

My Most Embarrassing Moment

*A*lmost everyone has their most embarrassing moment. Unfortunately, mine had to occur when I was with Elvis Presley, my super-hero since I was 14-years-old.

The clear pre-dawn Memphis sky fell in on me on an otherwise perfect summer night in 1961 at the Fairgrounds Amusement Park (now Liberty Land).

Elvis rented the park about once a week when he was home at Graceland. The management would close the park to the public about midnight, then reopen.

About a dozen of the nearly 50 rides were left operating, with a few of the concession stands and games that Elvis and his payroll buddies especially liked.

Elvis's entourage of boyhood chums and young men from his Army days who worked for him was dubbed "The Memphis Mafia" by wisecracking newspapermen, and they were always there. Some had girlfriends or wives with them.

But there were also others. The more devoted fans whom he or some of the guys recognized from the Music Gate; friends from Memphis; and friends of friends.

There were always some girls who came prettied up in heels and hose, hoping that Elvis would notice them. A girl fainted once and everyone got excited but Elvis and the boys. Girls often fainted to get his attention. He was used to it.

One or two of Elvis's full-time buddies stayed at the gate, and it was they who decided who could come in and who would be locked out.

In the early years it was easier for someone to work their way into the circle of young people who gathered around Elvis than it is today.

I had been accepted as one of the crowd for some time and went to the park with a girlfriend, whom I worked with at the Baptist Hospital in Memphis as an admission hostess.

Elvis wasn't at the Fairgrounds yet when my girlfriend and I arrived. But there was a crowd of other people already having a good time. Elvis usually arrived late.

My friend and I rode "The Whip," "The Tumblebug," and most of the other rides except "The Rocket." Cars on The Rocket spun rapidly on a tilted, circular platform base and the centrifugal force smashed riders against the back of the seats so hard that they could barely move.

It was too rough for me, but it was one of Elvis's favorite rides. The merry-go-round wasn't. It was never operating while Elvis was at the park. He liked the rides that you had to stagger away from with your insides churning and your heart in your mouth.

Anyone who climbed onto a ride that Elvis was on,

4

could usually expect to stay for awhile. Elvis controlled the rides, and he might stay on one that he particularly liked for an hour.

Sometimes he would take over the controls and operate The Rocket while others rode.

When he was at the Fairgrounds he was usually on The Rocket, The Pipin (the roller-coaster), or with the boys, roughnecking on the Dodgem cars.

Wearing soft leather driving gloves Elvis and the boys would keep the Dodgem cars going for hours, jolting each other back-and-forth as they smashed their hard-rubber-bumpered cars together. The Dodgems were off-limits to girls while he and the boys were driving. They were too rough.

He rode The Pipin almost as often as the Dodgems. Sometimes he would have it all to himself, and make as many as 20 circuits of the hump-backed, swivelled track before getting enough. Anyone else who happened to be riding just stayed there until Elvis was ready to stop.

Elvis also liked a concession called "Walking Charlie's," where he threw baseballs at dummies that moved. One night his buddy, Bobby "Red" West stuck his head in with the dummies. Elvis hit him in the eye with a baseball.

Elvis took chances that would have given his manager, Colonel Tom Parker, falling-down-fits.

More than once when the cars would hesitate at the top of the Pipin track, seconds before plunging almost straight down, Elvis would climb out of the front seat and scramble into one of the seats at the rear. Sometimes he would vault into another car.

At other times he stood up in the car or stopped it at

5

the top of the tallest hump and sat there looking over the relative handful of people in the spacious near-deserted park.

It was early in the morning and my friend and I were standing by a concession booth eating the last of some popcorn and candy as we watched Elvis ride the Pipin. We had just agreed that it was time to leave for home when Joe Esposito approached us.

Joe, a Chicago native, has variously worked as an accountant, road-manager, bodyguard and all-around aide for Elvis. He is the only one of Elvis's guys who isn't a native southerner. He was also the guy usually sent to deliver the message when Elvis wanted to be with a girl.

"Becky, if you're fixin' to leave, don't," Joe said. "Elvis wants you to ride with him." I looked up, startled. Then I glanced at the roller-coaster. Elvis was sitting inside the first car, waiting.

I had already ridden the Pipin a dozen times that night. But an invitation from Elvis was a command performance.

There probably weren't a half-dozen unmarried girls from 13 to 35 in Memphis, or all of the South for that matter, who would have said "no," because they had already ridden the Pipin.

Just about every girl was a fan of his, and I was like everyone else. Every girl I knew dreamed about marrying Elvis. I almost ran over Joe, getting to the roller-coaster.

The first time we went around the track I was in hog heaven. I was hardly aware of the unpleasant taste in my mouth and the uneasy feeling in my stomach the third time around.

I began to get uncomfortable as the car continued to

6

scream up-and-down the rickety wooden valleys of the roller-coaster. I was feeling slightly dizzy. The track ahead was melting into a hazy blur of lights, and there was a sharp, coarse acidic taste in my throat as we slowed, then began the labored climb to the top of the highest peak.

The car poised on the peak for only an instant before rapidly plunging for the bottom. Elvis tightened his arm around me. I opened my mouth to scream—and vomited all over him.

The car was jerking and hurtling up the next incline before we knew it. The air rushing past was plastering spray and vomit all over me, the inside of the car, and Elvis. Elvis was leaning away from me with a hand up between us.

"Becky," he asked, looking at me solicitously, "are you sick?"

I was. But I wasn't sick enough to go home, or to get off the roller-coaster. I wasn't about to leave until Elvis was ready to go.

He stopped the ride and we moved to another car. At that time I would have ridden to the moon in a garbage truck if Elvis would have looked at me and said, "Come on Becky, lets go to the moon."

We rode the Pipin another dozen times or so until Elvis was ready to move to the Dodgem cars with the guys.

Elvis sent someone to his car for a change-of-clothes. He always kept extra clothes with him because he wore his pants so tight they sometimes split.

I was cold and shivering when he returned so he put his clean jacket around my shoulders and told me to wait for him. My girlfriend had gone home.

I had seen Elvis ride the bumper cars before, so I knew that I would have plenty of time to clean up. One of the fans I knew was in the ladies' room, and because we had loaned grooming aides back-and-forth before, I asked to borrow her comb. She acted like she didn't hear me, and walked out.

The girls around Elvis and his friends were bitterly jealous and competitive. There was seldom loud quarrelling around Elvis, however. Everyone knew he wouldn't permit it, and the troublemakers wouldn't be welcome at the Fairgrounds or at Graceland next time.

Daylight was breaking over Memphis. The sky was lighting up in the east and red and white highlights were beginning to play over the flags, arches and peaked tops of the equipment in the amusement park by the time Elvis had enough of the bumper-cars for the night.

Joe drove Elvis and me to Graceland for breakfast.

A cook I knew as Christine from other trips to the mansion asked Elvis what we wanted to eat. A few minutes later, Elvis, Joe and his wife Joan, and a couple of the other guys and I were having a breakfast of ham and eggs, potatoes, hot rolls and coffee. A cook and a maid were on duty at Graceland around-the-clock.

I was tired and didn't say more than three or four words. But Elvis and the guys slept during the day and played at night, so they were wide awake. I just concentrated on my food and tried to keep from falling asleep as I listened to the guys talk and watched Elvis play with the butter.

He was showing the other guys a trick. He placed a piece of butter on the tip of his knife as he held the handle parallel to the table with a thumb and one finger. Then he bent the blade back into a bow, and suddenly let go. The butter flipped across the table, shooting past Joe and splattering against the wall.

8

The guys guffawed and screamed as the butter stuck on the wall a moment, then slowly oozed off, dropping onto the floor in a greasy puddle. There were five or six oily butter splotches on the wall and a slippery mess on the floor when Elvis tired of the trick.

After breakfast, Joe drove me home in a limousine. It was after 7 a.m., when I tiptoed into the house. I was married soon after my breakfast date and that was the last time Elvis took me out.

Later, when I was working for Elvis, I often arrived for work at 7:30 or 7:45 a.m., and saw Elvis and the boys just getting in. At other times Elvis and people were still sitting around having breakfast. Elvis was always a night person.

When Elvis dated a girl it wasn't like any other date. In the South at least, a girl expects a man to pick her up at her home when they are going on a date.

Elvis never did that. If he wanted to be with a girl, he told Joe or one of the guys to telephone her. Then he had someone pick her up. Or he would go with someone who was already at the mansion or at the Fairgrounds. Dozens of attractive girls were always available outside the Music Gate or in the mansion just waiting for Elvis to speak to them.

I first met Elvis in 1954 when my brother, Harold Hartley, and I talked our parents into taking us to the grand-opening of a new shopping center.

Elvis, Scott Moore and Bill Black were playing from the back of a flatbed truck behind Katz Drug Store. Elvis hadn't been singing professionally for long, and the first time I had heard him was a few weeks earlier when some girlfriends and I called Dewey Phillips. Dewey was a disc jockey on WHBQ, and I asked him to play, "That's All Right, Mama."

Elvis was already catching on with the teenagers in

Memphis, however. The shopping center was full of boys and girls when we got there. Elvis was wearing a pink shirt and tight black pants with a small patch on the bottom. His hair was combed back in the famous ducktail.

I was wearing a tight black skirt and pink sweater, and when I asked him for his autograph he said, "Sure. But who do I sign this for, Marilyn Monroe?"

Later I got a paper drinking cup, and Elvis autographed it for me. I threw it away because my brother kidded me so much about it. However, I became a devoted Elvis fan that day.

I saw him in person another time, when I was 16, and a girlfriend and I went to the Overton Park Shell in 1956 to a performance by Carl Perkins and several other musicians. Elvis was introduced but didn't perform.

My friend and I climbed over a railing, scrambled past a policeman and with a group of other fans ran after him as he started to walk backstage. I pushed in next to him for a moment, and the next day there was a picture in the Memphis *Commercial Appeal* of Elvis and me.

But it was five years after my first brief meeting with Elvis before I was invited to the mansion. That didn't occur until I met Alan Fortas, one of Elvis's guys for several years; and George Klein, a high school friend of Elvis and a disc jockey for WHBQ.

Alan, now a successful Memphis businessman, is a nephew of former U. S. Supreme Court Justice Abe Fortas, and joined Elvis as a bodyguard in 1958 while Elvis was filming *King Creole.*

He had the build for the job. He is a former scholarship football player at Vanderbilt University, and was one of Elvis's favorite teammates for the rough-and-tumble touch football games he and the Memphis Mafia played at Graceland and at the later homes in California.

He had barely joined the Memphis Mafia when Elvis was drafted. While Elvis was in the Army, Alan kept in shape by working on construction. He rejoined Elvis in 1960 and took over most of the planning and preparations for the trips by car between Memphis and California before they started flying.

All of Elvis's guys act as bodyguards when they are needed.

George was president of Elvis's class at Humes High School, and travelled with him during the 1950's before leaving to become one of the most popular disc jockeys in Memphis. Elvis reportedly paid for plastic surgery on George's nose, which was straightened to help his career.

Elvis's friendship didn't end when the guys leave to take other jobs, and George was always a regular visitor at Graceland, coming and going at will.

It was about February or March 1960 and Elvis had just returned from the Army when my brother, a friend of his and my girlfriend were riding past Graceland and saw a large crowd. We stopped and joined them.

The boys boosted my girlfriend and me up on the eight-foot-high stone fence so that we could see better. Alan Fortas saw me and walked over to talk. Then Elvis, who was standing by the gate signing autographs, came over and kidded me about my shorts, asking me if I was cold. I wasn't.

A few days later one of the guys with Elvis telephoned and asked me for a date. It would have meant an opportunity to see Elvis, but my mother said she didn't want me hanging around at Graceland.

It was a week later when a girlfriend and I were on

our way to a movie and decided instead to go to the Music Gate and try to get inside the mansion.

We asked Travis Smith, the gate guard and Elvis's uncle, to telephone the house and tell Alan that we were there. A few minutes later we were on our way up the sloping driveway. I didn't know it at the time, but after that I was to become a regular guest at the mansion and to come to know Elvis on a mutual first-name basis.

In those days it wasn't difficult to get inside the estate. If you knew someone who knew someone close to Elvis you could get in. Even if you just hung around the gate long enough so that some of Elvis's guys began to recognize you there was a good chance that at some time you would be invited inside. There was always a crowd inside the mansion at night when Elvis was home.

It was open house. People, many of them strangers to Elvis, wandered through the 16-room house, going anywhere they wanted to on the main floor and in the basement. People were always opening the refrigerator to get drinks and snacks. Only the upstairs was off-limits. Of course there were people who took advantage of him.

Elvis became suspicious of a young man who was a frequent guest, when he noticed that every time that individual was around something disappeared. One night Elvis told one of the guys to leave $10 on a table. Then they watched the suspect until he took the money. Elvis told him to keep the $10, but had one of the guys take him to the gate, and it was made clear that he could never come back.

Elvis eventually had to put stricter limitations on the people who were allowed into the mansion, because of similar experiences.

Fans who didn't really know anyone well, too often-thought they had to take a souvenir. They would have carried the house away if Elvis hadn't stopped it. Even some of the people that Elvis and the guys knew well took advantage of him.

George Klein began to call me at work after my first trip to the mansion and ask if I wanted to get together a group of admission hostesses from the hospital and come to Graceland. George would be at the mansion when we got there, and other people would be all over the place.

There were two dens in the basement, and one had a pool table with couches around it. The couches and chairs were always filled with people and it was almost impossible to find a place to sit down. I usually shot pool with Elvis's cousin, Billy Smith, because I had to stand anyway.

Elvis kept an organ in the room with the pool table, which he would play when just he and his closest friends were there.

People would talk and laugh until Elvis walked downstairs. As soon as he appeared everyone shut up. It was almost like turning off an electric light. There wouldn't be a sound until Elvis said something. Then people would talk softly or whisper, unless they were near Elvis. If they were close to him they just listened. Some people who were especially nervous put their cigarettes out. The pool players stopped shooting.

When Elvis was in the room no one laughed at anything unless he laughed. Then everyone laughed.

The tension in the room when he walked in made Elvis uncomfortable. Sometimes he would stay only a few minutes and leave. As Elvis's back disappeared outside the door everyone would start talking again. If he returned there would be immediate silence once more.

Elvis seldom danced at the parties. The few times he did, it would be a simple two-step or foxtrot. Everyone else stopped and watched when Elvis danced, so he couldn't be very relaxed. The other girls were always jealous of his partner.

Two girlfriends and I went to the Music Gate at about 11:30 one night hoping to see Elvis. We just got there when he and a couple of the guys whom we knew drove out in one of his Cadillacs. They saw us and stopped.

Elvis said something and one of the guys leaned out the window and yelled, "Hey Becky. You girls want to go to the movie?"

We did. I pushed in ahead of my friends and grabbed the seat next to Elvis.

They were going to the Avon Theatre in West Memphis. When Elvis wanted to see movies he usually rented the Avon, or the Memphian or Crosstown theatres in Memphis. He would show perhaps a half-dozen first-run films which he obtained from a film storage depot for the Malco Theatres in Memphis.

They were usually movies that were still five or six weeks away from public release in our area. He started the show at about midnight and watched the films until daylight or later.

Before his hitch in the Army, Elvis also rented the Rainbow roller skating rink in Memphis for private parties. He took it over about midnight, like the movies and the Fairgrounds, and he and the guys chose sides to play tag or battle each other until 3 or 4 o'clock in the morning. They put colored bandanas in their hip pockets to identify their teams.

Elvis rented the rink for eight consecutive nights just before he went in the Army in March 1958. The skating parties were primarily for his and the boys' rough-housing. He didn't let the big crowds in at the roller rink that he let in at the movies.

In the early 1960's as many as 200 people would watch movies with Elvis at one time. Strangers could walk in off the street. He became more selective eventually and only people he or one of the boys knew were permitted inside.

Anyone who attended Elvis's movie parties had to be satisfied to watch what he wanted to see. He didn't like off-color movies, and if he thought that a film was in bad taste, it was stopped. One of his favorites was *A Shot In The Dark,* with Peter Sellers and Elke Sommer.

He might look at a movie for ten minutes and decide that he didn't like it. If that happened he had one of the boys tell the projectionist to stop it and put on another one.

There were times when he was on a movie binge that he would go to the movies every night for weeks. Elvis had been crazy about movies since he got a job as an usher at a theatre shortly after his family moved to Memphis when he was a boy.

But trying to keep up with the vagaries of Elvis's mind could be frustrating for other movie fans.

After I was married, for example, one of the boys stopped in the office one day and said that Elvis was going to watch some good movies that night and my husband and I should plan to attend.

So we got a baby-sitter and had an early supper. Jerry called Graceland to check on which theatre they were going to use, and was told that Elvis had changed his mind. There were no movies that night.

The last three times we planned to go to the movie

parties we telephoned the boys at Graceland for confirmation at about 11 p.m. before driving to the theatre Elvis had designated.

About 100 people and the projectionist would be waiting . . . and waiting. Finally 12:30 or 1 a.m., one of the boys would telephone the mansion to ask when Elvis was arriving.

Each time they were told that Elvis had changed his mind and wasn't coming. Everyone was sent home and the doors of the theatre were locked.

But the night we went to the Avon, Elvis was in the mood for movies and it was daylight before we left.

Elvis always entered the theatre with his dates and the boys by the little door up front near the screen. As soon as he sat down, friends, relatives and employes scrambled for seats directly behind him. No one sat in front of Elvis.

If Elvis got up to go to the mens' room, eight or 10 other people would get up and follow him. He didn't do anything for himself.

The concession stand was always open when he rented the theatres, and when he wanted a snack he would merely snap his fingers at one of the guys, and say, "Hit it!" The guy would jump up and run for popcorn, soft drinks or candy.

I hadn't been to a movie with Elvis before, and I was nervous. I ate a couple of boxes of popcorn and drank a Coke, but I wasn't aware of anything that was showing on the screen. I couldn't remember the name of a single movie that was shown that night.

I kept my eyes on Elvis, and answered when he said something to me.

Although I said only a few words, one of my

16

girlfriends leaned over me and peppered Elvis with one question after another. Once she asked, "How does it feel to be with us, when you're used to dating all those movie stars?"

Elvis stared at her for a moment, then turned back to the screen and mumbled that he didn't date that many movie stars.

My little toe was starting to cramp and curl in. I was sure it was nerves. A pressure situation. It was miserable.

I was afraid to say anything to Elvis, but the pain finally got so bad that I excused myself and got up to go to the ladies room.

Another girl followed me inside. "Are you Elvis's girlfriend?," she asked.

"No," I said. "I just came in here to rest my toe."

I can remember hearing of only one time that Elvis watched one of his own movies, and he and the boys didn't let anyone else in that night. Not even other employees. He was critical of his acting, and disappointed in some of his roles.

At one time Elvis considered building his own theatre at Graceland, but eventually abandoned the idea because of the expense. It was one of the few projects that Elvis dropped because of high costs. But more about Elvis's spending in a later chapter.

He sometimes showed movies in one of the basement dens, however. He had soft drinks, potato chips and dip for snacks.

There was a jukebox in the patio upstairs, and during the early 1960's Elvis sometimes sang along with the records. He sang less frequently at home as time went on, and eventually stopped altogether when outsiders were around.

Early in 1962 I took my cousin and my brother with me to a party.

Several girls were talking about asking Elvis for a job as his secretary. The girls always talked about working for Elvis, and a couple had already asked for jobs but were turned down.

My brother and cousin had wandered into another room when Elvis walked into the den and sat down beside me to talk. I told him that I was uncomfortable because I was wearing heels and a party dress, and all the other girls were wearing slacks. "I think I'll go home and change," I said.

"Don't worry about it Becky. You look fine," he said. "But I know how you feel. I've been to parties where I was dressed different from other people too."

I looked down at my dress, then at Elvis. I was comforted—and suddenly bold.

"Elvis," I blurted out. "Do you need a maid?"

Elvis was startled by the sudden change in the direction of the conversation. And by the subject.

In the South there were few, if any, white maids. There never have been.

My question was half joking, half serious. But I knew that other girls had asked for jobs as his secretary and were turned down. This at least was a different approach.

"Well," Elvis finally replied, grinning. "I don't need a maid. But I might need a secretary."

He told me to come with him while he showed me around the mansion, and we would talk about it. As I followed him, Elvis talked. I listened. And looked.

Pictures of Elvis's mother and father were in his room

upstairs. There were no pictures of girls. A half-empty bottle of black hair dye was on a bathroom shelf. Everything was very neat.

He had a large fancy box full of jewelry; extra watches, bracelets and a handful of elaborate heavy rings with enormous stones which he said he wore only in Los Angeles and Las Vegas because they were too big and showy for Memphis. (They were small compared to some he bought in later years).

I was fascinated and thrilled with the personal tour, but I wanted to know more about becoming his secretary. I turned the conversation back to the job.

Elvis said he paid his secretaries $65-a-week (more than I was making at the hospital) and gave Christmas bonuses of $250. One year he gave employees $1,000 each, he said, and no one showed up for work the next day. Some didn't reappear for a week.

Elvis said he wanted the people who worked for him to be happy. In return he expected them to do their jobs well and not talk about him or his life at Graceland to outsiders.

"It always gets back to me," he said, "when people talk."

Elvis didn't promise me the job however, and when I left Graceland that night I didn't know for certain if I would go to work for him. He said he had to talk to his Daddy before he could be sure he needed a secretary.

I was sure that when he talked to Mr. Presley, I wouldn't get the job. Working for Elvis was something girls only dreamed about.

A week later Alan Fortas telephoned and told me to report for work Monday morning.

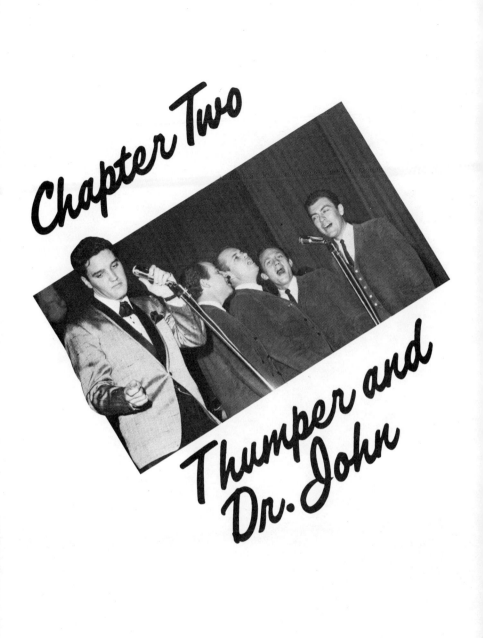

Chapter Two

Thumper and Dr. John

On the preceding
page: Elvis on stage
with a favorite back-
up group, the
Jordanaires

*T*he thirteen-and-one-half-acre estate and the wrought iron gates had never looked as imposing as they did the first morning I reported to work as Elvis's secretary.

I was nervous about the new job and afraid that Elvis's Uncle Travis might not recognize me and let me inside.

He did, of course. He just smiled, said "Good morning, young lady," and pointed up the driveway toward a small frame building.

Invisible from the gate, it was attached to a concrete block wellhouse about thirty-five feet east of the carport. The estate was supplied with water from its own well until the area was incorporated by Memphis a few years after I began working for Elvis and Graceland was provided with city water. The mansion was a few feet west of the building, hidden from the gate.

"That's where you'll be working." Uncle Travis smiled.

I had worried about the two secretaries already working for Elvis at Graceland. Perhaps, I fretted, they would resent me.

I needn't have worried. Maintaining communication with Elvis's hundreds of thousands of fans was a colossal job. The secretaries, Pat Boyd West and Bonya McGarrity, were pleased to have the extra help.

Pat married in 1961 to Bobby "Red" West, a song writer, movie stuntman, and one of Elvis' bodyguards. Red wrote, "If Every Day Could Be Like Christmas," one of Elvis's 1975 hits. "Holly Leaves And Christmas Trees," is another of Red's better known compositions. His songs have also been sung by Pat Boone, Ricky Nelson, and Johnny Rivers.

Bonya was married to a student at Memphis State University and had gotten her job through the Tennessee State Employment Agency. She left when her husband completed school and joined the Air Force not long after I began working for Elvis.

Pat West quit in 1963 to have a baby, and was replaced by Elvis's double-first cousin, Patsy Presley. Patsy Presley married Marvin "Gee Gee" Gambill, Jr., who took care of Elvis's wardrobe and chauffered for him.

Patsy's father, Vester Presley, is a brother of Elvis' father, Vernon, and a gate guard at Graceland. Her mother, Clettes Smith, is a younger sister of Elvis's mother. The Presleys and the Smiths were close, as poor people sharecropping on the red dirt farms and rich bottom lands of northeastern Mississippi could be. They neighbored, helped one another when there was sickness, and married into each other's families.

Patsy has the same slightly broad forehead and handsome Presley features as did Elvis. They played together as children in East Tupelo, Miss., and they wheezed together through asthma attacks.

Grandma Minnie Presley once told me that the asthma attacks got so bad, the parents of the two cousins took them outside, stood each of them against a tree, and then pounded nails into the trees a few inches above their heads.

According to local lore, when the children grew taller than the level of the nails in the trees, their asthma would be gone. Elvis and Patsy had no more asthma attacks after they outgrew the nails, Grandma Presley said.

During the childhood of youngsters who grew up in the rural South during the Depression years, as Elvis did, few of them learned much of expensive prescription drugs or fancy medicines doled out in doctors' offices.

They were more likely to come in contact with folk cures such as bloodwort, gathered in old pastures in late summer and made into a tea to break a fever or settle a troubled stomach; the bark of a chokecherry tree boiled into a tea for cough, colds, or measles; or asafetida, the evil-smelling resin of an Asiatic plant useful as a laxative or sedative and said to be effective for warding off colds and whooping cough when worn in a small bag around the neck.

But when I started to work for Elvis, Patsy West was handling all the bills for Graceland, and Bonya and I worked on the fan mail. We mailed form letters and autographed pictures to fans, and pasted clippings about Elvis in scrapbooks.

The girls I worked with were friendly, but the office and the furnishings were disappointing. There was nothing plush about them. Crammed into one little clapboard building were three metal desks, including mine, which was painted an ugly army green. The office was previously the servants' quarters, and some furniture, including the desk, went with the estate when Elvis bought Graceland in 1957 for $100,000.

There were file cabinets, cardboard boxes stuffed with books and papers, knick-knacks, and an old gas heater that turned white blouses charcoal gray in the winter. Later Mr. Presley moved his desk into the office, cramping it even more.

We always called Elvis's daddy "Mr. Presley." Later when Patsy came to work there, she called him "Uncle Vernon." We used first names for Priscilla and Mr. Presley's wife, Dee.

Elvis, of course, was always "Elvis" to everyone.

Mr. Presley and Dee were on vacation when I began work, so it was several weeks before I met either of them. Elvis was also gone, filming *Girls! Girls! Girls!* It was immediately after he had returned from the army, and he was churning out two or three movies a year.

Most had shallow plots, featuring fighting, dancing, womanizing, and of course ten or twelve songs sung by Elvis.

The era of Elvis formula films had begun. By the time *Kissin' Cousins* was produced by MGM in 1964, it was shot in only eighteen days. Critics said the films were abominable. The box office said they were good enough to justify paying Elvis a million dollars up front and half the profits for each film.

Although even his most devoted fans must concede that some of his weakest movies were turned out during that period, some of Elvis's biggest song hits came from the films—songs like, "Girls! Girls! Girls!" "Return to Sender," "King of the Whole Wide World," "Jailhouse Rock," and "Bossa Nova Baby."

26

But while Elvis was in Hollywood grinding out musicals, I was getting settled in my new job and meeting members of the extended Graceland family.

Grandma Presley lived in the main house with Elvis. Gene Smith, a cousin of Elvis's on his mother's side, and his wife lived in the garage apartment attached to the mansion.

Eventually the Smiths moved out and the apartment was kept up for the boys or anyone else who might stay over several days or weeks.

Several years after I was first employed, Elvis's Aunt Delta Mae Biggs, a sister of Mr. Presley's, moved into the mansion. She and her husband were driving in Alabama when he died of a heart attack. Elvis sent two of his sidekicks to Alabama to take care of arrangements and to bring his aunt back to Graceland.

Aunt Delta moved in and was put on the payroll as housekeeper and companion to her mother. She bought the groceries, paying cash. When Elvis was home the grocery bill was about five hundred dollars a week.

Aunt Delta always bought the groceries at the same store—until someone there turned Mr. Presley down one day when he tried to cash a personal check. Then they bought at other stores. Mr. Presley expected good service from anyone he dealt with. When an appliance dealer whom I had phoned told me that he couldn't get out to Graceland immediately, Mr. Presley instructed the staff never to deal with the store again.

I was to get to know all the relatives around Elvis very well, especially Mr. Presley, Aunt Delta, and Grandma Presley. But first, I had to learn the office routine.

Even though Elvis lived a few yards away in the main house, his personality dominated the office.

A pair of black-and-white shoes that Elvis wore at one

27

of his first performances was kept in the office for several years, until finally they were sent to the trophy room.

A huge photograph of Elvis, Colonel Parker, movie producer Hal Wallis, and the RCA dog was hanging on one of the walls. Elvis was signed to RCA Records. Initially he signed with Sun Records, but his contract was purchased by RCA-Victor in 1955.

For months a little toy phonograph on a block of wood sat by my desk. My husband came into the office one day, picked it up and fingered it idly. Then he noticed the inscription. It was a Grammy award. It too was eventually moved to the trophy room.

Many times awards would be dropped off at the office and left there for months, or years.

The work was easy enough, but I got into minor trouble with some of the sharper-eyed fans because I am left-handed.

Fan mail was answered with form letters made up to look like they had been individually written. They were actually run off on a mimeograph machine with "Dear ----." Bonya, Patsy Presley Gambill, or I would then fill in the recipient's name and sign Elvis's name.

Bonya and Patsy were better forgers than I was. My "Elvis" signatures never looked quite right, because Elvis is right-handed. Occasionally a fan would write back and want to know what was going on. Sometimes they would ask if Elvis had switched from right- to left-handedness.

Lunch hour at Graceland was pleasant. The secretaries could walk along the tree-lined paths or picnic among the flowers and shrubs of the carefully landscaped estate. More often, during the summer months, we would take our lunches to Elvis's commodious kidney-shaped swimming pool to eat and sunbathe or swim.

The pool was always available to Elvis's employees and their families. When my son, Jerry, Jr., was old enough, he would swim there occasionally with the children of other employees and of friends of Elvis.

Mornings we had coffee in the mansion. Aunt Delta made the best coffee I've ever tasted. Occasionally we would eat breakfast there with her and Grandma Presley. You could ask the cook for whatever you wanted.

Elvis seldom went to bed before six or eight in the morning and was rarely seen around the mansion again until about two o'clock or later. Occasionally he would get up early and sit in the living room in his pajamas and bathrobe drinking coffee and reading *The Commercial Appeal*.

Early one morning as I was going into the kitchen for coffee, I saw him in the living room and tried to slip by without bothering him. But he saw me, put his newspaper down, and told me to stop and talk.

Elvis did most of the talking because I was so nervous. I had already been working there about a year, but as long as I worked for him I got the shakes whenever he was around. He always noticed and tried to help me relax. Sometimes he would joke about it. But I was still a fan, and still nervous around Elvis. I always was.

My husband and I continued to socialize with Elvis and his friends after we were married. But we were reluctant just to get in the car and drive up to the mansion uninvited. I seldom went to his home at night unless it was for a special party.

Invitations weren't needed, and Elvis seldom extended

any. He and the guys adopted the attitude that if you were a friend—and most of his employees were friends or relatives—you should come to Graceland whenever you wanted to.

My husband and I met at one of Elvis' Fairground parties. Jerry already knew some of Elvis' side-kicks, including Alan Fortas; Lamar Fike, an almost three-hundred-pound hulk of a man who handled the lighting for Elvis's Las Vegas shows for a while; and Jimmy Kingsley, who worked for Elvis before becoming a Hollywood stunt man.

The guys used to complain that every secretary that came to work for Elvis, got married right away. I started working at Graceland in March and was married in September.

Elvis's buddies were right. But it wasn't so surprising that the girls got married so soon. The secretaries that Elvis hired were always in their early twenties—prime marriageable age.

A few months after I started working at Graceland, I was riding the Tumblebug at the Fairgrounds with one of the guys, when Elvis summoned him and told him not to fraternize with the secretaries. None of the guys rode with me after that.

Elvis wasn't always aware of what the people around him were doing. Running the office and dealing with the employees, except for the Memphis Mafia, was his daddy's job.

When he had returned to Memphis after filming *Girls! Girls! Girls!* Elvis looked over at me from a moderate distance at a Fairgrounds party and asked one of the guys who the girl was. "That's Becky. Your secretary," the guy said.

30

Elvis gave people just about anything they asked for, if they could get to him. But Mr. Presley was more cautious and demanding than Elvis.

Mr. Presley didn't think anything of telling one of the secretaries to clean his glasses. And he appeared to think even less, after walking through the pasture that runs between his house and Graceland, of telling one of us to clean the mud off his shoes. He had the secretaries washing windows and doing other cleaning in the office in addition to clerical work. His wife, Dee, was friendly to the secretaries and didn't give us jobs to do unless there was a problem at her home.

The secretaries were given one week's vacation with pay. I usually took an additional week without pay. For the first few years Elvis paid insurance for employees and their families. Then he agreed to a Blue Cross program, and employees had to pay for their families themselves. There was no retirement plan.

But there were ancillary benefits. For example, employees would be given time off from work to attend openings in Memphis of Elvis's movies. I was at Graceland only a few weeks before Bonya and I went to the opening of *Follow That Dream*.

We also got complimentary tickets when he first appeared at the Mid-South Coliseum in Memphis in 1974. By that time Pat West and Bonya McGarrity had left Graceland and Paulette Shafer Lewis was working as one of the secretaries. Paulette, who has since remarried, to Gene Williams, is the daughter of Paul Shafer, an executive with Malco Theatres, Inc. who obtained movies for Elvis's midnight theatre parties.

Paulette and I were in the office when Jerry telephoned and said he had heard on the radio that Elvis was going to give his first show in Memphis since becoming a superstar. That's the first we had heard about it. Paulette and I asked Mr. Presley if it was true, and he said it was news to him too. Colonel Parker handled all Elvis' professional commitments, and even Elvis' daddy had to telephone to the Colonel's office in Culver City, California, to confirm that the story of the Memphis show was true.

Mr. Presley eventually distributed about 20 tickets to relatives and employees, including Paulette and me. But when the news broke, we started getting telephone calls from all over the United States and Canada from people wanting tickets. Calls were even made to my home, some from people I hadn't heard from since I was in elementary school. I had forgotten some of the names, but they reminded me that they were old friends and asked for tickets.

Tickets, of course, were never handled from the mansion.

To fool his fans, Elvis stayed in a suite at the Rivermont Hotel between performances. Hundreds of fans gathered at the Music Gate. The driveway was full and some were standing on Elvis Presley Boulevard, which is also busy Highway 51 South. The fans waited all night and the next day for Elvis.

Off-duty Memphis policemen were called in to patrol Graceland and protect it and its occupants from the hysterical, determined fans. One officer said he'd never had more fun during his ten years on the police department, than he had the nights he spent patrolling the estate by golf cart. As we left work, one of the officers stationed himself on Elvis Presley Boulevard and stopped traffic for us. I felt like a celebrity.

Elvis's albums and singles records were routinely mailed to the office from the recording studios and promotion agencies, and the secretaries were given copies.

But most exciting of all was just being at Graceland in the center of all the activity.

We once spent two days going through boxes and boxes of Elvis's clothes, picking out items that could be cut up so that square-inch patches of material could be inserted in the jackets of one of his new RCA albums.

Before the clothing was cut up, Mr. Presley told the men who were helping us to pick out anything for themselves that they could use. Scarves, shirts, trousers, and socks, many of them articles mailed by fans as presents, were sliced up.

None of Elvis's famous jump suits have been destroyed. They have sold at charity auctions for thousands of dollars.

Paul Lichter, president of the Elvis Unique Record Club in suburban Philadelphia, acquired the famous red "Burning Love" jump suit by donating $5,000 and a rare original Elvis Sun label record at a Cerebral Palsy telethon in Nashville in March 1974. Knowledgeable fans agree that the suit might have brought as much as $10,000 if it had been placed on the market a couple of years later.

Elvis reportedly gave the jacket of his famous diamond-studded gold lamé suit to his personal hairdresser for many years, Homer "Gil" Gilliland. The suit had cost $10,000 when it was made for Elvis in 1957 and now would probably bring many times that much from collectors.

Gil began taking care of Elvis's hair in about 1967. He was given an American Airlines credit card so that he could fly to Las Vegas and on tour with Elvis. He once showed me a watch with valuable gems set in it, which he said Elvis gave to him.

Gil has several valuable pieces of Elvis' clothing. Many went to his full-time companions, men like Red West, Joe Esposito, and Charlie Hodge.

I lifted one of his jump suits once. It was so heavy, I was amazed that Elvis could move around so easily in it.

Elvis also sometimes exchanged gifts of personal jewelry with other people in show business. He once exchanged rings with Welsh singer Tom Jones while Jones was visiting at Elvis's beach house in Hawaii. Later Elvis gave away the Jones ring. He also gave to Sammy Davis, Jr., a valuable ring that he liked.

Many people in show business visited Elvis at Graceland, wrote letters to him or telephoned at different times. Mahalia Jackson, the late gospel singer, a favorite of Elvis's, telephoned for him at least once. Jerry Lee Lewis; Jack Lord, of *Hawaii Five-O;* Vince Edwards, who became famous on television's *Dr. Ben Casey;* and Jackie Wilson were a few others.

Jackie Wilson, who has been called "The Black Elvis," suffered a disabling stroke while performing at the Latin Casino nightclub in Cherry Hill, New Jersey in 1975. He and Elvis were close friends, and Elvis is said to have offered to help out with the hospital bills.

Elvis was always receiving presents in the mail from admirers—sometimes secret admirers.

One day a box with little breathing holes punched in it was delivered to the office. Inside was a pair of baby ducks. There was nothing to indicate who they were from, but the story around Graceland was that they had been sent by Ann-Margret.

Stories about a romance between Elvis and Ann-Margret were prevalent at that time, because they had just starred together in *Viva Las Vegas,* a MGM film released in 1964.

Certainly, they had developed at least a close friendship while working on the picture, their only film together. She often telephoned Elvis at Graceland.

Elvis, Mr. Presley, several of their business associates, and some of the Memphis Mafia used code names when they were traveling or receiving telephone calls at the mansion.

Ann-Margret called often enough to acquire a code name, "Bunny." Unless a code name was used, it might be possible for a fan to telephone and get through to Elvis by claiming to be Ann-Margret.

It wasn't long before "Bunny" became "Thumper," to Elvis's friends and employes when one of the guys recalled the name of the lovable rabbit in Walt Disney's classic animated cartoon *Bambi.*

After Elvis was married, his wife, Priscilla, dressed and, for a time, used make-up that made her look so much like Ann-Margret that in California she was sometimes mistaken for the auburn-haired actress.

Actress Ursula Andress also telephoned frequently for Elvis. They starred opposite each other in *Fun In Acapulco,* a 1963 Hal Wallis film. Instead of using a code name, she would ask, "Is Alan [Fortas] there?" If not, I would say that he wasn't available, and she would ask me to tell him, "Ursula called." Her voice was very recognizable because of the heavy German accent. Ursula was very friendly and would sometimes chat with one of the secretaries a few minutes before asking for Alan.

35

She had posed in the altogether for *Playboy,* and with her fantastic figure and vivacious personality, the brown-eyed blonde actress had a reputation as one of the most desirable women in the world. But she was married to actor John Derek, and Elvis was raised in the South with Southern values instilled in him by God-fearing parents. It wasn't honorable in Elvis's world to become involved with married women, not in Memphis and not in Hollywood.

Probably the biggest surprise was the call from Ron Ziegler, President Nixon's press secretary. He called and asked for Elvis's telephone number in Los Angeles shortly after the National Jaycees named Ziegler and Elvis among the ten outstanding young men of 1970. Ziegler met Elvis at the awards banquet. But he had to wait like everyone else until I telephoned Los Angeles for approval to give him the number.

"Brother" Dave Gardner, a comedian, an occasional supporting act for Elvis and his long-time friend, called frequently but never used an alias. "Is Elvis still making those B movies?" he would always joke. That was sufficient identification, and we always put his call through.

Fans, of course, were always telephoning and asking to talk to Elvis. Calls from as far away as South Africa, Australia, and England were not unusual. Usually the fans accepted gracefully when told that it was impossible to talk with him, and they eventually settled for a chat with a secretary or, infrequently, with one of the guys.

Elvis usually used the alias "John Burrows" for personal mail or telephone calls. His daddy was "Colonel John Burrows." Whenever Colonel Parker telephoned for Mr. Presley, he used the code name "Colonel Snow" to prevent someone else from getting through by dropping his name.

People who called for "John Burrows" or "John Burrows, Jr." were always put through immediately to Elvis, with no questions asked.

The same rule applied to mail. Mail arrived addressed to Graceland or to Elvis, and there would be another envelope inside with "Mr. Burrows" written on it. That mail would be delivered immediately unopened to Elvis. Otherwise all letters except routine fan mail were held for Mr. Presley, Joe Esposito, Charlie Hodge, or one of the other boys to look over.

Elvis's favorite name for reserving airline tickets was "Dr. John Carpenter." After his marriage we received countless billings for flights reserved to "Dr. and Mrs. John Carpenter."

There was no need for secrecy, however, when Elvis filmed his classic thirty-third movie, *Elvis On Tour,* for release in 1972. The Hollywood film makers came to Graceland.

There was very little work accomplished in the office the day that Mr. Presley told Elvis's cousin Patsy, Paulette, and I that we would be in the movie. But we calmed down long enough to sign releases. Then we anxiously waited for the day of the filming.

It was early morning and I was at home, getting ready for a routine day at the office, when one of the girls telephone to say that the film crew was there. Hurry and get to work, she said. The cameras were about to roll.

I had to dress all over again. My husband and I were both late for work by the time I was finally satisfied that I looked as good as I could. Still, Patsy, Paulette, and I were unnerved and fussing about our make-up, hair, and clothing.

We waited, almost afraid to breathe, as the film crew set up the cameras. A few moments later the lights set the ceiling afire. The fledgling blaze was quickly beat out, and we checked our hair, our clothing, our make-up again. No smudges.

One of the film crew, David Draper, a former Mr. Universe, advised us to "just relax, and act natural." We weren't relaxed, and we couldn't act natural. But the cameras finally rolled.

The postman lugged in two heavy bags of fan mail, and I got my first and only speaking part on film. "Hello," I said to him, startling myself with my own voice. There was only the slightest trace of a quaver.

Minutes later it was over. The crew broke down the cameras and lights and moved off to another area of the estate.

The movie was a hit. All Elvis's movies have been hits. But this was something new, an approach never before taken in his films. It showed Elvis at home as well as on tour, and cameras were allowed in areas of Graceland where they had never before been permitted.

But I never enjoyed the film. The portion that Patsy, Paulette, and I so much looked forward to and worried so about ended up on the proverbial cutting room floor.

Chapter Three

Fan Mail

On the preceding
page: A 1976 birth-
day greeting from
some fans in front of
the Music Gate.
(Photo by Jerry
Yancey)

*E*lvis fans are the most sincere, devoted, and generous of any fans in the world.

Letters and packages for Elvis flooded into Graceland from all over. There was an avalanche of mail, a seemingly never ending cascade of letters and cards and boxes. Nevertheless, every letter to Elvis that was delivered to Graceland was read and answered, and every package was opened and acknowledged.

Elvis's payroll buddies brought boxes full of letters with them when they returned from his shows in Las Vegas. Other boxes of mail were forwarded from the RCA offices, from the movie studios, and from Colonel Parker's office in Nashville.

Mail was filed in cabinets, stacked on the floor, and piled on desks and tables. The clutter was so awesome and confusing that one time a yard man carried an entire boxful of letters outside, thinking it was trash. Fortunately we found out about the mistake in time and rescued hundreds of letters from a garbage can before they could go up in smoke.

Had the mail burned, it's certain that about a hundred pictures would also have been destroyed. Some of them probably would have been of extremely beautiful females, teenagers and mature women. Some would have been nudes.

Most of the nudes mailed to Elvis were tasteful. Others looked like they could have been clipped from the rottenest publications available in those little stores where books and magazines are wrapped in cellophane and it costs a dollar to browse.

The nudes went in the bottom drawer of my desk, which I dubbed "the dirty file." Eventually there were two or three hundred photos of women in sexy negligees; see-through undies; pumps, hose and garter belts; or, more commonly, nothing at all.

The more tasteless the pictures in the dirty file, the more Elvis was turned off. He looked at the pictures occasionally and sometimes lingered a few moments over an attractive nude. But he laughed and made fun of the others and dropped them face down in the drawer.

Mr. Presley and some of the boys went through the dirty file periodically and looked at the pictures. Sometimes they would keep one.

More often, however, the boys would take a picture of some wholesome-appearing girl either fully dressed or in a swimming suit—especially if she was pretty and there was an address on the back. Elvis never took any of the pictures.

Bonya, Patsy, Paulette, and I also kept up albums of

photos that fans sent in, as well as the scrapbooks. Elvis didn't show any special preference, and liked pictures of blondes, brunettes, redheads, long-legged girls and petite girls. If they were slim, with a nice figure and pleasant face, he appreciated them.

Elvis usually sat on the edge of one of the desks, with one leg dangling, while he leafed through the albums, discussing the better features of the girls or talking about things that were happening at Graceland.

He didn't talk much about Hollywood with the secretaries. He seemed to consider that a separate part of his life, one that he shared with the guys or his friends in California. Sometimes he talked about his fans. He appreciated them and liked to keep abreast of their activities.

It was amazing that some of Elvis's mail reached Graceland. Much of it arrived addressed simply to: "Elvis, Memphis, Tenn." Those letters were easy enough to deliver. Everyone knows who Elvis is, especially people who work at the U.S. Post Office in Memphis.

Letters addressed to: "Elvis, U.S.A.", and "The King, Memphis, Tenn." were also easily deliverable to 3764 Elvis Presley Boulevard, thanks to Elvis's world-wide fame.

But fans are far more fortunate than they deserve to be when their letters are delivered with no formal address at all. Some fans substituted admiring couplets, such as:

Postman, Postman, don't be slow
Be like Elvis, go man go.

Not great poetry, perhaps. But the meaning was clear enough to the U.S. Postal Service and the letter was dutifully delivered.

Many letters were addressed properly but were impossible to read because of poor penmanship. Others were in foreign script. Mail arrived daily with letters written in Japanese, German, Korean, Portuguese, French, and other languages incomprehensible to the Graceland staff. During the critical days of the Cuban missile crisis in October 1962, a letter written to Elvis in Spanish arrived from Cuba. Somehow it got through Castro's censors and the American naval blockade.

Letters from foreign fans were answered like those from the United States, with mimeographed or xeroxed form letters. Occasionally one of the secretaries would write a personal answer to a fan she developed a particular interest in.

A nurse's aide from the Midwest wrote once a week, telling about her personal life, her boyfriend, what she had for dinner, and whether she was constipated or having regular bowel movements.

Our curiosity piqued by the flood of information, Bonya and I finally decided to pencil a "P.S." on one of the form letters we mailed to her, asking for a photograph of herself. About ten days later a letter was received with a photograph showing a rather plump, neatly dressed, middle-aged woman with short brown hair and a pleasant smile. She was feeding a caged parrot.

Polaroid pictures began arriving almost weekly with her letters. Periodically we would add a small personal note to the form letters we mailed back.

The day a package arrived from her, we were unusually busy and it was set aside and forgotten. It was three or four days before I noticed it again and opened it. As I slit open the top of the box, a stench escaped. The horrible odor got stronger as I leaned over to peer inside. The discolored corpse of a decomposing parrot was nestled in a pile of newspapers. I screamed.

A letter was enclosed with the dead bird. (Bonya said it must have been a carrier pigeon.) The note was from our friend, the nurses' aide. Her parrot had died, she said, and because she had loved the bird so much she wanted Elvis to bury it at Graceland.

Elvis never saw or learned about the parrot, but today it is resting in a shoe box a few feet under the sod at Graceland. One of the yard men buried it.

People mailed incredible presents to Elvis. Some showed genuine imagination. Others were just weird.

Enough warm clothing was received in the mail every year to outfit a regiment of Elvises. Somewhere in the world every day, woolen sweaters, scarves, and socks were being knitted lovingly for Elvis. Usually they were the right size to fit his six-foot, 175- to 185-pound frame.

Shirts, hats, and outlandish underwear were delivered to the office. Boxer shorts with luminous red hearts on them, shorts with pictures of teddy bears or tigers, and fancy men's net bikinis. One woman mailed him a musty old athletic supporter that had belonged to her late husband. Sporadically, Elvis would pick out some of the shirts or scarves to keep.

Elvis was nearsighted and loved prescription sunglasses. He had nearly three hundred. A few were sent to him by fans, but most were purchased at the Dennis Roberts Optical Boutique in Los Angeles for about two hundred dollars each.

Elvis bought sunglasses for the boys, and all were designed for him with "TCB" (Taking Care of Business) printed on the sides.

Most gifts mailed to Elvis were new and usable items

45

of clothing, knick-knacks, or food. Some he couldn't keep. Fans mailed diamonds and other precious stones to Elvis. A woman once sent her engagement ring. Dozens of high school class rings were received from young girls, some asking him to wear them around his neck on a chain. The rings and precious stones were always returned to the owners.

Vitamin pills were mailed to Elvis with detailed instructions about how and when to take them. The sender signed her name "Capricorn" and sounded as though she knew what she was talking about. But Elvis never took the pills.

The mail always brought many items from businesses that Elvis hadn't ordered and couldn't use. He received magazines, leather goods, everything imaginable. Bills were enclosed or mailed later. We responded, explaining that Elvis hadn't ordered the items and was not obligated to pay for them. At one time, dozens of items were charged to a credit card that was made out in Elvis' name but that we had no record of.

For his birthdays fans mailed cakes baked in the shape of guitars, the letter E, and various other forms that they believed had some special significance for him. Businesses mailed him complimentary cakes, candies, pretzels, and cheese. Enough food was mailed to Elvis during the holidays to feed Graceland for a week, and Graceland had a healthy appetite.

Fans celebrated his birthday with parties, some extremely elaborate. They sent congratulatory telegrams to Elvis, and later pictures of the celebrations would arrive. Each year on his birthday scores of fans made the pilgrimage to the Music Gate, where they gathered and paraded.

Elvis usually spent his birthdays quietly. There would be no special observance inside Graceland.

Fans often remembered to send presents to Grandma Presley. More of her years were spent in humble, hard times than in the good times after Elvis grew up. Grandma appreciated the fans' adulation of her famous grandson, and their gifts. Grandma says she was born on June 17, 1893, but other family members have said they believe her year of birth was 1888. Birth records were imprecise then.

There were difficult years back in Tupelo, probably the worst when she and her husband, Jesse, were divorced. In her middle years divorce was an uncommon occurrence among the hard-working folks of the deep South and was considered almost as tragic as the death of a family member.

Grandpa Presley visited Graceland a few times from Louisville. He and his second wife, Vera, stayed then with Mr. Presley and Dee in their home behind the mansion, and I don't know whether he and Grandma ever talked to each other. Coming to work early in the morning during his visits, I often saw him puttering about on the lawn or talking with the grounds keepers.

Grandpa Presley died in the early 1970's. Elvis paid the doctor bills and funeral expenses.

Grandma Presley's room in the east wing of the mansion was decorated with knick-knacks from fans. They were on stands, window sills, and the new color television set that Elvis bought for her. A china jar that Bonya and I gave her for Christmas was on a night stand.

Before Elvis and Priscilla were married, Grandma kept pictures of some of his girlfriends in her room. He had broken up with some of them months or years earlier, but if Grandma liked them their pictures stayed. Elvis never dated anyone for long until Priscilla and, later, Linda Thompson.

Grandma kept her television set going most of the day, watching the first soap opera of the morning through the last soap opera of the afternoon.

The high point of her viewing day was *As the World Turns.* Sitting at the kitchen table over coffee every morning with Aunt Delta, her granddaughter, Patsy, Paulette, and me, Grandma talked about the characters on the show as if they were real people and worried about their muddled lives, agonizing over the troubles of Dr. Bob Hughes and fuming at the nastiness of Lisa. Grandma said the Hughes family was like the Presleys. They stuck together in bad times and good.

We sometimes ate breakfast with Grandma when we were hungry or hadn't had time to eat at home. On those mornings we could expect food like ham and eggs, biscuits, gravy and coffee. All the Presleys except Elvis liked simple, solid food. He consumed great amounts of junk food, and seemed always to be eating.

An organ that Elvis bought for Grandma was kept in one corner of her room. Sometimes the old woman would sit at it in her long dress and matching apron, with back straight and forehead wrinkled in concentration, and play.

Her gnarled, thin fingers pressed the keys with surprisingly graceful movements, while her feet, always in soft black leather granny shoes, vigorously pumped the pedals.

All the Presleys liked music. People at Graceland recalled how before Elvis's mother, Gladys, died, the family loved to sing together. Elvis always played the piano, while his rich high baritone blended with the pleasant voices of his father and mother.

Grandma loved handkerchiefs. She got upset once when she learned that a young woman fan had come to the gate with handkerchiefs for her and the guard wouldn't let her inside. Grandma had one of the maids call the gate and tell the guards that anyone who showed up with a present for her was to be sent up to the house. She wanted anything that was coming to her, and she had a temper that surfaced when she felt she had been slighted. The temper could explode over something that happened on *As The World Turns,* or it could build over something that was going on in the house.

Usually she was warm and friendly to everyone. She fussed over Elvis. In the early years she would bake pies. Later, however, the maids and cooks took over all the housekeeping, cooking, and baking.

Elvis loved his grandmother, as he loved all members of his family. She stayed in her room much of the time, and Elvis would often go inside to talk for an hour or two, or just sit and watch soap operas with her.

Like many old people she caught colds and viruses easily, and doctors were called to the mansion for her several times. Elvis always worried and fussed over her then if he was home. If he was working on a movie or was in Las Vegas, he telephoned every day to ask how she was. She fell when Priscilla was pregnant and was bedridden with a broken hip when Lisa was born.

Fans remembered Elvis's mother and his deep, almost worshipful love for her. Always on the anniversary of her death on August 14, 1958, there were mounds of fresh flowers on her grave and around her ten-foot-tall monument at Forest Hill Cemetery. The Elvis Presley Tankers fan club (now defunct), headed by Gary Pepper, regularly placed flowers on Gladys Presley's grave on the anniversary of her death and at Christmastime. Pepper, a victim of cerebral palsy, is the son of Sterling Pepper, who worked as a gate guard on the night shift at Graceland.

Gary later was put on the payroll as Elvis's fan club coordinator and foreign correspondent. He operates a Memphis newspaper clipping service from his home at 1288 Dolan Street.

At one time Elvis was known to have five thousand fan clubs around the world. New ones are formed as old ones go out of existence. They vary in size from two people to thousands.

Elvis appreciated all his fans, but he had special regard for Gary, Gary's mother, Mrs. Gladys Pepper, and the Tankers. The Peppers, usually with other Tankers, were always welcome at the Fairgrounds and at the movie parties.

Elvis's best-organized fans in Europe are kept informed by *The Elvis Monthly,* a slick little magazine founded in England nearly twenty years ago by printer Albert Hand. The magazine rather immodestly identifies itself as the communication organ for "The Official Elvis Presley Organisation of Great Britain & The Commonwealth."

Before his death a few years ago, Hand visited Graceland and met Elvis. The magazine and club sponsored trips to the United States to tour Graceland and to see Elvis perform, and they held conventions, parties and dances for fans.

European Elvis fans are perhaps even more dedicated than American fans. American fans have periodic opportunities to watch their idol perform in person without traveling across an ocean. But Elvis has never given a European performance, and his fans there are understandably disappointed. Hundreds of letters used to be written to Elvis every year, begging him to come to Europe to perform.

Writer Alan Dawson disclosed some of the frustration felt by Elvis's European fans in a by-line article in *Elvis Monthly:*[1]

> For Elvis' management to keep the rest of the world waiting for 17 years and still waiting is absolutely ridiculous. Elvis himself promised . . . . in 1970 that he was coming to Europe no later than Spring of 1971. Tom Diskin (a top aide to Col. Parker) also promised the same. . . . It is after all, a bit of a farce when his fans have to think about getting a petition up to try to get Elvis over here. It is even more of a farce when fans have to think in terms of paying at least £225 to go and see Elvis in Las Vegas.

The situation was considered so critical by some Elvis fans in Europe that they emigrated to the United States to be closer to "the King."

In "El-Topics," the letters-to-the-editor section of the same issue of *Elvis Monthly* that Dawson's story appears in, a young woman named Susan wrote from Stockport, Cheshire:

> We are two Elvis fanatics who are planning to go to the U.S.A. some time next year permanently. We would like another girl around nineteen-years-old to accompany us, must be an Elvis fan and preferably living in the Manchester area. Object, to be near the King. . . .

51

Thousands of European fans have made pilgrimages to the United States to see their idol. Most of them, of course, returned to their homelands after viewing Elvis's act in Las Vegas or hovering around the Music Gate day and night, waiting to be rewarded by a glimpse of their hero.

Usually, if they waited long enough and Elvis was living at Graceland, they were titillated with a quick look at him driving through the gate. Lucky ones managed to exchange a few words with him.

A stunningly lovely French girl caught up with Elvis at the gate one day, as she was telling other fans that she had flown to the United States to become the next Mrs. Presley. Elvis, bundled in a heavy parka after a recent bout of illness, came roaring down the Graceland drive in a three-wheel motorcycle powered by a Volkswagen engine. His current girlfriend, Linda Thompson, was in the passenger seat. Two other motorcycles piloted by Elvis buddies, with their wives as passengers, were behind him.

As the vehicles waited for a break in north-bound traffic on Elvis Presley Boulevard, the girl pushed her way to him and desperately blurted out her name and why she was there.

"All right, hon," he replied. Then he chomped down on the cigar in his mouth and, tires screeching, pulled into the line of traffic, barreling toward downtown Memphis. The French girl turned away, sobbing.

Love-struck girls tried other means of winning Elvis.

Shortly after his marriage to Priscilla Beaulieu, in 1967, a girl telephoned the office. Speaking in a low, conspiratorial voice, she confided that she had a picture of Elvis and a few strands of his hair. She said that she liked Priscilla but couldn't live without Elvis, and she was going to use the picture and hair in a witch's spell to win his love.

Elvis once told me that he knew barbers swept up his hair and sold it in the days before he started travelling with his own hair stylist. He believed his hair was sold to fans as mementos, but perhaps more of it than he realized was used in love charms and spells.

Some of the more imaginative fans tried for jobs at Graceland. Some inquired at the gate. Others wrote letters.

Grandmothers write, worrying that Elvis isn't eating properly. They ask to come to Graceland to cook for him. Or they say they pray for him. One touching letter was from a woman who said she had prayed for Elvis since his mother died. Even celebrities, she said, need a mother to pray for them.

Fans often asked very personal questions about Elvis and members of his family. Sometimes the questions were about me or other employees. Some teenagers and older women asked for advice about their love lives.

A housewife from the Northeast wrote that a fire destroyed all the Elvis records and memorabilia she had collected since she was twelve. Consequently, she was replacing the lost treasures with money from her food budget, leading to bitter quarrels with her husband.

Another girl asked for advice about marrying a boyfriend who was handsome, intelligent, had a good job and was perfect in every way but one. He didn't like Elvis! I explained to her that no one is perfect, and said that despite the young man's failure to recognize Elvis's greatness, his other qualities made him sound like good marriage material.

One girl, who mailed pictures of herself with nearly every letter, would have been attractive except for a nose that was too long and eyes that were set too far apart. She claimed she was saving her money and was going to have plastic surgery, move to Memphis, and marry Elvis.

I recognized her once among fans at the gate. She hadn't had plastic surgery. And she never married

Male fans sent pictures of themselves as Elvis look-alikes.

There are dozens of Elvis imitators around the world. Alan Meyer, who has played Las Vegas and foreign countries with his "Tribute to Elvis," bills himself simply as "Alan" and is perhaps the best known and most successful of the professionals.

But there are and have been others who also put together entertaining Elvis acts. Bill Haney, of West Memphis, Arkansas; Johnny Rusk, Seattle; Rick Saucedo, Chicago; "Double El," Larry Blong, Philadelphia and Memphis; Rich Locknane, Carlsbad, New Mexico; Nick Paulichenko, Hamilton, Ontario, Canada; Bud Sanders, El Paso, Texas; Ron Hutchinson, Cheshire, England; and Eli Culbertson, another American, have all done Elvis acts or imitations at one time or another with varying degrees of success.

One impersonator, Johnny Harra, a preacher's son and former truck driver, was so good that in 1976 he was mistaken for Elvis and escorted by police into the McNichols Sports Arena in Denver, where fans were waiting for a performance by Elvis. A picture identifying him as Elvis was printed in *The Rocky Mountain News* before Harra admitted the hoax. He had been doing an Elvis act for fifteen years and said he often needed police protection from fans who were convinced he was the real thing.

Almost to a man, each impersonator insists he isn't "just another Elvis imitator," as the others are.

Fast-money operators are constantly writing or telephoning to offer investments and other financial opportunities for Elvis. Elvis has been asked to back inventions, build shopping centers, and finance trips to the Las Vegas gambling tables for half the winnings.

Letters proposing business deals are turned over to Elvis's daddy. Some of the letters are filed. Others are thrown away.

Many people wrote to Elvis suggesting that he buy real estate. A woman from a prominent, old-time Memphis family once telephoned and told me that if I could interest Elvis in buying the family farm, she would make it worthwhile to me. I turned her down, but I told Mr. Presley about the call. He wasn't interested.

A car dealer also offered me money if I could influence Elvis to buy at his dealership. The man offered me a fat commission on each car, and at the rate Elvis buys cars I could have considerably raised our family's living standards. But I explained that I was in no position to influence Elvis, even if I wanted to—which I didn't.

Mr. Presley once deposited several thousand dollars in a local bank, after the president came to Graceland to talk to him. But he didn't agree to make that bank the major depository for Elvis's money, as the executive had asked. I don't know that he ever followed up any of the other business proposals.

Churches called, wanting Elvis to buy bonds so they could build or carry out other projects. Everyone, it seems,

55

had some kind of deal they wanted Elvis to invest in. And they approached anyone they thought might have the slightest chance of influencing him. An old high school acquaintance once wrote to me from Hollywood, asking me to persuade Elvis to help him break into movies.

Mothers mailed Elvis pictures of their babies, asking him to help them obtain modeling or movie contracts. Hundreds of song lyrics and compositions were mailed to Elvis from would-be song writers, asking him to sing them or help get them published.

Of all the ways people concocted to get money out of Elvis and of all the mail he received in the years that I worked for him, there were only a few threatening letters. Mr. Presley turned them over to the police. Some were written to Elvis by husbands or boyfriends who were upset because their wives or girlfriends were too devoted to him. But Mr. Presley worried most about those from people who were obviously mentally unbalanced.

Elvis was fortunate enough to be handy with his fists. He could take care of himself in a fist fight long before he began practicing karate.

Probably the most celebrated instance of Elvis's mixing it up with someone occurred at a Memphis gas station on October 18, 1956, a few weeks before the opening of his first movie, *Love Me Tender*.

Station attendant Ed Hopper became angry because Elvis and his ten-thousand-dollar car drew such a large crowd that business at the gas pumps was being blocked. Hopper slapped Elvis on the back of the head and growled at him to leave.

Elvis leaped out of his car and staggered Hopper with a solid right. Aubrey Brown, another attendant on duty and a husky 220-pounder six feet four inches tall, came to his buddy's assistance. Brown got another Presley fist in the face.

Elvis was cleared of charges in Memphis City Court. Hopper and Brown were fined for assault and battery.

Most of Elvis's few other fracases have been with men jealous of their wives' or girlfriends' infatuation with him.

While Elvis was in the army, he beat up a marine who attacked him. The marine was jealous because his wife had a picture of Elvis in her billfold and none of her husband.

One of Elvis's most serious brushes with danger, however, apparently resulted over a thirteen-year-old girl's near-fatal infatuation with him.

According to writer May Mann, the superstar nearly had a gangland "hit" put out for him when a powerful mobster's daughter deliberately overdosed with sleeping pills and left a suicide note to Elvis.[2] Miss Mann wrote:

> After the doctor was able to restore his daughter, the father heard her cry, "I love Elvis and he will never marry me!" The mob man was set to give the word "to nail Elvis," when he learned, and his daughter readily confessed, that she had never had a physical encounter with the singer. She was a victim of the national hysteria of girls who wanted to die for the love of Elvis.
>
> "Who is this . . . . ham strung pig singer?" the father demanded. The report on Elvis came back within an hour: Elvis was the worldwide hero of teenagers; hands off!

Miss Mann went on to say that the New Jersey gang boss was only one of hundreds of angry males who would have liked to see Elvis dead because of the hysteria of their womenfolk. If that's true, it's surprising that Elvis didn't get more threatening letters.

One of the most upsetting came in January 1971, just before Elvis was to open at the International Hotel in Las Vegas. It was considered so serious that a surgical team and an ambulance were put on stand-by.

James Kingsley, a staff writer for the *Memphis Commercial Appeal* who was said to be the newspaper reporter closest to Elvis, later disclosed the threat in a front-page article. (James Kingsley, the journalist, should not be confused with Hollywood stunt man Jimmy Kingsley, Elvis's friend and former employee.) The threat was originally delivered in a letter to Colonel Parker at his home in Palm Springs, and he notified federal authorities. About a month later it was repeated by telephone to the wife of one of Elvis's guys, shortly after his group arrived in Las Vegas. She was told that Elvis would be shot during his performance. The assassination attempt did not materialize and I never heard of there being an arrest in the case.

Kingsley's disclosure in the article that Elvis at times carried a pistol in a shoulder holster on the Las Vegas tours, meant trouble for Shelby County Sheriff Roy Nixon in Memphis. Tennessee state law prohibits private citizens from carrying guns. But Nixon explained that he had sworn in Elvis as a special nonsalaried deputy sheriff on September 1, 1970 and thus Elvis could legally carry a gun in his home state.

Nixon's statement, however, added fuel to criticism of his department by county officials who were already complaining about law enforcement equipment and manpower supplied for guarding Elvis and controlling

58

traffic during the recent Jaycee Awards Banquet where Elvis was honored with other selectees.

Off-duty sheriff's men and equipment had also been called on when Elvis hosted his Christmas party. The furor over county funds spent protecting Elvis eventually died out.

The Las Vegas threat was taken more seriously than some others, and even though Elvis was away the tension at Graceland was obvious. Fans wrote to offer their personal services as unpaid bodyguards. Others telephoned, in tears, frightened for the safety of their hero.

A few days after we learned of the death threat, a young man about eighteen or nineteen walked into the office. "I want to see Elvis," he growled, glowering down at Paulette and me.

We were startled. We had heard the door open, but thought it was Mr. Presley or one of Elvis's guys and hadn't looked up from our work until he spoke.

The unsmiling, unshaven young man stared down at us. One hand was thrust suspiciously into the pocket of his rumpled trousers as he repeated his demand to see Elvis.

"Oh, my God," I told myself. "This guy's after Elvis and Elvis isn't here. We're going to be killed." I forced myself to ask what he wanted Elvis for.

"I wrote a song and I wanted Elvis to see it," he mumbled, pulling a grimy hand from his pocket and shoving a crumpled sheet of paper to us.

The gate guard had sent him to see us, he said. When I started to telephone the gate the young man changed his story. He admitted that he had climbed the fence the night before and slept on the grounds.

The crisis over, I explained that Elvis wasn't home and

wouldn't be back for weeks. I took the paper and promised to show it to Elvis when he returned.

Paulette was already calling the gate, and in a few minutes the young man was escorted off the grounds.

After that I kept the door locked whenever I was in the office alone. People were always sneaking onto the grounds.

1. *Elvis Monthly,* Issue No. 166, November 1963, "Could Elvis Have Been Greater?"
2. *Elvis and the Colonel,* by May Mann. Drake, New York, 1975.

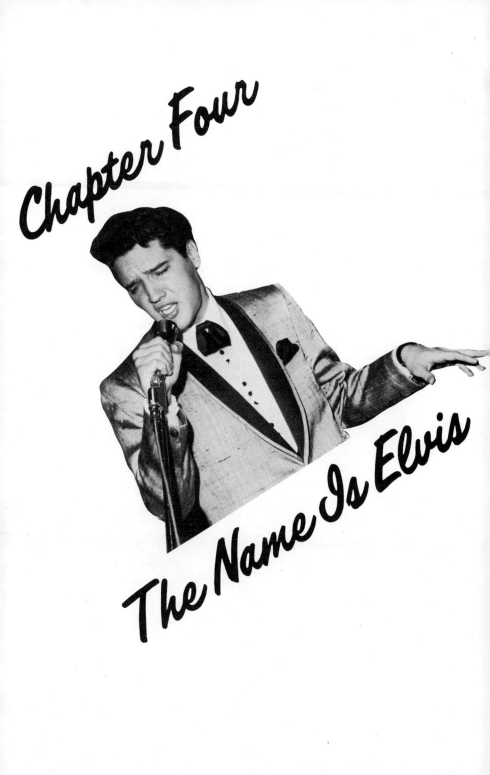

Chapter Four

The Name Is Elvis

Fans knew Elvis in a jump suit, the front of it open almost to his waist, sweat glistening and plastering his black hair to his chest as he belted out "Burning Love" or "Thinking About You" under blistering stage lights.

It was a different Elvis who wandered downstairs at Graceland wearing floppy pajamas under a loosely tied robe at two or three o'clock in the afternoon.

A spot of shaving soap he'd missed with his washcloth was still clinging to one sideburn one afternoon when I encountered Elvis.

"Hi. You're looking good, Elvis," I said.

"Well Becky, you're looking good too," Elvis replied, turning his head and stifling a yawn with his hand.

That was our "looking good" routine. No matter what Elvis looked like, no matter what I looked like, we always told each other we were looking good before we said anything else.

But the afternoon I met him at the bottom of the stairs, I was speaking honestly when I told him he was looking good. He was also looking for Aunt Delta to tell her what he wanted for breakfast.

Elvis was always eating. He had a refrigerator upstairs, which was kept filled with soft drinks and ready-to-eat snacks. He insisted that a maid be on duty day and night to cook. There were so many people around that it seemed someone was always eating, just as a telephone was always ringing and a television set was constantly playing somewhere in the mansion.

Elvis snacked constantly on such things as meatball sandwiches, peanut butter and mashed banana sandwiches, and ice-cream with Pepsi-Cola. He seldom ate candy, so the other secretaries and I ate most of the candy mailed to him by fans. The few times when he sat down to a serious meal he liked good, simple, stick-to-the-ribs food such as roasts or steaks with potatoes and gravy, bread and butter. Potatoes and a small steak were an elaborate meal for Elvis. There was nothing that a fancy French chef could do for him that a good Southern cook couldn't do better. But not even a skilled cook was needed to slap together a plateful of bacon and eggs or a jelly or peanut butter sandwich, the kind of eating Elvis liked best.

He never fixed his snacks himself. He would always have someone do it for him. He always calls on the telephone or intercom for one of the guys or a maid when he wakes up hungry.

Occasionally in later years, he still wandered downstairs before rounding up someone to arrange his breakfast. Someone like Aunt Delta. Elvis found her easily enough the day I met him at the stairway, and while

64

she was telling the maid what to fix for breakfast he asked me to have coffee with him and talk. A couple of minutes later we were seated on a green velvet couch in the den, talking and sipping cautiously at cups of steaming coffee. Elvis's was doctored with a teaspoonful of sugar and a dash of cream; mine was black.

In the kitchen a few feet away, Mary Jenkins, one of the maids, busied herself breaking eggs in a bowl, as bacon fried in a skillet and two slices of bread were browning in the toaster. Two oranges to be squeezed for fresh juice were arranged on the cabinet top in front of her with a carton of milk, a bottle of ketchup, and other ingredients for Elvis's Spanish omelette.

Elvis started eating Spanish omelettes at one of the hotels in Las Vegas and liked them so well he had one of the boys get the recipe. He insisted that the cooks at Graceland fix them the same way. Regardless of how the eggs were seasoned, Elvis always smothered them in black pepper.

He ate enough Spanish omelettes for a while to put half the hens in West Tennessee on double time. The omelettes were always served with King Cotton bacon. Elvis liked the brand so well that he had it flown to the West Coast when he was working in Hollywood.

He was like that. He would get on kicks with everything—giving away cars, taking up new hobbies, going on movie binges, buying new wardrobes, and picking a favorite food and eating the same thing for weeks. Whenever he took a liking to something, he pursued it until he was satiated. Finally he would have enough and drop it.

For a while he couldn't get enough ice cream. Anyone who walked into the den for coffee in the middle of the afternoon might find Elvis on the couch hunched over a copy of the *Memphis Press-Scimitar* as he scooped huge spoonfuls of vanilla ice cream into his mouth.

There was a craze for watermelon, and when that died out he went after cantaloupe. There were diets, and there were vitamin pills. It wasn't surprising that Elvis got on a vitamin pill craze. He has always been concerned about his health and physical appearance.

Afternoons just before Elvis got up, a rainbow array of vitamin pills would be lined up, like ranks of silent soldiers, with a glass of freshly squeezed orange juice on the coffee table in front of the sofa or at the table in the den just off the kitchen. Elvis would take them all. He said they made him feel better.

It seemed as though Elvis and everyone around him was preoccupied with his health and physical appearance. When he wasn't feeling good, everyone was depressed and worried.

Usually during these times he would stay in his private rooms upstairs, sometimes for weeks. The upstairs is his private domain and the only place he can go when he wants to be away from everything and everybody. Only Priscilla, his best girlfriends or, occasionally, one of the guys was allowed upstairs.

Karate is one of the means Elvis used to keep in shape. Bobby "Red" West, who at one time operated the Tennessee Karate Institute in Memphis, once said that "Elvis's whole life is singing and karate. In that order."

That may be exaggerating a bit, but not much. Elvis made no secret of the fact that he was devoted to the sport. He worked out in karate nearly every day for twenty years, whether he was in Memphis, California, or Las Vegas.

66

Elvis could talk about karate for hours without stopping, and one day he was telling me why I should take it up. Paulette and I finally took some Judo lessons at the YMCA but lost interest and quit after a while. Elvis later got Priscilla involved in the sport.

Elvis insisted that karate is not basically violent and said that it is equally good for physical fitness and for building character in men and women. "It's a way of life," he said, "not something that you use to beat people up with. Its so much more than a sport. It teaches discipline, patience, and makes you more spiritual."

As I've mentioned, he was good enough with his fists so that he usually didn't need karate for self-defense. And, of course, Red and his other bodyguards were always with him when he was in public.

However, Elvis reportedly used karate on February 19, 1973, when he was rushed by four men from the audience as he was performing at the Internationale Showroom in the Las Vegas Hilton Hotel. More than seventeen hundred fans watched as Elvis neatly disabled one of the men. Red, his cousins Sonny West, and other bodyguards moved in and took care of the others.

At Graceland we heard that Gene Dessel, the hotel security chief, said that the men, who were drunk, claimed they were only trying to shake Elvis's hand.

Elvis used karate to loosen up and relieve tension before performances. He had so little private life that there were few times when he could be just himself. One of those times was when he was practicing karate.

Elvis's blue eyes sparkled when he talked about karate. He sometimes struck fighting postures, shifting his feet suddenly to demonstrate the importance of balance, or weaving his flattened hands at chest level in front of himself. His karate movements were graceful, almost like ballet, as he shifted and turned.

Elvis watched the television series *Kung-fu,* starring David Carradine as a master of the ancient Chinese martial art. He enjoyed the show, but said that kung-fu could never stand up to karate. "If a kung-fu master was pitted against a master of karate," he said, "the karate master would win."

Some people have the idea that Elvis became interested in karate through his association with Red West. Not so! It's just the opposite. It was Elvis who got Red and some of the other boys involved in karate. Elvis and Red each have black belts.

Elvis took up karate in the army, but he became really proficient at the sport after he was discharged. He was an avid reader, and many of the books and magazines he bought were about karate and other fighting arts. He had almost as many books about the martial arts as about music, and more than about medicine—another of his reading passions.

"It's affected my whole life," Elvis once said of karate. It's certainly affected his performances. He believed that karate training in proper breathing helped his singing. His karate training also showed up in his movements on stage. The karate influence was especially obvious when he performed and sang, "If You Talk in Your Sleep." The song was written for him by Red in 1974.

He also executed karate movements during instrumental breaks in other songs. The graceful, fluid movements of karate lent themselves easily to music, following the beat.

Elvis worked out at Graceland when he didn't want to

drive downtown to the Institute, where he often practiced before he and Red had their falling out in 1976. American and Tennessee state flags are draped above a huge mirror on the wall of the red carpeted practice area at the karate center. Elvis liked that. He loved Tennessee, and he loved his country.

I was told by a friend at Graceland that Elvis wasn't satisfied with the work that Red and Sonny were doing and that he was also upset because their rough handling of people was getting him into too many lawsuits. So he fired them. David Hebler, one of the newer members of Elvis's clique, was reportedly fired when he sided with Red and Sonny.

One night years before their disagreement, Elvis and Sonny gave a karate and judo demonstration in the entrance hall to the mansion. People were sitting in the dining room and the living room. Others were lined up on the stairs when Elvis and Sonny walked into the room in their loose-fitting white karate uniforms.

The two men squared off from each other, moving lightly on the toes of their feet. Suddenly Elvis leaped into the air, bellowing as his bare feet grazed the neck of Sonny's uniform. Several of the girls screeched when Elvis yelled.

Then Elvis and Sonny were leaping, thrusting and chopping at each other, never quite connecting with their punches but coming so close that it looked as though they were going to be seriously injured.

When Elvis threw one jab, Sonny sidestepped, grabbed Elvis's arm, jammed a hip into him and tossed him onto his back. Elvis landed with a thud, but bounced back onto his feet and in seconds was measuring Sonny with the palms of his hands. Sonny and Red have said many times that Elvis took his falls and jabs as well as the next guy.

It was Red who disclosed that Elvis was hurt using karate while he was doing his own stunt scene in *G. I. Blues,* his first movie after discharge from the army in 1960. He broke a bone in his left hand.

Elvis specialized in two forms of the art: *tae kwan do,* a form developed in Korea that emphasizes the feet; and *kem-po,* which relies more on chopping or jabbing blows with the flattened hand.

A Korean, Kang Rhee, who teaches the movements of *tae kwan do,* was one of Elvis's favorite instructors in Memphis. Ed Parker has instructed him in *kem-po* during workouts in Las Vegas.

Elvis could almost be described as a physical culture freak. The sense of natural balance, rhythm, and coordination that so greatly complement his music would undoubtedly be just as helpful if he had decided to become a professional athlete.

Althought his payroll buddies—most of whom were pretty good athletes—deferred to him in other ways, they didn't pull any punches when it came to their rough-and-tumble play. Whether he was practicing karate or playing touch football, Elvis took his lumps just like the others. He wouldn't have it any other way.

Some of the guys genuniely loved Elvis. Nearly all of them mimicked him in his actions, habits and dress. Elvis was fascinated with words, and when he heard one that was unfamiliar to him he would ask for a definition and make sure he knew how the word was used. His interest wasn't confined to components of the English language accepted by the academic linquists. Elvis loved slang as it

70

evolves on the street and among musicians. He used new words, conventional and slang, over and over again until he finally tired of them or heard new ones that captured his imagination.

For a while everything at Graceland was "burnt." If it was good, great, pretty, or fortunate, it was "burnt." Elvis might be talking about Self-Realization, shake his head and say "Burnt!" The guy next to him would say, "Yeah, man. Burnt!" All around the room guys would nod and repeat, "Burnt! Burnt!"

Many of the expressions came from California and, like fashions, eventually made their way to Memphis. But Elvis and the guys brought them home first, and they were impressed with their own sophistication.

Their clothing styles were far ahead of or different from Memphis fashions. Men in Memphis were dressing in overalls, bluejeans, or conventional business suits when the boys were coming home from California and strutting around Graceland in sleek continental suits and flashy boots.

The first year I was at Graceland, Elvis and the boys were already dressing like The Beatles, whom no one in Memphis had yet heard of. They wore tight black pants, silk shirts with monograms on the sleeves and collars, and custom tailored jackets. Most of Elvis's clothes were custom made. He bought boots at Hardy's in Memphis until the manufacturer quit making them; then he bought the pattern.

There have been perhaps twenty or more men who have at one time or another been on Elvis's payroll as one of his companions. He was seldom seen anywhere without them.

When Elvis was at Graceland the boys stayed with

their wives and girlfriends in other buildings or trailers on the grounds, in nearby motels, or in homes of their own in Whitehaven. When Elvis was in California the boys stayed with him in his house and in near-by apartments or motels. When Elvis traveled on tour or played Las Vegas, his entourage required entire floors and suites of rooms.

Many of Elvis's guys had drifted away by the time he died and the football games had been replaced by racquetball. Like everything else Elvis did, he went wholeheartedly into the sport.

He not only built a court at Graceland but also, early in 1976, became an investor and for the first time authorized use of his prestigious name for a commercial venture.

The Presley Center Courts, Inc., was formed in Memphis by Elvis's physician, Dr. George C. Nichopoulos; Joe Esposito, Elvis's road manager; and Michael McMahon, a local real estate developer. Elvis was named chairman of the board of the new corporation, which constructed its first court in Nashville. But he bowed out of the business before the end of the year and the company was renamed. Mr. Presley said Elvis was too busy with his singing career to devote time to the racquetball business.

A $150,000 damage suit was filed against Elvis in early 1977 on behalf of Center Courts, Inc., by his former partners in the corporation. They claimed he backed out of the venture without giving a reason and reneged on an agreement to loan money to the corporation to get the business underway.

Elvis admired good athletes, and heavyweight boxer

Muhammad Ali was one of his favorite sports personalities. Elvis had a robe made for Ali when the champion fought British boxer Joe Bugner. "The People's Champion" was stitched across the back. Ali wore the robe the night he lost in an upset to Ken Norton. He reportedly never wore it again because he considered it bad luck.

A statue of Muhammad Ali, with a tiny body and a nearly life-sized head, stood in our office for more than a year. It was a present from Paul Lichter and, according to the Elvis superfan, is one of only two in existence.

It was finally moved to the trophy room after the other secretaries and I complained that it made us feel creepy because the eyes always seemed to be following us.

Elvis was a football fan and spent hours with the guys watching the Los Angeles Rams games on television. But he also used to slip into the press box in Memphis to watch the Memphis Southmen play.

He and the guys played a bone-jarring brand of touch football at the Graceland School in the Graceland subdivision in the early years and later, for privacy, moved the games to the mansion grounds. A black panel truck was always driven onto the field with refreshments when games were being played at the estate. Elvis occasionally climbed inside and drove away before anyone realized what was going on. His buddies then sometimes found him at Forest Hill Cemetery with his head bowed, quietly standing at his mother's grave.

Elvis's love for vigorous sports was matched by his addiction to motor vehicles. He was attracted to anything with an engine and wheels.

When customized van trucks became popular after I left Graceland, Elvis spotted one of the vehicles created by an Elkhart, Indiana, firm for a country singer Conway Twitty. Elvis ordered a van for himself because he liked Twitty's so well.

Luther Roberts, president of Van Man, Inc., said that when fans learned that a Dodge van was being customized for Elvis, they converged on the company plant with their children and cameras. One female fan planted a wet kiss on the steering wheel.

Elvis's van was painted brown, with pictures of his horses on the side and back. (More about Elvis's horses later.) The van is equipped with brown carpeting, a davenport bed, built-in television, cupboard, refrigerator, sink, coffeemaker, citizens' band radio, and hi-fi system with a tape deck. It is air conditioned and has a burglar alarm. The cost, Roberts said, was between fifteen and twenty thousand dollars.

Elvis drove everything fast, whether it was cars, buses, trucks, motorcycles, golf carts, go-carts, or people movers. I'm sure there is a better name for the machine, but all Elvis ever called it was a "people mover," and that became its official title at Graceland. It was descriptive enough.

One day when Elvis wasn't home, Aunt Delta and I drove it around the yard. It was a short ride. After nearly crashing into a couple of trees and then heading in a suicide dash for the swimming pool before we managed to veer away at the last minute, we turned the key to the "off" position and left the machine for Elvis and the boys to play with.

Elvis and the boys sometimes gave us rides on the motorcycles and golf carts. There was always something in the yard with an engine running, and the poor yard men spent half their time repairing tire tracks and deep ruts in the grounds.

74

Elvis crated his motorcycles and sent them back and forth between Memphis and California. He especially liked Harley Davidsons. He also liked snowmobiles, and there were enough of them so that he and most of the guys could ride around the grounds together. There was hardly ever any snow in Memphis, so Elvis had tires mounted on the machines. He and the boys played so rough with them that they were always breaking down or being busted up when the guys rolled them over while attempting to turn them at high speed. We kept a parts catalogue in the file to pick out replacements because there was no place to buy parts in Memphis. Elvis never liked to wait when he wanted something, so Mr. Presley usually took one of the employees with him and flew to Nebraska to buy parts when they were needed.

Elvis didn't do things like other people. One day after he'd decided to tear down an old house on the grounds, he rented a bulldozer and pushed it over himself. During his army years the building was the home for his uncle Travis Smith, but it was being used for storage when Elvis decided to get rid of it.

After he knocked it down he set the wood on fire. A few minutes later fire trucks from Memphis roared up the winding Graceland driveway. After the ashes had settled, Elvis parked house trailers where the old building had stood.

Elvis learned to love dune buggies while he was making movies and kept at least one at his home in Palm Springs, California. He seldom talked about his activities in California, but he occasionally discussed actors and actresses he appeared with in movies.

Shelley Fabares was Elvis's favorite actress, of those he worked with. They were together in three of his movies—*Girl Happy, Spinout,* and *Clambake,* released in

1965, 1966, and 1967. Shelley later appeared a few times in the television series *Love American Style*, and it was (with *Combat* and *Shindig*) one of Elvis's favorite shows. There was never a romance between Elvis and Shelley that I was aware of, but he said he liked her as an individual and enjoyed being with her. They had fun together.

Elvis didn't make any secret of his admiration for Ann-Margret, but she wasn't the only one of his female co-stars he was romantically linked with or dated. Juliet Prowse, who appeared with Elvis in *G. I. Blues*, was one of the leading ladies he was linked to. Mary Ann Mobley, the gorgeous one-time Miss America from Mississippi who appeared with him in *Girl Happy* and *Harum Scarum*, both released in 1965, was another. He once predicted that Mary Ann would make the big time in movies. He observed that Ann-Margaret was emphatically there. Referring to her talent during an interview with James Kingsley, he asked, "How are you supposed to act or sing with her around?"[1]

As a Southerner and as a gentleman, if Elvis couldn't say something good about the girls he dated or the actresses he worked with, he usually didn't say anything at all. But he did concede that the actress he liked working with least was Joan Blackman. She was in Elvis's *Blue Hawaii*, released in 1961, and in *Kid Galahad*, a 1962 release. Elvis didn't say why he disliked working with her, just that they didn't get along.

Elvis was friendly with several other actors and celebrities. Nick Adams, who played the lead in the television series *The Rebel*, visited at Graceland. He was one of Elvis's closest celebrity friends before the young actor's death. Buddy Hackett was one of Elvis's favorite comedians.

Elvis regularly broke up in laughter when he was watching Buddy's routines.

The Beatles were one of his favorite singing groups in the 1960's, and he bought most of their records. He collected records of almost every kind of music from country and gospel to classical; his taste in music was limitless. I heard that during the Beatles' first American tour he sent them a toy water pistol, implying they could use it to play Russian roulette. They were, after all, competitors. Elvis thought it was a good joke and was sure they would accept it that way. He said they were a terrific group of musicians, and was pleased to have them visit him at his home in Los Angeles.

Elvis's friends learned quickly to call him by his first name. He hated to be called "E," or "El," and no one who cared about him or wished to remain his friend called him by anything other than his full first name. The Presleys apparently picked Aron as his middle name simply because they liked the sound. Neither Elvis nor his father ever mentioned either name belonging to anyone else in the family. The name "Elvis" apparently stems from an old Norse name, "Alviss," which means "all wise."[2]

An identical twin, born dead after Elvis's birth in East Tupelo, Mississippi, was named Jesse Garon. The first name was the same as Grandpa Presley's.

Some say the Presleys, and probably Elvis's maternal ancestors, the Smiths, came originally from England. Could be. But when that was suggested to Mr. Presley years ago, he just remarked that as far back as he knew most of his and his first wife's kin were from northeast Mississippi.

Elvis didn't worry much about where he was from. He

knew where he was going. And he knew who he was. He was Elvis, and he wanted his friends to call him that. If the name was good enough for his parents, millions of fans, and the ancient Norsemen, it was good enough for his friends.

1. *The Mid-South Magazine*, the Sunday magazine of *"The Commercial Appeal."* Memphis, March 7, 1965.
2. *Name Your Baby*, by Lareina Rule. Bantam Books, New York, 1963.

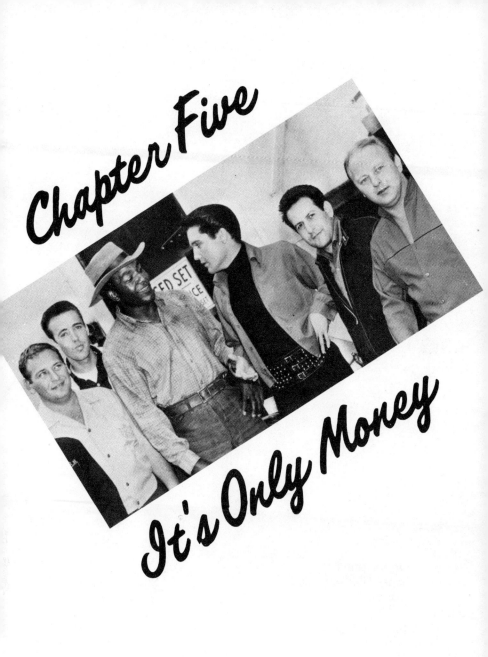

Chapter Five

It's Only Money

On the preceding
page: Elvis in Holly-
wood talking to
football immortal
and film star Jim
Brown, as members
of the Memphis
Mafia look on.

*A*mateur and professional psychologists have theorized about why Elvis spent so extravagantly and showered such expensive gifts on family, friends, and strangers.

One of the most popular conclusions is that he was trying to buy friends.

Another theory blamed guilt feelings of a man who was suddenly catapulted from extreme poverty to millionaire status.

Whatever the reason, it was true that Elvis spread his money around lavishly enough to make a Croesus jealous.

Elvis gave away so much over such a long period of time that it's difficult to separate the truth from the fables that crop up about his generosity.

One of the stories I considered the most touching was the experience of two English teenagers who stood outside the Music Gate crying all night. Elvis heard about it the next morning. He brought them into the mansion to feed them breakfast and learned that their mother had just died. They were penniless orphans.

Elvis not only paid their fare back to England, but arranged for the body of their mother to be shipped home and picked up the funeral expenses.

It was just the type of thing that Elvis would do. But he didn't. It was just a story. Fans wrote to Graceland about it, however, and I'm sure that many still believe that it happened.

People probably believe it because they know the story is typical of Elvis. And the true stories they have heard about his impetuous generosity are often equally fantastic and dramatic. Elvis was born poor and he knew what it was to want things. So he gave money and other gifts to people.

I started paying bills and writing checks for Elvis in 1966. One of the first checks I wrote was for thirty thousand dollars. It had so many zeros that I didn't know where to put them. Mr. Presley showed me.

That didn't shake me as much as the day I totaled up Elvis's purchases of cars and trucks. In one month he had bought thirty-three vehicles, an average of more than one a day.

They went to everyone imaginable. His buddies, their wives and girlfriends got some. Four of his house maids, and doctors from Memphis and Los Angeles got others. He gave one car to a well-known movie director.

But many went to chance acquaintances or strangers who just happened to be there when Elvis was feeling generous.

When he once wanted to go motorcycle riding with

the boys, he had Alan Fortas contact a Memphis Triumph dealer and order a dozen motorcycles for the boys so they could ride with him.

Elvis told me one day that he thought he'd go for a ride on a Harley Davidson motorcycle he liked, and I told him that it had been sold a long time ago. His jaw dropped. Then he grinned. "I just got so many, Becky," he laughed, "that I can't keep up with them."

That was in the 1960's, and Elvis's lavish spending hasn't changed.

In January 1976 he made national news when he gave away three Cadillacs and two Lincoln Continental Mark IV's while he was on a skiing vacation in Vail, Colorado. Three of the cars were given to police department employees, and two to a doctor and a television newsman. Each was valued at thirteen thousand dollars or more.

Many of the gifts never made the newspapers. But stories written about Elvis's generosity always brought hundreds of requests to Graceland. Fans would write and telephone asking for cars, houses, cash, credit cards, and everything else they could think of. Some claimed to be long-lost relatives and wanted to come live at the mansion.

Elvis would give away as many as ten cars at a time. He would buy them as casually as other men buy a pack of cigarettes.

It's not surprising that the car dealer asked me to influence Elvis to buy from him. Elvis went on car buying binges, and many of the binges were in Memphis. Sometimes Elvis would take the old cars when he bought new ones for people, and give the exchanged vehicles to someone else.

After I left Elvis, Mr. Presley's girlfriend, Sandy, told

me at lunch one day that Elvis had given one of the maids a house. "Elvis is just giving away so much that it has Vernon worried," she said.

One of the few times Elvis ever got in trouble with his fans occurred when he went on a kick buying Mercedes-Benzes. A newspaper story told about Elvis's giving his personal Mercedes to Shelby County Sheriff William Morris. Almost immediately he started getting letters from fans complaining because he didn't buy American cars. The unemployment rate in this country was very high at that time.

Elvis loved Mercedes, just about every one of his cronies received one from him, and several of the doctors he knew. He gave away so many that people wouldn't believe that everyone who worked for him didn't have a Mercedes. My husband and I were at a party during the Cotton Carnival in 1968 and a woman told me that I was lying when I insisted that I didn't have one.

One of Elvis's most famous gifts of a car involved a more modest new Ford Mustang he bought for an actress when he was filming *Double Trouble* in 1966. Elvis heard she had to walk half a mile to the studio because she didn't have a car, so one day when she got there, he was waiting for her with a set of keys and registration papers.

He handed them to her, pointed to the car, and strolled away after telling her, "I sure hope you can drive."

Elvis's giving, however, wasn't limited to cars. A cape he threw to the crowd while he was doing his Hawaii special cost about eight thousand dollars. Another time he gave a security guard a ten-thousand-dollar ring in Las Vegas.

84

Elvis didn't begin spending large amounts of money on jewelry until his Las Vegas tours. Then he would spend nearly thirty thousand dollars for a ring to use once on stage.

Fans weren't above trying to help themselves to gifts. Elvis told me that he almost lost one of his big diamond rings when he leaned over to kiss a girl during a performance and she tried to pull it off his finger. After that he always kept his fists clenched when he was kissing fans, so they couldn't pull his rings and watches off.

Elvis was as inconsistent as he was generous about his gift giving. I had worked for him for about six months when Jerry and I were married. There was no card and no gift from Elvis. The only acknowledgment came several weeks later when he walked into the office, stopped, looked at me, and said, "Becky, why'd you get married?"

Before I could reply, he shook his head and said, "Aw, that wasn't a fair question." He turned around and walked out.

But people learned that if Elvis was approached in the right way he would give away just about anything.

The way I got my job is a good example. If I had asked for a job as a secretary, he probably never would have hired me.

Other people learned to get things from Elvis by mentioning how much they admire something, without asking for it outright.

If someone approached Elvis and said, "Hey, Elvis, how about buying me that car?," He would probably tell them to jump in the lake.

But if they saw a car they liked and said, "Oh, what a great car. I've never seen anything so beautiful." Elvis would probably buy it for them.

Jimmy Kingsley admired a jeweled watch Elvis was wearing once and Elvis simply slipped it off his wrist and gave it to him.

Elvis gave fourteen-karat gold identification bracelets with their names on them and necklaces emblazoned with the letters "TCB" split by a lightning bolt to all the guys. His girlfriends and the wives and girlfriends of the guys were given gold "TLC" necklaces. (TCB stands for "Taking Care of Business," TLC for "Tender Loving Care.") The lightning bolt, Elvis said, symbolizes the West Coast Mafia.

Most of the necklaces cost one hundred and fifty dollars each, but a few very special pieces were made with ruby and diamond sets and were considerably more expensive. Elvis ordered dozens of sunglasses from a Hollywood optician with the TCB insignia on the earpieces and his initials across the bridge.

Almost everyone was getting jewelry from Elvis for a while. His doctors, lawyers, musicians, and everyone around him had either TCB or TLC necklaces. Everyone but Paulette and me. Elvis had been passing out necklaces for two years but we were set off from the mansion in our little office and had been left out. Our feelings were hurt because we were overlooked. We complained about it to a couple of the guys one day and it apparently got back to Elvis.

That afternoon when we went into the mansion for coffee, Elvis was watching *Love American Style* on television. He asked us to sit down and talk awhile. As we were talking, one of the boys walked downstairs with a couple of TLC necklaces. Elvis put them around our necks and kissed us. "See," he said, grinning his lopsided smile as he fastened the clasp on my necklace, "I don't forget."

He did forget. Elvis never intentionally slighted any-one, but if people didn't mention things to him he some-times forgot. There was so much competition for his at-tention that there were always some hurt feelings, no matter what he did or how careful he tried to be to treat everyone with equal consideration.

Some of the girlfriends and wives of the guys made more money in presents from Elvis than I made working for him. Not many of them truly appreciated the gifts.

I know girls at Graceland, not girlfriends of Elvis, who were given thousands of dollars in cash, expensive jewelry, furs, and new cars.

At lunch one day I was discussing a trip to Lake Tahoe with the wife of one of Elvis's cronies. Elvis was footing the bill for her and her husband. He had already bought her a Pontiac Grand Prix, a diamond ring with sapphires, a watch, and a mink coat. Unfortunately, the more people get from Elvis the more they want. Even while telling me about the Lake Tahoe trip and the other gifts, she couldn't help wondering out loud what Elvis would buy for her next.

Elvis, of course, knew this, and he let his frustration surface once while drinking coffee with me in the den. Suddenly he slammed his cup down on the table, spil-ling the hot coffee on his hand, and muttered angrily, "Damn! Damn! I give these people everything and still they're not happy."

Another of the guys' wives complained to me once that if she had only been around at the right time she would have been given a car. She started hanging around the mansion again, and it wasn't long before Elvis gave her a valuable ring. Then she complained pri-vately that he had given more expensive jewelry to other people.

The guys were given motorcycles, cars, horses, furniture, down payments on houses, jewelry, and clothes. Some had their rent paid. Several of them got ten-thousand-dollar checks as gifts.

Stories of Elvis's giftgiving away from Memphis often reached us as gossip among the guys and their wives when they returned from Hollywood or Las Vegas.

Elvis was generous to other performers, whether they were already successful or were still struggling to make it.

In 1975 he gave to country singer T. G. Sheppard a converted Greyhound bus that sleeps eight and has a television set and a sitting room. Sheppard, who had in 1961 hitchhiked to Memphis from his home in Humboldt, Tennessee, to launch a career as a singer and picker, had the hit singles "Devil in the Bottle," "Another Woman," and "Tryin' to Beat The Morning Home." The bus certainly made it easier for him and his band to travel around the country for performances.

Elvis is also said to have given J. D. Sumner, a white gospel singer, many valuable gifts. Elvis had idolized him since boyhood. Bass singer with the group J. D. Sumner & The Stamps, he backed Elvis on records and at live performances.

It wasn't at all uncommon for Elvis to buy jewelry for the different groups who sang or played with him. Sometimes Elvis would decide he didn't like the way his group was dressed, and he would buy new clothes for everyone. We got the bills at Graceland.

Most of the time that I worked for Elvis, he was backed by The Sweet Inspirations, a black female group; and by Voice, a male group. Every month I wrote checks for approximately nine thousand dollars for Voice.

The guys with Voice came into the office once, and I also met The Sweet Inspirations, when they visited in the mansion. Elvis's backup groups didn't show up that often at Graceland, although The Jordanaires sometimes came to the mansion and Elvis sang gospels with them there.

Elvis was ripped off a lot. Businesses sent bills to Graceland several times for goods charged in Elvis's name by people who claimed they worked for him. They were imposters, and the bills were not paid. At other times we received medical bills for treatment of people who said they worked for Elvis, and no one at Graceland had ever heard of them.

Elvis's daddy was affected differently than his illustrious son was by the hard years of the past. He didn't believe in sharing the luxurious living with people outside the family.

When I left Elvis in 1974 I was earning $125. Some secretaries in other jobs in the Memphis area were making $200 a week.

But Elvis's daddy set the salaries for the secretaries, and he was of the old school. To me, it seemed clear that he didn't think women should make much money, no matter what they did. If any of us asked Mr. Presley for a raise, he would tell us to wait. "We just ain't making that much money now," he would say.

One time after Mr. Presley announced that we were getting five-dollar raises, I got my check on payday and the money wasn't there. I asked him about it. "Forget it," he said. "We're not giving them out."

A week later we heard yet another story about Elvis's buying a new Cadillac for someone he had never seen before.

In 1967 the girlfriend of one of Elvis's buddies was

hired as a secretary at a salary twenty dollars higher than Patsy and I were getting. We complained about it, and Mr. Presley said he would raise our pay to the same amount.

Patsy and I were excited about the raise, and to celebrate we went out and bought a bunch of new clothes. Then Mr. Presley changed his mind and didn't give us the raise. Since then, I've never spent money I didn't have. The new girl left after a few weeks to return to the West Coast.

Most of the people who worked for Elvis didn't have to depend on their salaries alone. They took expensive presents from him and borrowed money they never paid back.

A bulky file of people who owed Elvis money was kept in the office. Some of the loans were set up so that payments could be deducted from paychecks. Elvis never charged interest, but it didn't make much difference because he never saw most of the money again anyway.

Elvis once called all the employees into the dining room and announced that he was clearing the books. Nothing had to be repaid.

One Christmas he summoned all the employees who owed him money and told them he was wiping the debts clean. I'm the only one I know of who wasn't at the meeting. But I was around when everyone else walked out, smiling and laughing.

I never asked to borrow from him, because I knew how easy it was to take advantage of his generosity and I didn't want to be tempted. There were times when Jerry and I could have used some help just like anyone else, but we never went to Elvis for it even though we knew he would have given us the loan.

I read once that the Rockefellers never lend money to friends because people have the idea they don't have to repay rich people. It must be true, because it worked that way with Elvis.

Every year before tax time I had to get out the files on loans that hadn't been repaid. They were written off as tax losses.

It was easy enough for those close to Elvis to wheedle money and gifts from him, but he was an absolute pushover for charities. His father and the employees screened charity requests as best we could before forwarding the most deserving to him. Elvis gave about $100,000 annually to registered charities.

On Christmas or a day or two before that holiday, he or his father would walk into the offices of the Memphis newspapers, the *Commercial Appeal,* and the *Press Scimitar,* with one hundred or more checks for various charities. The checks were usually made out for five hundred or one thousand dollars each.

But Elvis gave throughout the year, and the annual total of his gifts to the needy was staggering.

Some of his favorite charities were Father Flanagan's Boys' Town, Father Tom's Indian School, Salvation Army, Girls' Club, Boys' Club, YMCA, YWCA, Muscular Dystrophy, Cerebral Palsy, March of Dimes, and the Motion Picture Relief Fund.[1] He also helped local charities in Memphis and in California communities where he lived or had other personal or business ties.

We kept in the office a photograph of actresses Janet Leigh and Barbara Rush shining Elvis's 1964 $35,000 Rolls Royce, which he presented to SHARE, a Hollywood womens' group. The luxury car was auctioned for funds to support their charities.

Elvis gave a $55,000 yacht, the *Potomac,* to St. Jude's Children's Hospital in Memphis. The yacht was once owned by President Franklin Delano Roosevelt. The March of Dimes and the Coast Guard Auxiliary in Miami had earlier rejected the yacht as a gift.

Some charity requests went through Colonel Parker, and you could be sure that if they got past him they were worthwhile.

Most requests had to be turned down. There were too many and they couldn't all be forwarded to Elvis. One woman wrote and asked him to pay for her four-hundred-dollar set of false teeth. I'm sure she needed them, but Elvis never saw the letter. It went into the files.

Newspapers carried a story after I left about a fan, Mrs. Jeannette Erickson, who was bitter because Elvis didn't send her a get-well card when she was hospitalized. Mrs. Erickson, a Seattle widow on welfare, was founder of the eighty-eight member Elvis Presley Flaming Star Club. She said she had offered to donate one of her eyes to him when she heard that he was losing the sight in his left eye. She further claimed she had spent about a thousand dollars buying him birthday presents and telephoning long distance to wish him well.

Elvis never responded, so she took his pictures off her walls, disbanded the club, and switched her allegiance to an Elvis imitator, Johnny Rusk.

I'm sure it was true that Elvis didn't send the woman a get-well card. He probably didn't know there was a Jeannette Erickson. He has hundreds of thousands of fans and he can't get to know each of them individually. If he were to chat with everyone who telephones him, he would never get anything else done.

However, Elvis did telephone some sick children and

adults. He also mailed cards, pictures, and anonymous gifts of money to needy people. But even with his great wealth and earning capacity, he couldn't help everyone. Not even the U. S. government can do that.

People are quick to see the commercial opportunities surrounding anything that can be considered an Elvis memento. Articles of his personal clothing are always being auctioned as fund raisers for charity.

Early in 1976 the manager of a Holiday Inn in Bristol, Tennessee, donated bedsheets Elvis slept between, for auction to raise money for the local Episcopal Church Day School. Manager Jack Trayer said that aluminum foil put over the windows to shut out the light while Elvis slept was also donated to the Bristol Humane Society and cut into strips for sale. Flowers from Elvis's room were given to crippled children.

Fans were constantly writing to Graceland asking to buy suits, shirts, or trousers as personal mementoes of Elvis. I've been offered a thousand dollars for a pair of Elvis's socks.

More of Elvis's charitable acts were anonymous than even his most devoted fans might suspect.

One of these was a large check that he mailed to Tennessee Sheriff Buford Pusser after the lawman's home was burned while he was fighting organized crime. Elvis admired Pusser for his one-man fight against corruption.

Few people have heard of the expensive slot-car track and cars that Elvis gave to a Memphis charity for boys.

Elvis went crazy over slot-cars for awhile. He rented a little track in Memphis initially, but he finally got so involved in running the cars that he decided to build his own racecourse so that he and the boys could play with them anytime they wished.

To accommodate the track he spent about eight thousand dollars building a fifty- by eighty-foot room connecting the house with the swimming pool. Lush blue carpeting was laid, with eight leather-covered stools, a Pepsi-Cola fountain, and cigarette, candy, and gum machines. None of the machines required coins. Elvis and the guys played with the cars four times before he tired of them. The cars and track were then given away, and he converted the room to a trophy display area.

generosity was misleading and that most of the money and valuable gifts he gave away were part of a calculated plan to reduce his declared income and get a tax break.

It's not true. Elvis didn't look for all kinds of tax loopholes as many wealthy people do, his accountant told me. He just made money, lots of it, and paid taxes on what he made, also lots of it. Elvis may have paid some of the highest personal taxes of anyone in the country, the accountant said.

He considered it part of his duty for the privilege of living in this country. It's the same attitude he took when he was drafted into the army. Elvis didn't fight it or join the National Guard, as many professional baseball and football players did, to avoid active military service. He was an American and proud of it, so he served his time.

People are always wondering how much money Elvis really earned and how much he was worth. But I'm not sure that he could have told them. Elvis never seemed very much interested in what he was earning, or where the money was going. His daddy and Colonel Parker handled his business.

I never saw the money that was coming into Graceland. Just part of what was going out.

One year in the early 1970's, a ledger sheet was left lying in the open, showing net earnings of about four million dollars. Writers for newspapers and magazines have claimed Elvis was earning five million dollars or more; it was probably more than that. As long ago as 1970, he was receiving $200,000 a week at Las Vegas. While other big-name performers were hurt by the country's economic recession a couple of years later, Elvis was, as always, packing in customers at Las Vegas. And he was being paid accordingly.

Royalties from his movies and records are, of course, a constant source of new income.

Elvis made a few investments. He bought a small amount of real estate, but most of it was unimproved land. Several years ago he bought two hundred feet of frontage directly across Elvis Presley Boulevard from Graceland.

Some of his business interests included full or part ownership of the Elvis Presley Music Company, Whitehaven Music Company, Gladys Music Company, and Hill and Range Music Company.

Since leaving Graceland, I've been told that Elvis and the Colonel set up their own record label, Boxcar, in Madison, Tennessee, near Nashville.

There were rumors that Elvis owned stock in RCA and other companies, but in the years that I worked for him I never took a telephone call about stock, saw a letter from a stockbroker, or paid a broker's fee. There was no communication through me from stockbrokers for either Elvis or Mr. Presley. And Mr. Presley insisted that all the business not involving Elvis's performances was handled at Graceland.

Colonel Parker, of course, was Elvis's professional manager. And for that he got twenty-five percent of Elvis's earnings. I know, because I made out commission checks.

Checks were also made out to the William Morris Booking Agency, headed by Abe Lastfogel, Elvis's personal agent.

Stories cropped up periodically about feuds between Elvis and Colonel Parker, rumors of splits and that sort of thing. They may have quarreled, but I think they realized that they needed each other and continued to honor their partnership until Elvis died.

Elvis and Colonel Parker had a disagreement in 1974 over a ninety-minute gospel show on television. Elvis didn't want to do the show, and the colonel said that he should. Elvis grumbled about getting a new manager, but I don't think he was serious. Mr. Presley dictated a letter to Colonel Parker and the problem was worked out amicably.

I never saw Colonel Parker at Graceland, although I talked with him by telephone occasionally, and my husband saw him there once. Jerry, in fact, was a bit peeved about his brief brush with the outspoken colonel. ("Colonel" is, in Parker's case, an honorary title bestowed by the State of Tennessee.)

Jerry, with Joe Esposito, Lamar Fike, and John Kingsley, had driven to a near-by lake to bring Elvis's boat back to Graceland. While Jerry and John were unhooking the boat from the trailer they heard a bull-horn voice boom from under the canopy at the mansion: "Who the hell are them damned guys? Get them sons-of-bitches out of here."

It was Colonel Parker, and he was standing with Elvis. Elvis didn't say anything until Colonel Parker calmed down, and then he explained that it was two friends of his helping bring in his boat for the winter.

That was the end of the incident, but Jerry and John weren't happy about it. No one likes to do someone else a favor and then get cussed for it.

I handled bills for Elvis's Memphis and California expenses and for his ranch in Mississippi. I also worked on the payroll, employees' insurance, and helped make up total-sheets of monthly expenditures.

Expenditures sometimes ran more than $100,000 per month on the "Elvis Presley Payroll and Expense Fund." This didn't include checks written on a separate "E. A. Presley" account. As Elvis's executive business administrator, Mr. Presley kept the E. A. Presley checkbook, which was reserved for the largest checks.

Some of the boys also had checkbooks to handle expenses while Elvis was performing away from Memphis.

Mr. Presley often toured with Elvis, and before leaving he would instruct me to take care of the office until he returned. The accountant was authorized to sign the checks, which I would fill out while Mr. Presley was away. (Costume costs alone were about eleven thousand dollars while Elvis was performing in Las Vegas.)

I've filled out checks for telephone bills for just one line at Graceland that totalled sixteen hundred dollars for one month. Elvis's American Express charge would sometimes run six thousand dollars a month.

Some of the American Express charges were for clothes the guys bought for Elvis. They would pick up a dozen pair of pajamas at a time for fifteen or sixteen dollars each. They seldom purchased one of anything if it was for Elvis.

Elvis regularly bought jumpsuits for eight hundred dollars each from the I. C. Costume Company for his Las Vegas tours. Some costumes were as expensive as $2,500 each. The scarves he threw to girls at his performances cost twenty dollars each. Later some were found for five dollars.

Despite, or probably because of, the hundreds of thousands of dollars Elvis spent every month, his daddy tried his best to keep an eye on every penny that went out. That's no exaggeration—every penny!

At Mr. Presley's direction, I made telephone calls and wrote letters about bills that appeared to be a penny or a dime too much. Mr. Presley pays his bills, but he expects to receive his money's worth. He can be unpleasant if he thinks he has been cheated.

1. Elvis donated more than $250,000 to the Motion Picture Relief Fund during a two-year period when he was making movies. The fund provides medical and extended care facilities for elderly veterans of the film industry.

Chapter Six

Mr. Presley

On the preceding
page: Mr. Vernon
Presley and his wife
Dee.

Vernon Elvis Presley knew how to enjoy the good times. But he never forgot the hard times.

Mr. Presley and Elvis's mother, Gladys Smith, were married during the worst days of the Great Depression. It was 1933, and seventeen-year-old Vernon was working with his father on a neighbor's farm, cultivating cotton and vegetables for a share of the profits from the crop. Four years older than her teen-aged husband, Gladys was working as a sewing machine operator at the Tupelo Garment Company in Milltown.

Things didn't get a whole lot better for the Presleys for a long time. Vernon and Gladys always managed to put enough food on the table for themselves and, later, for Elvis. Mr. Presley said his wife was the best cook he had ever known. She cooked meals with greens and burned bacon, mashed potatoes and brown gravy, and black-eyed peas with salt pork and corn bread. Gladys Presley loved cooking for her men.

She made do with what she had. But there wasn't much left over for embellishments.

Elvis didn't talk much about his early life in East Tupelo. It could be that it hurt too much to be reminded of his mother. Gladys Presley was forty-six when she died, and it was the worst thing that ever happened to Elvis. Worse than his divorce. Worse than anything else.

But his daddy talked about her. And he talked about the hard times they shared before Elvis was born and when Elvis was growing up. Mr. Presley would travel miles for a day's work. He told us he once found work several miles away in New Albany, Mississippi, and rode a bus back and forth, starting out before daylight and getting home after dark. One night he didn't have enough money for the return bus fare and had to walk the whole way after working all day. When he finally got home he was worn out—and it was almost time to start back.

Vernon moved from job to job during the Depression, taking whatever work he could get. As most of the men around north Mississippi did at one time or another, he did farm work. He also sorted lumber, worked as an apprentice carpenter, was a foreman for the federal Works Progress Administration (WPA), and for a time delivered milk door to door in East Tupelo.

He was working the milk route when he asked his boss, local dairy farmer Orville S. Bean, to finance a house for him. Bean paid for the lumber and then rented the house to the Presleys. It was the house that Elvis was born in.

Vernon said that he and his daddy built the house themselves. Two box-shaped rooms under a roof, it was thirty feet long and about fifteen feet wide. Plenty of

102

other poor folks in northern Mississippi and other parts of the South lived in houses just like the one that Vernon and Jesse Presley built. They called them shotgun houses because someone could fire a shotgun through the front door and it would go out the back without hitting anything in between. Most folks didn't own much to put between the doors, unless it was a bunch of ragged little kids.

It was tiny but it must have looked like a mansion to the young couple, who had been squeezed in first with Gladys's folks and then with Vernon's kin. The house has been preserved and stands near a community center in Elvis Presley Park in East Tupelo.

The little wood frame house is furnished with items said to be authentic to the period, if not necessarily to the Presleys themselves. On the twelve acres of wooded Mississippi hill land that surround the house, there are now tennis courts, a swimming pool, a lake for fishing, and picnic grounds.

Elvis left that house when he was thirteen. His folks packed up their few belongings in paper sacks and cardboard boxes and, in an old 1939 Plymouth, headed for Memphis. Mr. Presley had heard he might have a chance of finding a steady job there. It was 1948.

Mr. Presley said they were worse off at first than they had been in Mississippi. They were still dirt poor, and Mr. Presley crammed his family into a one-room apartment in one of the most run-down sections of Memphis about a mile from the Mississippi River. They cooked on a hot plate and shared a bath with three other families.

Patsy asked Mr. Presley once if he remembered having roaches in that apartment. He did. "They were the biggest roaches I have ever seen," he said, his mouth turning down in disgust. "Some of them were a couple

103

inches long at least, and there wasn't nothing we could do to get rid of them. You could kill a few, but before it got dark they would be right back." There were dozens of people living in cut-up cubicles in the old house on Poplar street, and there was no way you could clear the roaches from one room since they infested all the others.

The Presleys learned to live with them, as they learned to live with other discomforts. It was just another of the disadvantages of being poor.

Elvis was a few weeks away from completing his freshman year at Humes High School when his family was approved for public housing. They moved into a two-bedroom apartment in the Lauderdale Courts, part of a 433-unit project just across the street from the shanties of some of the city's poorest blacks.

Mr. Presley remembered that the apartment had a lot wrong with it. But the problems were nothing compared to the wretchedness of the shoebox apartment they had been living in on Poplar street.

There were endless reports to make out, however, and someone was always inspecting their apartment and everyone else's. When Mr. Presley talked about that, his voice would get lower, gruffer, and dimmer. He seemed to come from somewhere deep in his chest. He hated those reports.

The worst part of it, he said, was that every time it looked as though he and Gladys might be about to improve their family situation by making a few extra dimes or saving a few dollars, someone with the housing authority would decide they had too much money and should move out. It wasn't good enough to be poor, he said; you had to be flat on your back, and if you tried to get up someone told you to lay down again. It was put up with that, or get out.

104

By late 1951 Mr. Presley had found himself a steady but low-paying job, making about two thousand dollars a year with the United Paint Company in Memphis. Mrs. Presley got a job as a nurses' aide and began chipping in four dollars a day to the family funds. When Mr. Presley got a ten-dollar-a-week raise it boosted the family income well over the three-thousand-dollar eligibility limit established by the Memphis Public Housing Authority for remaining in the project. The Presleys were told they would have to move. Mr. Presley recalled that the housing authority agreed to let them stay only after his wife quit her job. "They just wouldn't let you get ahead," he said, shaking his head as if he still couldn't understand the bureaucratic reasoning. Mr. Presley was thirty-nine when he left public housing, the paint factory, and poverty behind thanks to Elvis's first successes in the music business.

For the most part, when he talked about the hard times, Mr. Presley didn't look as though the memories were all that distasteful to him. They were, after all, memories he shared with Elvis's mother, and I never heard Mr. Presley or anyone else say anything bad about her. Everyone who knew her said the same thing: She was a kind, gentle, loving woman devoted to her family.

Mr. Presley and Elvis were also devoted to each other. I quickly learned that if you had trouble with one you couldn't expect to go to the other and say his son or father had done something wrong. That was a good way to find yourself permanently standing outside the Music Gate. When Elvis talked about his father he called him "Daddy," and it was always with respect.

Mr. Presley had power of attorney for Elvis and took over a lot of his son's business affairs, shielding him from people who would interfere with his privacy. His job wasn't always easy. He was expected to deal with lawyers, bankers, politicians, doctors, and all types of professional people. He was at a disadvantage because he had only an eighth grade education. But he had a perceptive, shrewd mind and he was able to grasp concepts and solve problems that could be expected to be far too complex for an individual of his educational background. He studied the problems until he figured them out. If he needed help he contacted professionals who could obtain or explain information for him.

For years Mr. Presley and Elvis were legal clients of E. Gregory Hookstratten, a West Coast attorney who also represented other celebrities, such as comedians Dan Rowan and Dick Martin, and sportscaster Vin Scully.

There were some mistakes and poor investments in handling of the Presley money. Everyone in business picks a loser sometimes. About the biggest business disappointment Mr. Presley had was an investment in Texas cattle. Most of the cattle apparently died, and the entire affair ended in court. Mr. Presley and his attorney had to fly to Texas to testify.

I was matron of honor at the wedding of Mr. Presley's niece Patsy. When she forgot to give me the ring for the ceremony I got so nervous I could hardly stand. Mr. Presley told me later not to feel bad about it. He said he had been just as nervous when he went to court, and was shaking so much during the oath that he could hardly hold his hand on the Bible.

The pressure affected him, and there were times when he was obviously worried about his responsibility for such large amounts of his son's money. And there were times when he worried because of the amounts Elvis was spending.

Those were times when he would take his worry out or the staff. Whomever he had given the most responsibility to in the office got it the worst. If he gave one of the secretaries a job to do and was asked when he wanted it completed, his stock answer was always "Yesterday." He never smiled when he said that.

He was a hard taskmaster. I once became ill at work with the Hong Kong flu and told him I had to go home. He said if I would type a couple of letters first he would drive me. I was so sick and dizzy I could hardly see, but I typed the letters. Then he drove me home. I was in bed for three days.

There were days when he grouched at everyone. On those days he would push open the door to the office and the first thing he would say would be, "What's the matter, y'all dead or something?"

He could complain one minute because we didn't keep the office clean enough to suit him, and the next minute he would spit on the floor.

Or he might ask if we had seen a certain television show the night before. It made him angry if we hadn't watched it. "What do y'all do at night, anyway?" he would growl. We knew those days were going to be difficult and tried to keep out of his way. He, like Elvis and Aunt Delta, had an explosive temper.

The other secretaries and I, including his niece, Patsy, were scared to death of getting on the bad side of him. Bonya and I were sitting on lawn chairs sunning and chatting with Uncle Travis at the gate during our lunch break one day when Mr. Presley drove by. It upset him. He said he didn't like seeing us sitting by the gate, and we never did it again.

We chanced getting fired a few times on some of

Memphis's hotter summer days. Bonya, the other secretary and I began sneaking naps on the couch in our air conditioned office after getting the guard to promise to call us if Mr. Presley drove through the gate. He forgot to call us one day. Suddenly we heard Mr. Presley just outside the office window, yelling something to one of the yard men. Both of us rolled off the couch and onto the floor and crawled to our desks on our hands and knees so he wouldn't see us. We made it just in time.

Mr. Presley didn't have to be angry to throw the mail at us. As he sorted it he tossed the bills and letters at me. Some of them landed on my desk, some on the floor. Others struck me in the face, some coming dangerously close to my eyes. He could be an exasperating man to work for.

He always went through the mail first if he was in the office. At other times when one of the other girls or I sorted it, we found all kinds of pornography. He liked to show the magazines to us. His name was on more than one mailing list.

It wasn't alcohol that made Mr. Presley moody and difficult at times. He didn't drink much during the years I was at Graceland. He was a borderline diabetic and couldn't safely drink. After I left he had a heart attack. My mother cared for his girlfriend's children while he was hospitalized.

Mr. Presley had always appeared to me to be reasonably healthy before his attack. He wasn't skinny, but neither was he grossly overweight, and he hadn't shown any signs of possible ill health. He appeared to take good care of himself and was extremely careful about his grooming and appearance. His eyebrows and mustache were dyed or tinted periodically by Elvis's private hairdressers.

108

Mr. Presley appeared to be happiest when he was tinkering with his cars. He loved cars and engines as much as Elvis did, and like Elvis he had a Mercedes-Benz for a time. He drove it for a while before selling it to opera singer Nancy Tatum. He later got a new silver Fleetwood Brougham Cadillac.

For a time he went into business with a Memphis used car dealer and established the "Doc" Hayes/Vernon Presley Motor Sales. The partnership was dissolved after a while, and the secretary, Doris O'Neal, transferred to Graceland and went on Elvis's payroll. She left after a few weeks when her husband was transferred to a job in Arkansas.

Elvis's daddy liked fixing old cars better than selling them. We never knew what we would see being towed up the drive, and I told him a few times that I wouldn't have been surprised to see a locomotive parked on the lawn when I came to work.

More than once I watched through the window as Mr. Presley bent over an old car, his head hidden under the hood, his shirt collar open and his sleeves rolled up while he messed with the engine. Or the other secretaries and I would be jolted by the ear-shattering popping of an engine as Mr. Presley sat in the driver's seat with his foot pressing the accelerator to the floor.

Mr. Presley often crawled under an old car in an impeccable business suit.

He didn't do the serious work himself; mostly he tinkered. One of his favorite vehicles was a Ford built sometime shortly after World War II. He took it to two men to restore and they sent him a bill for $9,942.05.

The day the bill arrived was one of Mr. Presley's bad days. He was willing to pay honest fees for honest work, but he wouldn't knowingly permit anyone to take unfair

109

advantage of him. His face flushed and he slammed the bill down on the desk when he saw the charges. He was furious and refused to pay. The bill was finally settled for less than $2,000.

The penny-counting, the struggle to save and the buying on credit ended when Elvis's leg-shaking, pelvis swiveling style of music made him world famous. But Mr. Presley still wouldn't stand for paying inflated prices for something just because he was Elvis's daddy.

However, neither the father nor the son forgot people who had been good to them before Elvis became famous. Elvis probably bought more single pieces of jewelry from Harry Levitch Jewelers in Memphis than from any other jeweler in the country. My husband and I were having coffee with the owners, Harry and Frances Levitch, after a wedding, and Mr. Levitch told us how they first met Elvis.

Elvis was just beginning to sing professionally when he walked into their store and picked out a piece of jewelry he wanted. Elvis hadn't established credit, but the Levitches sold him the item on time. "For some reason," Mr. Levitch said, "I just liked and trusted him. He looked like the kind of young man who would pay his bills." The Levitches have kept a large picture of Elvis in their office for years.

Amazingly, considering the large amount of jewelry Elvis owns, it wasn't insured at the time I left Graceland. There had once been a policy, but there were so many clauses and so many exceptions that could prohibit payment that it was decided it wasn't worth renewing the coverage.

Mr. Presley has spent a lot of time in jewelry stores since Elvis made it big. Once, a jeweler waiting on him

110

in Las Vegas told him about the terrific show that Elvis was putting on and advised him not to miss it. Mr. Presley hadn't identified himself as Elvis's father. He said the compliments about Elvis were some of the nicest he had ever heard, because he knew they were sincere.

He went to Las Vegas and on most of Elvis's tours. I was always instructed at those times to take care of the office and to telephone twice a week to keep him informed about business matters.

On the set of one of Elvis's movies in Hollywood, he once approached a well-known star of a television western and introduced himself as Elvis's father. "I don't care who the hell you are," the actor growled, and continued walking. Mr. Presley was hurt by the star's reaction and said he was merely trying to be friendly.

Most of the actors and actresses were nicer, and Mr. Presley always enjoyed meeting movie stars and other celebrities. He had a nonspeaking part in one of Elvis's 1968 films, *Live a Little, Love a Little.* Elvis's mother also appeared as a member of an audience in *Loving You,* a 1957 Paramount picture about a young truck driver who makes it big as a singer. There were so many parallels with his own career it must have been an easy role for him to play. But for years after his mother's death, he wouldn't watch the film because she was in it.

Mr. Presley's status as Elvis's father didn't hurt his own reputation with the ladies. Not long after Mrs. Presley died, Elvis was transferred by the army from Fort Hood, Texas, to Germany for duty. Ironically, both father and son met their future wives there.

After a suitable period of mourning, Mr. Presley met a pretty blond American, Davada "Dee" Elliott Stanley, just then in the process of dissolving her marriage to an army sergeant. By the time Elvis was discharged from the army on March 5, 1960, the relationship between Dee and his father had ripened. On July 3, Dee became the new Mrs. Vernon Presley in a secret ceremony at the home of her brother in Huntsville, Alabama.

The new Mrs. Presley, with her three young sons, moved briefly into Graceland. Not long after that the Vernon Presleys moved into a house on Hermitage Street, then into a new $23,000 five-bedroom white brick, Dutch style home on Dolan Street in the Graceland subdivision at the rear of Elvis's estate.

Walking into the Vernon Presley home was an experience. It had the same little-of-this, little-of-that sort of decorating as the mansion. Pictures of Elvis and later also of Lisa were on the walls and shelves of nearly every room. Most of Dee's things were ultramodern. Most of Mr. Presley's were western. The huge living room was dominated by an outsized, egg-shaped television set that looked as though it belonged in the twenty-first century. It was made especially for Elvis by RCA, which was producing his records. He gave it to his father and Dee.

The big surprise was in the main bedroom. Mr. Presley and Dee had an eight-foot-square, tiled swimming pool installed there. Air jets in the sides converted it into a whirlpool for muscle relaxation. A more conventional swimming pool was built at the rear of the house, overlooking Elvis's mansion and estate.

Mr. Presley's house was run like Elvis's. Dee is an ebullient and gregarious woman, and lights were on in the house all night. Someone seemed always to be up, just as someone was always up across the way at Graceland. A thirty-cup coffee pot was almost always perking, and snacks were kept in the icebox and on tables for the

112

older Presleys or their guests. Mr. Presley had insomnia and would often stay awake all night.

Vernon and Dee ate when they were hungry and went to bed when they were tired. They didn't serve regular meals but snacked or had food brought in. They often ate out.

Dee keeps active with business and self-improvement projects. With her calls and Mr. Presley's business calls, telephones were ringing almost constantly. The atmosphere was like an organized madhouse, if there is such a thing. It could be hectic at the mansion too, but the chaos there wasn't as noticeable because Elvis's house was larger and fewer people lived there full time.

While I was at Graceland, Dee's sons were still young and living at home. Elvis immediately hit it off with Richard (Ricky), Billy, and David, and the three boys followed him around like admiring puppies. Elvis and his buddies roughhoused and played touch football and softball with them. Two of the boys eventually began playing the drums and guitar; they were going to become famous musicians like their celebrated stepbrother.

Dee was protective of the boys. She did what she could to shield them from too much publicity. A movie magazine quoted her as complaining several years ago that fourteen- and fifteen-year-old girls were sending "terrible notes" to the boys while they were in Las Vegas. Whenever they were recognized as Elvis's stepbrothers, they were besieged by fans. Pretty girls, older and more experienced than they, would do almost anything on the outside chance that it could lead to a meeting with Elvis.

Dee knows how to have a good time, but she is a regular churchgoer who has taught Sunday school and vaca-

113

tion Bible school, and she is sincere about her religion. She was also sincere about the job of raising her boys properly.

She tried to keep them from being overly influenced by Elvis's unique station in life. Still, there were times when it was impossible to pretend that they were part of a normal family leading a normal life. Elvis showered them with expensive gifts, just as he did everyone else close to him. The boys grew up to know they were step-brothers of the most famous performer in the world. Eventually Billy, Ricky, and David went on Elvis's payroll with the older guys.

There was nothing Dee could do to shield her son Ricky from publicity in 1975 when he was arrested and accused of attempting to obtain drugs (Demerol) from the Methodist Hospital Pharmacy in Memphis with a forged prescription. The charge against Elvis's twenty-one-year-old stepbrother was eventually reduced to malicious mischief, and he was fined fifty dollars, given a six-month suspended jail sentence, and put on supervised probation.

Police Lieutenant J. L. Vaughters said that Elvis appeared at the Memphis police headquarters at five o'clock in the morning to lecture the young man.[1]

"He gave Stanley a piece of his mind and told him to go to a hospital and see a psychiatrist," Vaughters said. "He told him that is the one thing he hates—anything to do with drugs. He said he thought Stanley was disturbed to get into any trouble like this."

The policeman said that Elvis explained to Ricky that he wanted to help him, but insisted that the youth accept medical assistance. Elvis didn't ask for special police handling of his stepbrother, Vaughters said.

114

There was one other part-time occupant of the Vernon Presley household during Mr. Presley and Dee's years together—Dee's stepmother, Ma Elliott. Elvis was fond of the old lady.

She was in her late seventies and weighed about ninety-five pounds, but when it snowed, if Elvis was home the two of them would have a snowball fight. Elvis started it when he tossed a snowball at her one day, and she scooped up a handful of snow and winged one back at him. Elvis was like a playful bear when he and the old lady were sneaking around in the snow trying to catch each other by surprise.

Ma Elliott had another daughter she stayed with part of the time, so she wasn't always with Mr. Presley and Dee. But when she was staying there, you knew she was around.

She spotted a house guest cautiously peeking at the nub of her missing finger once and told hm, "I got it chopping stove wood, Sonny." Ma Elliott speaks out. She also insists on keeping her hands close to the earth, and most of the time in the summer she would nurture half a dozen tomato plants or some other vegetables in a little patch of ground near the house. Members of the household discussed the health of her tomato plants with the same concern they showed for million-dollar deals.

In some ways Dee was like Elvis. She was one of the most vivacious human beings I've ever met, and when she was around her presence dominated. Elvis impressed people with a different kind of charm. Despite all his popularity and fame, he could still be shy, reticent, and cautious around strangers. But even when Elvis was at his quietest, his personality made itself felt on everyone around him.

115

Dee acted as though there were no strangers in the world. She enjoyed being Elvis Presley's stepmother and lived the role to the hilt. She wore around the house dresses the likes of which other women couldn't have afforded to hang in their closets for the fanciest parties. They were simply housedresses to Dee. Her taste in clothes was flamboyant. At social functions in Memphis such as the annual Easter Seal benefit, she might show up garbed in an ankle-length white fur coat, a sequined dress, white boots, and shades. At her best she doesn't merely enter rooms—she sweeps into them with the practiced grace and self-assurance of a movie queen.

An attractive woman when she and Mr. Presley married, she did everything she could to keep herself that way. She went to a plastic surgeon for a face lift and later had her breasts lifted. She was meticulous about her grooming and kept a wardrobe as stylish as any in Memphis.

Dee kept busy and always had some new interest she was involved in. She once trained to become a laboratory technician, but I believe she switched to something else before completing the course. There were never enough hours in the day or enough activities for her.

She once signed with a Memphis modeling agency and modeled street clothes at fashion shows and clubs. That also ended after a few months. Like Elvis, she could get excited about all kinds of projects or hobbies, spend a pile of money on them, and then lose interest. She could give the impression of being a lovable scatterbrain. But her sometimes scattershot approach to things merely reflects her zest for living and her naturally inquisitive mind. Dee can be a good friend and a pleasant, exciting person to be around; but it would be a mistake for most people to try and match the frenetic pace she keeps.

116

Music seemed to hold her interest the longest. She began writing songs, and when she completed one that she was particularly fond of, she would telephone the office to play a tape of it for the other secretary and me. Many of the people around Elvis, including Mr. Presley, tried song writing at one time or another. He also taped one of his songs and played it for us.

Dee was in a position to get her foot in the door to music producers, other song writers, and performers. And she wasn't shy about using the Presley name to gain entree. After his marriage to her started going sour, Mr. Presley told another secretary and me that Dee had said she didn't want a divorce because she didn't want to give up her "title." She wanted to be recognized for her own accomplishments, yet she was aware of the enormous advantage of being Elvis's stepmother.

Mr. Presley filed in a Memphis court in May 1977 for a divorce, citing irreconcilable differences. They had been separated three years. Mr. Presley told reporters he regretted that they "could not reconcile our differences because of my travel." Dee also said she regretted that the differences couldn't be worked out.[2]

I learned how concerned Dee could be about her image and Elvis's when a man hired to work on a temporary basis as a grounds keeper was discharged and decided to use me to get even with the Presleys. I had rejected a couple of his passes, so he also had reason to involve me in the plot. When he was told that the employee he replaced had recovered from illness and was ready to return to work, he was so angry that he went to Dee's house and told her he had seen Mr. Presley and me kissing in the office.

The first I heard anything about the grounds keeper's accusations was when I returned from lunch and Mr.

117

Presley was waiting in the office. He was standing at the window staring outside when I walked in and began slipping off the light spring jacket I was wearing.

"Becky," he said. "You're going to have to go in the house and talk to Dee. Tell her we weren't in here kissing each other." Mr. Presley didn't turn from the window, and he had his back to me.

I couldn't believe what I was hearing. "What did you say?" I gasped. "Tell Dee *what?*"

"Tell Dee that we haven't been in here kissin'," he said, turning around and looking at me. "This guy we let go told her he saw us kissin' in here. I told her it wasn't true, but she still wants to talk to you."

It was incredible. Mr. Presley and I hadn't even been getting along well. I thought he had been especially grouchy lately, and I knew he wasn't satisfied that I was working hard enough. I couldn't see either one of us kissing the other. But there was nothing to do but go talk to Dee. I could feel my knees trembling, and the palms of my hands were damp as I walked into the house.

Dee was waiting for me in Grandma's room. She was terribly upset, and her voice was shaking so much that she could hardly talk.

"Dee, I didn't do it," I said. "I just wouldn't do anything like that." We were both standing, facing each other. Grandma was sitting in her rocker, quietly watching the two of us.

"It's going to be in all the newspapers. It's going to be in all the fan magazines," Dee moaned.

"Dee, we didn't do anything . . . I didn't do anything," I said. "My God, I haven't even been married to my husband for very long. I'm not looking for an affair with a married man."

118

Dee groaned. Grandma could see that I was getting upset. It was frustrating, frightening, to be denying the whole thing and watching Dee act as though she hadn't heard me. How could I defend myself? Grandma got up and put her wrinkled old hand on Dee's shoulder.

"Dee, Honey," she said, "Becky's a good girl, and I know you don't have nothing to worry about." She didn't say Mr. Presley was a good boy.

I let Grandma do most of the talking, and she finally got Dee calmed down. I don't think Dee was so much jealous of me as she was horrified at the thought of a scandal. She didn't want anything to hurt Elvis or the family.

When my husband came to pick me up that night, Mr. Presley told him about the accusations and the trouble with Dee. Jerry laughed about it.

The former yard man was still upset, and a day or two later he showed up at the gate, demanding to see Elvis. Elvis came to the gate, there were a couple of sharp words exchanged, and Elvis punched him in the face. Not long after that Elvis's pink jeep was mysteriously damaged by fire.

It wasn't I that Dee had to worry about. It was Sandy Miller, an attractive blond divorcée and operating room technician from Denver whom Mr. Presley met while he was in Las Vegas with Elvis.

Early in 1973 or shortly before, I noticed that Mr. Presley was hanging around the office more than usual. Sometimes he would stretch out on the couch and relax or nap. Several times while he was there he would take telephone calls from a woman. But that wasn't unusual. Mr. Presley took business calls every day and most of them were placed by secretaries.

As I was driving home from work one afternoon, however, I saw Mr. Presley riding in a car with a blonde who wasn't his wife. The telephone calls and the office naps suddenly became significant. By 1974 he was treating his relationship with Sandy as an open secret, referring to her by name and occasionally playing in the office some of the tapes that he was recording and mailing to her. Sometimes he read her letters to Paulette and me. It didn't sound as if he left any details out.

Early in 1974 Mr. Presley rented an apartment and Sandy moved to Memphis. He sent Paulette and me to the apartment on two different days to wait for the telephone company to install the phone and for the electric company to turn on the lights.

We carried a portable television set to the apartment to watch while we waited. We were ready to plug it in and then realized that it wouldn't work without electricity. Later that day a new television set arrived anyway. Mr. Presley bought new furniture for the apartment.

Early the day Sandy was to arrive, Mr. Presley bought groceries and told Paulette and me to take them to the apartment and wait for her. He gave us three dollars for lunch.

"Two of us can't eat on that, Mr. Presley," I complained.

He dug into his pocket, pulled out two more one-dollar bills, and handed them to me.

We dropped and broke a gallon of milk on the way to the house and had to spend more than a dollar of our lunch money to replace it.

Sandy and I became good friends. We are nearly the same age, and I found her to be a considerate person and fun to be with. I also liked Dee, but Sandy was more like a friend than my boss's girlfriend or wife. She didn't know anyone else in Memphis at that time, and I guess it was natural that she looked to me for companionship when she wasn't with Mr. Presley.

Mr. Presley didn't like the apartment. He had gotten enough of living in two or three rooms when he was poor, and he didn't have to put up with it any more. Sandy had a little girl and two boys, and three young children can make even a large apartment seem small. So Mr. Presley bought a house on Old Hickory Street.

He was in Las Vegas when Sandy decided to paint the interior of her new home. Jerry and I said we would help.

We got started early that day. About ten o'clock Jerry was in the bedroom painting, and Sandy and I were in the kitchen, with our hair pulled back and held with rubber bands, wearing bluejeans rolled halfway to our knees and men's worn shirts. We were cleaning out cabinets and stacking canned goods.

We heard rapid footsteps approaching through the carport.

Dee was wearing bright silver pants, a black see-through top with silver fringe, and no bra. Delicate-looking sandals were on her feet.

"You're Sandy," she smiled, flashing her teeth and glancing down at Sandy's ragged tennis shoes. "I've been wanting to meet you and see your home."

Sandy was stunned. She stood there a moment, oblivious of the water dripping to the floor from the wet cleaning rag in her hand.

"It's lovely," Dee said, pivoting slightly and glancing

at the paint-smeared newspapers on the floor, the shelf paper, the paper sacks, and the boxes stacked on the table.

"It's nice to meet you," Sandy mumbled.

Her little girl, Laura, had wandered into the room. "What do you think of Vernon?" Dee asked, looking down at Laura and smiling. "He's nice," said Laura.

Dee asked me what I was doing there. "I just came over to help Sandy with the painting," I said. Dee acted as though she were disappointed, as though I had somehow double-crossed her. She didn't see Jerry; he'd heard her talking and stayed in the bedroom. But he peeked out the window when she left and saw her getting into a car with a man. It was someone from outside the Presley circle of friends and employees.

Sandy and I continued our friendship. Before my parents moved to Mississippi, my mother sometimes stayed with Sandy's children when Sandy was with Vernon in Las Vegas or on tour. Dee ultimately moved out of the house behind Graceland and Sandy moved in.

The incident at the house was upsetting for Sandy, but she and Dee later became friends and appear to have a good relationship. They sometimes have coffee together. It isn't difficult to guess who they talk about.

1. *National Star,* September 2, 1975.
2. The *Commercial Appeal,* Memphis, May 6, 1977.

Chapter Seven

Priscilla

On the preceding
page: Priscilla Beau-
lieu Presley. (Blue
Light Studios)

*M*ajor Joseph P. Beaulieu stood militarily erect and seemed to tower over the five-feet-two girl beside him.

Dwarfed by the officer's size, she shyly smiled acknowledgment as Mr. Presley announced, to the secretaries "This is Major Beaulieu and his daughter, Priscilla. She'll be staying here as our house guest."[1]

It was the end of summer and I had been working at Graceland for about six months when I first met the pretty teen-ager who five years later was to become Elvis's wife.

She was carefully dressed in a neat white suit with black shoes and wore her dark hair in the short bouffant that was so popular in those days.

She got over her shyness about as soon as her father left Graceland for his new assignment at Travis Air Force base near San Francisco.

125

Although I'm five years older than Priscilla, Patsy Presley Gambill and I were closest to her in age of the women at the mansion. The only others were the maids and Grandma Presley. Elvis's Aunt Delta didn't move in until a few years later.

Her second day there, Priscilla popped into the office and stayed a couple of hours chattering about Graceland, Memphis, what it was like to be an Army brat—and Elvis. Her vists became a nearly everyday occurrence that both Patsy and I looked forward to.

She would wander into the office wearing slacks, blouse, and ballerina shoes, often rubbing her blue-green eyes or stifling a yawn. She regularly attended late-night movie parties with Elvis, and sat up into the wee hours of the morning at informal gatherings of his court at Graceland.

As she became more comfortable, she began to confide in us.

I mentioned one day that I thought her father must be very impressive and handsome in his uniform. "I guess you must be proud of him," I said.

"Oh, sure," Priscilla replied. "But you know, he's not my real father. Just a minute and I'll show you what my real father looks like." She jumped up and ran into the house.

She took a faded picture of a man in a uniform from her billfold and held it up, making a half-frame with her thumb and forefinger. "That's my real father," she said. "He died when I was four years old."

Priscilla told us that she was still a small child when her mother married Lieutenant Beaulieu. Her mother's new husband adopted her. Priscilla did not talk publicly about the adoption, and it has not been generally known to Elvis's fans.

"Mom and Dad raised me on military bases with my sister and brothers," she said.[2]

Major Beaulieu brought her to Graceland when he was transferred to Travis from his previous duty station in Wiesbaden, Germany.

It was in Germany that Priscilla first met Elvis. It was almost their last meeting, Priscilla said.

"One of the airmen, Curry Grant, knew Elvis and said he would introduce us," Priscilla recalled.

Grant picked up the then-captain's fourteen-year-old daughter and, after promising to have her home before midnight, drove to the near-by army base at Bad Nauheim to introduce her to the twenty-five-year-old jeep driver and internationally known performer.

"Elvis was just wonderful," Priscilla remembered. "He sang and played the piano. He was very charming. Would you believe it, he got up and shook my hand when I walked in and said, 'Hi. I'm Elvis Presley.'"

Elvis was charmed by the impish beauty of the petite girl in the crisp little sailor dress. He kept the party going until after midnight, despite Grant's nervous pleas that he had to get the captain's daughter home.

"They were waiting up for us when Curry got me home, and Dad was mad," Priscilla said. "I told him there was nothing wrong, that three or four of Elvis's friends were there with their dates and a couple of other girls. It was all so very informal and natural."

Grant also assured the Beaulieus that the party was properly chaperoned, and they were somewhat mollified.

"But Mom and Dad said I was too young to date Elvis," she said. "Well, I didn't think it made much difference anyway because I figured that I would never see him again. Then he called, and I couldn't have been more surprised."

Captain Beaulieu said there would be no date. "But Mom talked him into letting me go." Priscilla smiled. "She said I might never get a chance like this again."

Priscilla was permitted to see Elvis again, but only after her acceptance of strict ground rules established by her parents. She was to observe rigidly the midnight curfew, and she was to get another escort instead of the young airman who had brought her home late from the first party.

The Beaulieus were a military family with strict codes of behavior for their children, and they insisted on chaperones who met their exciting standards.

Elvis's daddy and his fiancée, Dee, stepped in and offered personally to escort Priscilla to and from the parties. Several meetings followed between Mr. Presley and Dee, and the Beaulieus and they soon became close friends.

So when Elvis invited her to spend Christmas vacation at Graceland after he was discharged, the Beaulieus consented.

Shortly after that, they agreed Priscilla could stay and finish high school in Memphis. Raised as a Catholic, although as an adult she has turned to Protestant denominations, she finished her last year-and-a-half at Immaculate Conception High School, graduating in 1963.

Nothing could have been more proper than the circumstances under which Priscilla and Elvis were seeing each other in Germany. But the relationship between

Elvis and the sixteen-year-old beauty was more relaxed at Graceland. Considerably more.

The arrangements called for Priscilla to move in with Vernon and Dee, who were married by that time, and with Dee's three small sons in the Presleys' house at the rear of Graceland.

Priscilla had been at Graceland only a couple of days when I met her one midmorning coming down the stairway from the second floor. I was going into the den for coffee. There was no school and Priscilla had slept late. She was still wearing a pink shortie nightdress, with a light robe thrown over it. Elvis didn't come down until a couple of hours later.

Privacy was not one of the benefits of living at Graceland. Even though Elvis's privacy and that of others living at the mansion was respected in their own rooms, little could be kept secret.

And Elvis was surrounded by relatives. Not only his father and stepmother, but his grandmother, aunts, and uncles were all over. It was obvious to everyone that Priscilla was not sleeping at the Vernon Presleys.

A few months after Priscilla moved in she said that there had been some gossip and she was going to have to start parking her car in front of the Vernon Presleys' house on the nights Elvis was home.

As far as the outside world was concerned, Priscilla spent her nights at the Vernon Presleys'. Anything even hinting at a less chaste arrangement would have been bad for Elvis's image with his fans.

But when Elvis was home Priscilla slept upstairs. She moved into Grandma Presley's room and slept with the old lady when Elvis was traveling or in Hollywood. Only occasionally did she stay at the Vernon Presleys' or visit with her parents in California.

It was not until after the divorce that Priscilla made even the most oblique public reference to her relationship with Elvis having been less than pristine during their courtship.

Discussing Elvis's proposal of marriage in a *Ladies' Home Journal* interview, she remarked that even though they were content the way they were, at that time it wasn't considered nice for unmarried people to live together.[3]

When Priscilla first arrived she occupied herself with her school work and with exploring Graceland, getting to know all the people who were there constantly. And, of course, there were the parties with Elvis at the mansion, the amusement park, and the movies.

Elvis's strange lifestyle didn't change when Priscilla moved in. The parties went on. It was understood that she was Elvis's girl, and no one else among the people hanging around courted trouble by making passes at her.

Elvis could be jealous. If he thought that some guy was paying too much attention to Priscilla, his blue eyes would turn cold and he would stare at them. The guy would always remember someone else he had to talk to and move away from her.

Priscilla said she always felt perfectly protected by Elvis and would have felt that way even if he hadn't been a celebrity. Elvis, she said, was a natural leader. "I like a strong man who will take charge," she once said. "I couldn't respect a weakling who let a woman boss him around. Elvis is strong and forceful. But he's also gentle and considerate."

I'd gotten married not long before Priscilla arrived, so we didn't go out together nights. But we had lunch to-

130

gether and rode around Memphis during the day when she was out of school.

Priscilla liked to go to lunch with Patsy and me, especially in the early years. We usually went to inexpensive restaurants.

Priscilla wasn't a spendthrift, although if she wanted money while Elvis was away, all she had to do was ask Mr. Presley for it.

He always gave her as much as she needed, and he was nice about it. But she was embarrassed to ask for money because she knew how people used Elvis's generosity. So she would often wait until she was broke or almost broke before approaching Mr. Presley.

For some reason Patsy stayed at the mansion one day while Priscilla and I went to lunch with Mrs. Luke Kingsley, Sr., the mother of Jimmy Kingsley, one of Elvis's guys, and with her daughter-in-law, Lilly, the wife of Jimmy's twin brother, John.

Mrs. Kingsley had invited us to the Beef and Liberty Restaurant, but Priscilla and I were worried. We weren't positive that Mrs. Kingsley had meant we were to be her guests, and we were worried about who was going to pay the check. Priscilla and I were both broke. She had told me the day before that she was out of money and was going to have to ask Mr. Presley for some. But I knew she hadn't gotten around to asking yet; and it was the day before payday, so I didn't have any money.

Mrs. Kingsley, of course, picked up the check. But Priscilla and I laughed about it later. Here we were, the girlfriend and secretary of the most famous entertainer in the world and one of the richest men in Memphis and we didn't even have enough money between us to tip the waitress after having lunch with a couple of friends.

When anyone but Elvis had lunch with Priscilla, there

131

was always a good chance that she would order tuna salad. She was crazy about it, but she never ordered it when she was with him. "He doesn't like any kind of fish," she told me. "He doesn't even like it on somebody's breath. So I only eat fish when he's gone."

Priscilla ate tuna almost every day that Elvis was away. When he was in California or on a tour she would fix a big tuna salad with soda crackers and hot tea for lunch. When Patsy and I ate with her at the mansion, we ate tuna.

In the last few weeks before my son was born, I stayed in the house much of the time with Priscilla and Grandma Presley. I filled up on tuna salad then.

But I was standing on a chair washing the office windows one day when Grandma walked in. She threw up her hands: "Lordy child, what are you doing up there?" she yelled, rushing to the chair and grabbing me around the legs.

"Just washing windows, Grandma," I said.

"Well now you just get down off there and come in and lie down on my bed," she demanded, pulling me off the chair and pushing me into the house ahead of her. "You do that kind of work while you're pregnant, girl, and you're gonna' hurt that baby."

I lay down. People didn't argue with Grandma Presley. After that she saw that I took a nice long nap every day. And I didn't do any more house cleaning until after Jerry, Jr., arrived. Grandma said not to worry about Mr. Presley. "That's my boy, and I'll take care of him," she assured me.

Mr. Presley never said anything to me about the naps, and I worked right through Friday, the day before I went to the hospital. My son was born Sunday afternoon, May 31, 1964.

132

Elvis had kidded me a couple of times about being so big, and he sent flowers when I was in the maternity ward. One of the boys was always assigned to keep track of births, deaths, marriages, and other special events involving people in the Graceland family and to see that flowers were provided in Elvis's name. Priscilla later took some of the responsibility for sending flowers and cards on special occasions. She was careful and, to my knowledge, never forgot anyone.

Priscilla said before she was married that she didn't want any babies because she was afraid it would mess up her figure. But after she had Lisa there was no noticeable change in her shape. The wife of one of Elvis's guys said that Priscilla had plastic surgery on her ears in Los Angeles to make them lie flatter. It could be true. Priscilla is very concerned about her appearance.

She never seemed to have trouble keeping her weight down, but then she didn't eat as much as Elvis did. And there's no question that her devotion to dance classes, and later to karate, helped keep her slim.

We were in the office one day answering fan mail when the door flew open and Priscilla bounded inside, leaping and pirouetting gracefully around the desks. We stopped work as she continued gamboling around the room. Finally she shifted one leg, swept one arm behind her, and ended the impromptu performance with a bow.

"Ballet!" she explained. "These are some of the steps I've been learning."

Priscilla stopped by the office nearly every day after that to demonstrate dance steps for us. She studied with the Jo Haynes School of Dancing. After her marriage Priscilla was in two or three dance recitals. But she used an assumed name and hardly anyone there knew that she was Priscilla Presley.

133

She also managed to model incognito at fashion shows in Memphis. She attended the Patricia Stevens Finishing School and modeled for a while at the Piccadilly Restaurant not far from the mansion, and at a local store. All most diners were aware of when she glided out to show an outfit was that she was a lovely, dark-haired model. Patsy and I went to the Piccadilly to eat several times so we could watch her.

An older model about thirty once advised her, "Your tummy is showing, Honey. You need a girdle."

"There's no way that I'll ever wear one of those things!" Priscilla fumed when she told Patsy and me about it.

Elvis was away so much that Priscilla looked for all kinds of self-improvement courses to keep herself busy. She's bright and talented, and she learned quickly. She attended one drama class. That was all it took to start stories in the gossip magazines about her desire to be an actress.

It wasn't true. Priscilla had movie offers, and Elvis said she could take them if she wanted to. But she knew that he didn't like the idea, and she was more interested in her husband and her home than in acting, so she turned the offers down. She made the decision.

Lisa was just a baby then, and that was also a factor.

Priscilla's ability to create imaginative fashions is well known, and she was quite successful after her divorce as a co-owner with Olivia Bis of a Beverly Hills boutique called Bis and Beau.

Olivia, a professional designer, had made Priscilla many of the outfits that Priscilla rough-sketched for herself. It was an easy and natural partnership when Priscilla decided that she wanted to go into business. They established their shop at 9650 Santa Monica Boulevard. Priscilla had started concocting many of her own creations before she was married, and a woman in Whitehaven sewed them for her. She even designed a few of Elvis's outfits.

The clothes Priscilla had designed for herself were original and strikingly inspiring. They had to be, to compete with Elvis's costumes.

One of the few "iffy" Priscilla Presley creations was a dress she wore to the wedding of one of Elvis's guys, Sonny West, to Judy Jordan. It was a long lavender dress with a hood. "It looks like something a monk would wear," Priscilla fretted when she tried it on. "It's ugly." But she wore it anyway. She looked lovely in it. Priscilla is so poised and beautiful that she could wear anything and look good.

Elvis dressed in black, wore shades, and carried a police-type flashlight.

Priscilla didn't design all her own clothes, of course, and most were bought on shopping trips. Elvis would have one of the boys call a store in Memphis and say that they would be in after hours. He took her shopping at LaClede's, an exclusive ladies' wear shop where some blouses sell for $150 each. One of the guys would drive Elvis and Priscilla to the shop. Someone was always waiting at the door to let them in and to assist them as Priscilla picked out a new wardrobe.

Elvis gave her everything she wanted. I made out checks for a black El Dorado, a blue Impala, and a Toronado in addition to the Corvair that he gave her during their courtship.

He once bought her a little pink motorcycle. A few times my husband and I were driving home when Elvis would roar around us on his big Harley Davidson, laughing and waving. A few seconds later Priscilla would go putt-putting by on her pink motorcycle.

After they were married, Elvis bought matching motorcycles for them to ride in California.

Priscilla was still in high school when she walked into the den one day as I was drinking coffee. She fixed herself a cup of tea and sat down beside me.

"Becky," she said, "would you do me a favor?

"If I can," I said.

Priscilla dug into a pile of papers she was carrying and finally pulled out a magazine with an ad from Frederick's of Hollywood. "I'd like to get this catalogue," she whispered, leaning over the desk and pointing to the ad as she looked over her shoulder at the doorway. "I don't want anyone else to know I ordered it. Especially Elvis and Mr. Presley. I want to use your name."

"Well, sure, Priscilla," I said, trying not to sound puzzled. You know it's okay with me. But it's okay to use your own name. You don't have to be twenty-one to send for a catalogue."

But Priscilla insisted she preferred to order the catalogue in my name. Frederick's specializes in the nation's most provocative, come-hither styles for women. Priscilla felt that she was too young to be ordering from Frederick's and didn't want anyone else at Graceland to know. I let her use my name.

Priscilla never demanded things of me or other employees at Graceland, but always asked if we would do her "a favor" when she needed something. She didn't throw her weight around or take the attitude that she was the mistress of the mansion and everyone had better jump when she called. Priscilla wasn't like that.

Elvis liked Priscilla to stay at the mansion and wouldn't allow her to attend most of his concerts. He would go on the road and she would stay in Memphis. It was that way the first two or three years. Later, he began allowing her to travel with him.

As Priscilla began to exercise more freedom, she took shopping trips to New York, always using assumed names for airlines and hotel reservations.

Styles in Memphis are always about six months to a year behind those in California. When Priscilla would return to Graceland wearing the latest fashions from California, Patsy and I and the wives and girlfriends of the guys would want to wear the same styles. Just as the guys let Elvis be the pacesetter in their clothing styles and in many of the things they did, the girls copied Priscilla.

I think Priscilla's hair is naturally brown. But she liked it dark, and although she once dyed it auburn she usually dyed it black. So the other girls and I dyed our hair black.

Priscilla like hairpieces. So we wore hairpieces.

Priscilla favored heavy eye shadow with upsweeping eyebrows, Cleopatra style; we, too, played Cleopatra.

An Avon Lady who lived in the Graceland subdivision stopped at the mansion every few weeks and Priscilla, Patsy, and I bought most of our cosmetics from her.

As a young girl Priscilla wore much heavier make-up than she does today. Elvis seemed to like it. He told her how he liked her to dress and to wear her hair.

Boots were just beginning to become stylish on the West Coast when Priscilla returned from Los Angeles wearing a pair.

The rest of us had to have boots like Priscilla's. I made two or three long distance calls from our home telephone to order two pairs of boots, black and white.

Not long after they arrived I was all dressed up in my new ensemble and was browsing at a shopping center when I noticed two other women watching me. It was obviously the first time they had seen accoutrements like mine; the new styles hadn't yet reached Memphis from California. My hair was dyed black, my lashes and brows were drawn out in heavy, sweeping curves, my leather jacket fitted my sleekly, and my green corduroy pants were bloused into new black glove-leather boots mailed from the West Coast. It was a striking costume.

My bubble burst as I walked past them and heard one say to the other in a stage whisper, "My God, would you look at that poor girl."

Until the boots became popular in Memphis, people stared at Patsy and me as though we were streetwalkers whenever we wore them.

As a teen-ager, of course, Priscilla wasn't as sophisticated as she was to become. But even then she was poised. Priscilla has innate class, and I believe that, as much as her beauty, is what made her stand out, among so many other lovely girls, as special to Elvis.

Priscilla had had hardly any experience with boys or dating until she met Elvis. She was just starting high school then and he was an international celebrity, ten years older than she and the prince charming of thousands of girls all over the world.

Talking about it one day, she said that about the only date she'd had before meeting Elvis was when some boy took her to a school dance. She got all embarrassed because someone told her she had dirt on her face.

138

Priscilla said she had never written a love letter until she started writing to Elvis. While she was in the office helping to read fan mail one day, she discovered some of his old love letters in a file cabinet. Some that she had written to him from Germany were among them. But she was most excited about the letters from other girls.

Patsy and I started to read the letters with her, giggling at some and passing them around to each other. There was a lot of baby talk in some of them.

Priscilla set her own letters aside and didn't open them for Patsy and me.

"Oh my God," I suddenly remembered. "What if Mr. Presley came in here and caught us?"

"Somebody better watch for him," Priscilla said.

I walked to the door and opened it slightly so that I could see the driveway leading from the gate. Patsy took her turn at the door after a few minutes, and we continued to trade off until we had read most of the letters. Priscilla took her letters back to her room.

After Priscilla was married and started traveling with Elvis, she got in a line of girls waiting in front of the stage at the Showroom Internationale in Las Vegas one evening. Elvis kissed her and started toward the next girl in line. He stopped suddenly and turned back to Priscilla. "Don't I know you?" he asked.

She never appeared to be jealous of the beautiful women hanging around the gate or in the mansion at the constant parties. She understood that the adulation of Elvis's female fans was something she would have to put up with. It was the way it had to be.

Elvis never dated or dallied with any other girls at Graceland after Priscilla arrived. There were stories that he dated stars in Hollywood while he was making

139

movies, but at least some of that was studio promotion for his films.

I first became aware of trouble between Elvis and Priscilla when I started getting bills for airline tickets, charged to Elvis, for other women. Then the rumors started about trouble between Elvis and Priscilla.

But it wasn't other women—or other men—who broke up the Presley marriage.

1. He is now Colonel Joseph P. Beaulieu. The Beaulieus live in New Jersey.
2. Priscilla's brothers and sister are all younger than she. They are Donald, Michelle, Jeffrey, and twins Tim and Tom.
3. *Ladies' Home Journal,* August 1973.

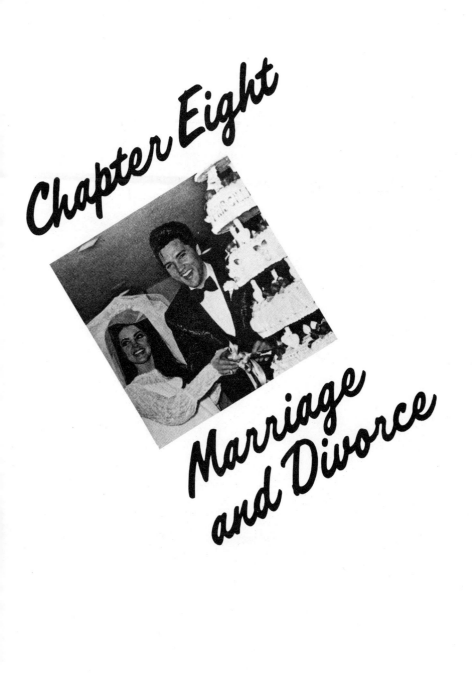

Chapter Eight

Marriage and Divorce

On the preceding
page: The official
wedding picture of
Elvis and Priscilla.

*E*lvis's Graceland family is good at keeping secrets, but no secrets were kept any better than plans for his marriage to Priscilla.

Priscilla had been Elvis's girl for one third of her life, including the nearly five years she lived with him at Graceland. Some people thought they might never marry. Many Elvis watchers were not even aware in 1967 that Priscilla was still at Graceland.

But a surprise announcement on May 1 made the world very much aware that "Cilla" (Elvis's pet name for her) was still very much his best girl.

Priscilla Beaulieu had become Mrs. Elvis Presley in a double-ring ceremony at the Las Vegas Aladdin Hotel.

I was one of the few—even at Graceland—who weren't caught by surprise. I had typed the abbreviated guest list of fourteen people a couple of days earlier. I

143

later wrote a check for nearly four thousand dollars for Priscilla's ring—a three-karat diamond surrounded by twenty smaller diamonds.

Elvis bought the ring from Harry Levitch. Levitch and his wife, Frances, flew the ring to Las Vegas and were in the wedding party.

The Levitches were in select company. Joe Esposito and Marty Lacker, who did Elvis's accounting work, were dual best men at the ceremony. Gee Gee and Patsy Gambill and George Klein and his future wife, Barbara Little, were also there. Most of the Memphis Mafia and their wives or girlfriends were conspicuously absent. They hadn't been invited.

They were some of Elvis's closest friends, and their feelings were hurt. Alan Fortas telephoned me five times on the day Graceland officially learned about the wedding.

"I just don't know why Elvis didn't tell me, why he didn't invite me," Alan groused. "I should have been at the wedding. I'm one of his best friends."

I didn't feel slighted because I wasn't invited. I realized that Elvis couldn't fly everyone to the wedding and couldn't make a big announcement beforehand. His wedding would have become a circus. And there were other reasons why the boys weren't invited, which I'll go into later.

The plans were so secret that Priscilla's parents didn't even tell her youngest brothers, Jeffrey, eight, and twins Tommy and Timmy, five.

Priscilla later said Elvis was disappointed that Grandma couldn't be at the wedding. He had always promised her, "Grandma, when I get married you'll be there." But when he offered to have her flown to Las

144

Vegas, the seventy-six-year-old lady wasn't up to making the trip. Grandma cried about it.

Elvis flew Priscilla's parents and her sister, Michelle, thirteen, and brother Donny, seventeen, from Major Beaulieu's new post at Fort Ord, California, to Palm Springs, where Colonel Parker has a home, two days before the wedding. The youngest boys stayed at home with a maid. "Their flight was a wedding present from Elvis," Priscilla said. "I think Mother was happy to get out of the house for a few days. One of my brothers had just gotten out of the hospital, the washing machine went out, and the plumbing wasn't working right when they left home.

"Of course they were happy for me. They were starting to wonder, because Elvis and I had been dating for years."

How did Elvis propose? "It was very relaxed," Priscilla said. "He just told me about the ring one day and asked if I wanted to marry him. 'More than ever,' I told him."

Although not quite as simple as the proposal, the wedding was relatively uncomplicated and modest, considering who the bride and groom were.

Holding off the rush of newsmen and fans as long as possible, they signed for their license around three-thirty on the morning of the wedding, in the Clark County, Nevada, Clerk's office.

At 9:41 a.m., in the private suite of Milton Prell, the principal owner of the hotel and an old friend of Colonel Parker's, Judge David Zenoff, Justice of the Nevada Supreme Court, began reading the marriage ceremony.

The thirty-year-old groom, wearing a black brocaded coat and vest and dark pants; and his twenty-year-old bride, in a traditional white wedding gown, promised to

145

"love, honor and comfort" each other. Priscilla did not use the word *obey*. Eight minutes after the ceremony began it was concluded.

Michelle was her older sister's maid of honor when Elvis slipped the ring on Priscilla's finger. Priscilla gave a plain gold band to Elvis. He later lost the ring on the grounds at Graceland and it was never recovered.

Elvis and Priscilla cut a six-tiered wedding cake. Decorated with red and pink hearts studded with pearls, it had been finished only minutes before the ceremony.

As they sat down later with more than eighty guests at a champagne breakfast and reception featuring everything from oysters Rockefeller and suckling pig to southern fried chicken, a band played "Love Me Tender" and other songs Elvis had made famous. Colonel Parker hosted the event, and for once the press was welcome.

Priscilla bought her wedding gown in California for about three hundred dollars. She laughed later about stories in fan and gossip magazines that said she had designed the dress.

She didn't, although she had a few alterations made, such as adding a six-foot train. The gown was made of plain white organza, trimmed in seed pearls, with lace sleeves. A double-tiered crown of rhinestones held a three-quarter-length tulle veil.

After the wedding they flew back to Hollywood. There Elvis spent two days finishing work on a film before he and Priscilla returned to Memphis.

They had a reception for their friends, relatives, and employees on returning to Graceland. It helped ease some but not all the hurt feelings among those who had not been invited to the wedding.

The new bride and groom wore their wedding finery and had a new cake to cut. There was a formal receiving line. Tony Barrasso, an accordion player from the Memphis area, circulated among the crowd playing requests and a band provided dance music. It was no surprise that many of the gifts opened at the reception were silver.

A huge buffet was provided by Monte's Catering Service, and butlers roamed the Blue Room (which later became the trophy room), refilling glasses with champagne before they could become half-empty. At one time I was in a group of about a dozen people who were standing at the bar talking, and each of us had his or her own bottle of champagne.

Guests arriving for the shindig drove past hundreds of adoring fans at the gate and up the torch-lit drive to the front door, where men were waiting to park the cars.

If there was anyone who didn't have a good time, it must have been Elvis. He was obviously finding it hard to loosen up.

Although he was surrounded by his closest friends and his family, many people had been invited for business or professional reasons. The gathering wasn't restricted to Elvis's usual comfortable crowd, and his actions showed it. Elvis drinks an occasional rum and coke, but I didn't see a drink in his hand all night. He just walked around or sat on a sofa looking as though he couldn't wait for the party to end.

Priscilla was her usual vibrant self. "You look beautiful, Priscilla," I said as I approached her in the receiving line.

"You think this is beautiful," she laughed, raising a

glass of champagne. "Wait until I've had a couple more of these." But she probably didn't have two more drinks. Like Elvis, Priscilla is a conservative drinker.

We paid for the night of fun on the next day. Although almost everyone showed up for work, hardly anyone got anything done. When Mr. Presley finally wandered into the office, his eyes were sunken and red-rimmed. He was pale. He said he had fallen asleep in the bathroom.

I didn't know that you're not supposed to drink water after drinking too much champagne. So I drank about half a gallon before someone mentioned it to me. By then it was too late. I sat around the rest of the day feeling bad until Jerry picked me up at quitting time.

Dee and a friend, Mrs. Charles E. Kyle, gave a shower for Priscilla at a Memphis restaurant a few days later, and she received presents about like those that any other bride would receive. I gave her Corningware.

At the reception in Las Vegas, Prell had given Elvis and Priscilla expensive white-gold watches with diamonds in the faces. After the divorce, Priscilla mailed hers to Patsy Gambill as a gift.

Fans mailed thousands of gifts and cards to Elvis and Priscilla. Priscilla asked the secretaries to keep all the cards because she was going to paste them in a scrapbook. They were still sitting in a cardboard box in the office when Priscilla and Elvis were divorced.

Many of the gifts mailed by fans were taken inside the house and used. Others were given away.

Some people around Elvis were worried that the marriage would damage his swinging image. There was no need to worry.

Many of Elvis's female fans are married and have children or grandchildren. They were thrilled when Elvis married. And most of his teen-aged followers were under-

148

standing. Priscilla was barely out of her teens herself, and as Elvis's young wife she was someone with whom many of the young girls could identify.

We received letters from many of the girls pledging their continued loyalty to Elvis and condemning any fans who deserted him now that he was a married man.

There were a few, of course, who reacted less gracefully to Elvis's marriage.

On May 1 when it was learned that Elvis and Priscilla were married, the telephone lines at Graceland were jammed with calls from the news media and fans.

Most fans just wanted to talk about Elvis's marriage to someone at Graceland for a few minutes. Quite a few cried over the telephone, even some of the men. It was an emotional time.

One girl was screaming and bawling when she called. She was so hysterical that it was a couple of minutes before I could understand her. I knew, of course, what she was upset about, but I didn't know what to do when she screeched that she was going to commit suicide.

"I'm going to kill myself," she bellowed. "If I can't have Elvis, I don't want to live. I'm going into the bathroom and slash my wrists."

I finally calmed her down enough so that she would listen to me.

"You really love Elvis so much that you're going to kill yourself?" I asked.

"Yes. I do. I love Elvis and I'm going to kill myself," she blubbered.

"Well, if you love someone, you want them to be happy, don't you?"

"Yes," she sniffled after a moment. The weeping had begun to subside to soft whimpers.

"Well honey, that's why Elvis got married—so he can

be happy," I said. There was a short silence. My God, I thought, I'm getting through to her. I think it's going to work. Then I jerked the receiver away from my ear as she wailed:

"But I want him to be happy with *me!*"

The girl finally agreed that it wouldn't be an act of love to saddle Elvis with a suicide on his conscience. She said she would try to carry on, but she would never marry.

An older woman who called was less easy to sympathize with.

Her voice dripped poison as she snarled, "He would have never married that woman if she hadn't let him get her pregnant."

"You have a nasty mind. Elvis doesn't need fans like you," I said, and hung up.

When Priscilla returned to Graceland as Elvis's wife she was the mistress of the mansion. It wasn't long before the intensely masculine surroundings that had for so many years characterized Graceland began to show a feminine touch.

Priscilla was careful, however, to do her redecorating with consideration for the tastes of her famous husband. As much as possible she worked around favorite pieces of Elvis's and incorporated his things into her over-all decorating. The house had been cluttered with all sorts of little trinkets, things that Elvis had bought and presents from fans. The Presley clan doesn't like to throw things away.

One of the most incongruous touches was the dainty crocheted doilies, lovingly knitted by fans, mailed to Elvis and placed on tables by the maids. They were out of place among the expensive, masculine furnishings.

150

Priscilla got rid of the doilies and the mismatched ash trays and table lamps. She gave away boxes of knick-knacks and cleared the attic of junk that had been stored there for years.

She was still a teen-ager when she told me one day that a wife should never overlook her husband's tastes when decorating, especially when doing the bedroom. "The bedroom for a husband and wife should never be too feminine. It's better for it to be more masculine," she said. "It's important to please the man. Elvis would never be happy with anything pink and lacy," she said. "And I couldn't be happy living with him if he's not happy."

When she was changing the decor at Graceland, Priscilla didn't depend on exclusive shops or put everything into the hands of any of the several fine decorators doing business in Memphis.

The blue drapes for the living room and dining room were bought at the Sears Roebuck and Company store in Memphis. She made selections from the same furniture stores that employees shopped at. A chair she picked out for $125 was a twin to the chair Jerry and I had purchased for our home. She wasn't extravagant with her decorating, yet her taste was good. Her decorating style was traditional. At Priscilla's direction, china cabinets were bought for the dining room to hold their silver.

The kitchen was carpeted, new cabinets were built, and a new stove—a gift from Mr. Presley—was installed. Priscilla picked out half a dozen pictures of food and cooking utensils, a new clock, and other smaller items to give the kitchen a more homey look.

Her dressing room and bath were done in both pale and deep pink.

Priscilla was reasonably cost conscious in decorating

Graceland, but she loosened up when she undertook the job of beautifying their homes in California.

At the time of his marriage, Elvis had the homes at Graceland, the ranch in Mississippi, and his house at 1174 Hillcrest in Trousdale Estates near Los Angeles. Soon after the marriage they moved from the Trousdale Estates home to a luxurious new house at 144 Monovale in Holmby Hills.

Elvis paid $400,000 for the fashionable home, and they rapidly invested another $200,000 in decorating and furnishings.

Elvis had several homes at various times, and those that Priscilla shared with him were filled with antiques, which she developed a love for. In California, Priscilla had help from professional decorators.

Of course, she had domestic help in California as well as in Memphis. Although she cooked a few favorite dishes for Elvis and fixed his breakfast now and then, she usually let the maids do the cooking. She was satisfied with planning the menus.

A few days after the reception at Graceland, Elvis and Priscilla flew to Palm Springs in California.

Elvis had just finished making *Double Trouble,* with John Williams and Yvonne Romaine, and had to return to the West Coast to begin work on *Clambake,* with Shelley Fabares. Much of the new film was shot on location.

Consequently, the first days of Elvis's and Priscilla's married life were not that much different from the years they had been dating. The only difference was that this time Priscilla was sitting at home in California waiting for Elvis instead of in Memphis.

But she didn't complain. She was used to Elvis's home-again, gone-again routine.

152

"Sure, I wanted to go with Elvis when he would leave for location to work on a new movie or go on the road for a series of performances," she admitted to me one day. "But I understood that I had to make adjustments. Elvis had to learn to live with his work, and so did I."

It's true that Elvis was away from Priscilla for long periods, but there were other times when they lounged and played together for days at a time.

They were like honeymooners when Elvis was home. They would ride out to the pool on golf carts to sunbathe, and the maids would follow with soft drinks and a telephone. They sometimes talked baby talk to each other when they didn't notice someone else was around.

At other times they vacationed in fun-spots like Hawaii, the Bahamas, and Aspen, Colorado.

The Bahamas trip was a last-minute decision; they already had passports for an excursion to Europe when they changed their minds. Priscilla laughed about the Bahamas trip when she told us that Elvis was almost turned away from a posh gambling casino there because of improper attire before someone recognized him and loaned him a necktie.

It was probably on the trips that the first signs of strain began to show in the marriage.

The guys and their wives went with Elvis and Priscilla on vacations. Elvis, as usual, paid the bills and bought whatever equipment was needed, such as skiing gear for Aspen.

Priscilla complained more than once in my presence that she didn't get to spend any time alone with Elvis. "Somebody's always there, everywhere we go," she grumbled. "A bunch of guys and their wives are always around. We never have any privacy."

I was having coffee in the den one morning not long

153

after that, when Priscilla walked in to get a cup of tea. As she dipped the teabag into the boiling water, she turned to look at me and said, "After Elvis finishes filming *Blue Hawaii*, he's going to rent a bungalow with a private beach so we can have a vacation." She smiled. "Just the two of us."

It would be the first time since their marriage, she added, that she would be alone for more than a few hours with her husband.

Elvis and Priscilla went to Hawaii. So did the boys and their wives. There were about a dozen people. Priscilla's cozy little family holiday was spoiled.

I didn't see her for a few weeks after they returned, but I heard from others that she had been upset and had quarrelled with Elvis about it. Soon afterward the guys and their wives started moving out and getting their own apartments.

Eventually only Joe Esposito—whose wife, Joanie, was one of Priscilla's closest friends—Charlie Hodge, and one or two others were left. Both Joe and Charlie met Elvis in the Army and they had been with him as long as any of the Memphis Mafia. Joe is one of the brightest, hardest-working members of Elvis's circle of guys. Charlie is from Decatur, Alabama. He was Elvis's shadow on stage and off when they are on tour. He blew Elvis's hair dry before performances; and during performances it was he who handed Elvis the scarves that were tossed to fans. Charlie saw to it that Elvis had water when he was performing, and he clowned around during the breaks in the music.

The guys were shifted to the sidelines and it seemed at last that Priscilla had taken a permanent place as the focus of Elvis's home life.

154

It was obvious that some of the guys and their wives blamed Priscilla for causing them to lose their meal-ticket buddy. Several were still smarting over the snub at the wedding.

They didn't have to feel defeated long. Elvis began bringing the guys back, one by one. Soon the old crowd was around, and although a few of Elvis's older buddies were missing, there were new faces to take their place. Alan Fortas didn't come back to work for Elvis after the ranch was sold, and is now in business for himself in Memphis. He and Elvis remained good friends.

There were other strains on the marriage, problems that are typical and all too familiar to celebrity families.

Like other famous Hollywood stars and entertainers before him, Elvis was finally slapped with a paternity suit. He beat it, and Priscilla stood beside him, but it couldn't have been a happy time for either of them. More about the suit later.

As early as 1969 the movie magazines and gossip columns were printing stories that Elvis and Priscilla were splitting up or had already secretly separated.

Every time that Elvis was seen with another woman, whether it was an actress he was co-starring with, a business associate or a friend, the rumors would start about another love in his life. It just wasn't true.

Girlfriends for Elvis and boyfriends for Priscilla didn't show up until the marriage had already begun faltering.

The total lack of privacy that destroyed any chance for true emotional intimacy between husband and wife was one factor in the weakening of the marriage. And Priscilla needed companionship to make up for the days and weeks when Elvis was away. Although she made friends easily enough, she and Elvis never moved with the Hol-

155

lywood crowd. Their friends were his buddies from back home and their wives or girlfriends. Priscilla was sometimes very lonely.

In the office one day she was idly thumbing through fan mail. But she wasn't looking at the letters and pictures. I could tell something was bothering her. Finally she looked up at me, the fingers of one hand still toying with the stacked letters: "Do you know, Becky," she said, "marriage seems to change everything. People seem to forget about the other person's needs after they've been married for a while. They don't do things because they want to any more, or because its fun, but because they have to or they're expected to. Elvis and I were so happy together before we got married. It's more fun being a girlfriend than a wife."

I didn't know what to say. I just stammered something about marriage being the way it was supposed to be when two people were in love.

Priscilla didn't seem to be listening. She continued shuffling through the letters, a faraway look in her eyes.

Priscilla was developing a need to become an individual in her own right. She enjoyed being photographed and being the center of attention. But she wanted to be more than an extension of Elvis and a rich ornament. She wanted to be important.

Mike Stone made her feel important.

Stone was a rugged thirty-year-old karate expert whom Priscilla met shortly after she began training at one of five karate schools operated in the Los Angeles area by Chuck Norris. Elvis, like Stone and Norris, is a karate black belt, and urged Priscilla to take up the sport.

Bored and looking for something to do, Priscilla took readily to karate. It wasn't long before her trim brown

156

Mercedes-Benz was seen parked regularly behind the Norris School on Ventura Boulevard in Sherman Oaks in the San Fernando Valley.

As Elvis's wife and because she was so strikingly beautiful, Priscilla was disturbing to some of the other students. Consequently, she usually worked out in a far corner of the gym with Norris, away from others in the class. She quickly earned a green belt and was ready to take the test for her brown belt when she dropped out.

"I decided ballet is more feminine," she explained. "But I still like to watch the guys work out."

Despite her relative isolation from the other students she soon began to meet other black belts.

After workouts a group would sometimes go to a near-by restaurant for snacks and conversation. The swarthy, Hawaiian-born Stone was in the gathering.

Priscilla eventually invited Norris and Stone to her home, where they met Elvis. Pleased that she was becoming so dedicated to the sport he loved and anxious for an opportunity to talk karate with other black belts, Elvis was happy to entertain.

He even invited the karate crowd to be guests at one of his Las Vegas shows. Norris, his wife, and Stone reportedly accepted the invitation. But Stone's wife, Fran, was unable to go because the couple's second child was only two weeks old.

Priscilla and Mrs. Stone were said to be so friendly for a while that they went shopping together.

On March 31, 1972, the budding friendship between the two wives was shattered for good. Mrs. Stone brought a divorce suit against her husband of six years. He was served with the papers on April 6.

At a hearing on June 5, Mrs. Stone was awarded the

family home in Huntington Beach and custody of the couple's two young children, Shelley and Lorie. Stone was ordered to pay each month two hundred dollars for each child and another two hundred in alimony. Later, Mrs. Stone reportedly went to work as a waitress to supplement the family income.

By that time it was obvious that Priscilla was involved and that she and Elvis were caught in the marital tangle.

Priscilla and Stone had frequently been seen together at karate matches and other events. The gossip magazines were having a field day. And rumors back in Memphis were flying.

One story had Priscilla waiting until Elvis was asleep and then slipping out of bed, dressing, and sneaking out to see a karate instructor boyfriend named Steve—not Mike. Another had Elvis hiring a detective to shadow her.

Some of the tales were preposterous. But there was too much happening to dismiss everything as rumors.

One day in December, Priscilla walked into the office while I was alone answering fan mail. She stopped in front of my desk and stood there for a moment until I stopped typing and looked up.

Priscilla usually came into the office smiling, kind of bouncing, as though she were bringing sunshine in with her. But this time she was different. She was obviously bothered by something.

"Becky," she said, "would you do me a favor?"

"Well sure, Priscilla. You know I'll always do anything you ask me to," I said.

"I'd like for you to mail a couple of things," she said, dipping into the sack she was carrying and pulling out a fat brown envelope and a couple of packages wrapped in bright Christmas paper. "Beau," Priscilla's pet name for herself, was written across one corner of the envelope.

"I don't want anyone to know you mailed this," she said, laying the packages on my desk and handing me the envelope. "Please take it to the post office yourself."

The envelope was addressed to Mike Young.

A couple of weeks later at the New Year's Eve party, Priscilla walked to the table where my husband and I were sitting and asked if I had mailed the package.

"The same night you gave it to me. I went home, put some stamps on it and took it to the post office. Jerry drove me," I said, nodding at my husband.

"Well, I wonder what happened," Priscilla mused, frowning slightly. "I had a picture of myself inside, and Mike said he never got it."

"Mike Stone, of course," she said.

Patsy Gambill had already told me about Mike—and Priscilla knew that. It was Patsy who had told Priscilla that if she had anything private to mail, and Patsy wasn't available she should give it to me. She said I could be trusted.

Although Patsy was Elvis's cousin, she and Priscilla had become very close. Patsy would skip work every once in a while to accompany Priscilla on trips to California, Las Vegas, or New York.

Priscilla later gave me a couple of other cards to mail for her. Mike had finally received the picture.

She was becoming more open about her relationship with Mike. At the party, when Jerry walked to the bar to pick up fresh drinks, she told me that I should come to California. "There are a lot of handsome karate instructors there," she said. "Come on out and I'll introduce you to some of them. They're not as handsome as Mike," she teased. "But they're all good-looking guys."

Priscilla said that Mike was like Elvis in some ways. "He's very masculine. He treats me like a woman, and he never lets me forget that he is a man," she said. I couldn't help but think that it wasn't so long ago that Priscilla was talking about Elvis and said almost the same thing. After the divorces Priscilla broke up with Mike and began dating her hairdresser.

One of the nicest things about Mike, she said, was that he had so much time to spend with her. "When we're together, it's just the two of us," she said. "We don't have a gang of other people around all the time."

By then bills with the names of other girls on them had started arriving at the office for limousine service and airplane tickets.

In his biography of Elvis, Jerry Hopkins claimed that Elvis had big parties on the West Coast and that the boys would sometimes get girls in trouble. Elvis would pay the bills, Hopkins said.[1]

I don't know who got who in trouble, or if it ever happened at all. But I know that we paid doctor bills for some girls who weren't married to the guys and who were not, to my knowledge, dating Elvis.

With so many guys around Elvis all the time it was hard to say that any of the girls was his.

I once mentioned the airline and limousine bills to Patsy while we were having lunch at Howard Johnson's. She was traveling with her husband and Elvis at that time and wasn't working in the office.

"Who are the girls?" she asked.

160

I remembered one was a girl who later married an Olympic athlete, and I named her.

"Oh sure, she's a model," Patsy replied. "Elvis thinks she's real cute."

Patsy said she found her husband's little black book one day and it was full of girls' names. "They're mostly just some girls we know in Palm Springs," he said. Then he reminded her that the wives couldn't go there.

Shortly before my chat with Patsy, I walked into the kitchen about nine-thirty one morning for coffee and Aunt Delta rushed up to me, flapping her arms. Surprised, I set the coffee cup on the table. She snatched it up again and shoved it at me.

"You better get back to the office, honey," she wheezed, pushing me out the door. "I don't think you should be in here now." As soon as I got back to the office I peeked out the window. A skinny girl with long brown hair was slipping out the kitchen door.

Another girl, much prettier, used to leave the mansion at about the same time some mornings. She was a nurse, and a couple of times I saw her in her uniform. She must have been working in Washington, D. C., because we paid for her air fare back and forth between there and Memphis.

Priscilla moved out of Elvis's California home on February 23, 1972, and rented a two-bedroom apartment near the Pacific Ocean. Almost a year later she moved to a three-bedroom apartment in the same building. She was only a few blocks from a karate school Mike had opened. There were no servants at the new apartment.

Stories about a separation started almost immediately, but at first even friends and employees at Graceland didn't know if it was true.

Reporters and fans trying to check out the rumors tele-

161

phoned Memphis and said they were told in California that Priscilla was at Graceland. They wanted to know if it was true.

I told them, "Yes, Priscilla is at Graceland. No, you can't talk to her."

Even I began to worry seriously when we began getting bills for all kinds of household goods delivered to Priscilla at a strange address in California. She was buying everything—new sheets and pillowcases, pots and pans, dishes and ash trays.

I was once holding a handful of bills that I had to write checks for, when I jokingly told Patsy, "Priscilla must be fixing up an apartment before the divorce." Patsy didn't laugh. She just looked at me very seriously, without saying a word. I knew then, althought I didn't want to admit it to myself, that the stories were true. Elvis and Priscilla's marriage was on the rocks.

On January 8, 1973, nearly eleven months after their separation, Elvis filed for a California divorce, citing "irreconcilable differences" that had caused an "irremedial breakdown" of the marriage. It was his thirty-eighth birthday.

Elvis agreed that Priscilla was to have custody of their daughter, and the petition was uncontested. They had lived together as man and wife for four years, nine months, and twenty-two days.

The divorce was granted on October 11, 1973. Elvis kissed Priscilla good-bye outside the Los Angeles courthouse.

Two months later I wrote a ten-thousand-dollar check for a new Jaguar that Elvis gave Priscilla for Christmas. She picked out the sports car in Los Angeles.

He was performing at Notre Dame University in South

162

Bend, Indiana, shortly after that when he saw an ad in a newspaper and telephoned jeweler J. R. Fox. He asked Fox to bring a selection of bracelets to his motel.

Fox was quoted as saying he sent a salesman eighty miles to Chicago for four bracelets ranging in price from $21,000 to $11,000. When Fox reached the motel with the jewelry, Elvis was sleeping and Joe Esposito picked out the $11,000 bracelet. It had seven blue oval sapphires, each surrounded by diamonds and set in separate squares. The squares were linked by platinum hooks. We were told that Elvis gave the bracelet to Priscilla.

Other stories continued to circulate about Elvis and Priscilla exchanging presents after the divorce. Some, including a story that Elvis gave Priscilla a new coat and she gave him a Rolls Royce, got into the movie magazines.

Throughout the separation and for some time later, Priscilla bought and charged anything she wanted to Elvis accounts or to credit cards he got for her.

The separation and divorce were amicable—but not quite as amicable as Elvis and his friends would have had his fans and the public believe.

On May 29, 1973, acting on behalf of Priscilla, the law firm of Tankel, Toll and Leavitt filed in Los Angeles Superior Court a petition charging that their client was a victim of "extrinsic fraud" during one-sided settlement negotiations with her estranged husband. Elvis, it was claimed, had failed to make full disclosure of his assets to Priscilla.

"The rule is well settled in California that the failure of a husband to fully and fairly disclose the nature of the community assets constitutes extrinsic fraud in relation to settlement agreements," the attorneys maintained.

163

If Priscilla had challenged the divorce or settlement within six months, the court could have been petitioned to change the agreement on grounds of "mistake" or "excusable neglect." But according to California law, after six months an allegation of fraud had to be made in order to seek relief.

Listing her occupation as housewife, and Elvis's as entertainer, Priscilla complained in the legal documents that she was tricked into accepting a $100,000 property settlement, $1,000 monthly alimony, and $500 monthly child support. Elvis had also agreed to furnish the new apartment and to pay the rent.

"She was not told by her husband or by their family lawyer, E. Gregory Hookstratten, that, as a matter of law she had a right to one-half of the community assets," her lawyers asserted.

Priscilla said that at the time she signed the property settlement and alimony agreements, she was told they were fair.

"Since I was sixteen years old I have been living with my husband's family, and during that time I developed trust and confidence in my husband, his father, and other persons associated with them," she said.

Priscilla insisted that throughout her marriage she was never told the amount of Elvis's income or the amount of property they had accumulated.

Priscilla lived as many southern women did. Her husband, or in this case his managers, took care of the family business affairs. She was more fortunate than most southern women, however. She explained that she had been supplied with an unlimited checking account.

Priscilla had put the same childlike trust in Hookstratten that she had put in Elvis and his father. She had allowed Hookstratten, who was representing Elvis, to obtain Robert Brock to act as her attorney.

She said Hookstratten instructed her to say that she was fully informed about Elvis's finances if Brock started to discuss money with her. She did as she was told.

Believing that she was being fairly treated, she permitted the divorce to go through uncontested.

It wasn't until later that she started to feel the money squeeze and realized that she couldn't live on $1,500 a month in the style she had become accustomed to as the wife of a multimillionaire entertainer.

A more generous settlement was worked out after Priscilla went to court with new attorneys demanding a bigger chunk of the property: $20,000 monthly alimony, $2,500 monthly child support, and $37,500 in attorney fees. Another $37,500 in court and other litigation costs was added to the bill.

All told, Priscilla wound up with a two-million-dollar settlement. Half was paid by Elvis in 1972 with the remainder to be paid over a ten-year-period. In 1977 Elvis placed a $494,024.49 lien on Graceland. Mr. Presley explained that the lien action was taken to meet collateral requirements for the settlement required by California divorce courts. He said Elvis had decided to pay off the remainder of about $462,000 in the next three years. He stressed that Elvis had no intention of giving up the mansion.

The settlement provided $4,000 monthly support for Lisa, and there was talk that Priscilla also received a five percent interest in two of Elvis's music publishing companies.

I didn't see the legal papers, but after the settlement I began writing two $6,000 checks every month for Pris-

165

cilla and a $4,000 check for Lisa. After a year one of the $6,000 checks was stopped.

At the time she filed the court action, Priscilla listed total monthly expenses, for herself and Lisa, of:

Rent or mortgage on residence	$ 700
Property Insurance and taxes on home	$ 100
Maintenance of residence	$ 500
Food and household supplies	$1,000
Utilities	$ 150
Telephone	$ 400
Laundry and cleaning	$ 300
Clothing	$2,500
Medical	$ 200
Insurance (life, health, etc.)	$ 300
Child care	$ 500
School	$ 300
Entertainment	$ 500
Incidentals	$1,500
Transportation	$1,000
Auto expenses (gas, repair, etc.)	$ 500
Installment payments	$1,350

Explaining the installment payments, Priscilla listed creditors and balances for clothing purchases.

She also claimed outstanding business expenses of $2,000, and furniture and furnishings costs of $1,000, for a total of $14,900.

In an income and expense statement, she listed her entertainer husband's estimated monthly income as "in excess of $200,000." She listed no income for herself.

She and her attorneys stated that the nature and value of the property at stake was unknown, but in excess of $1 million.

It was obvious to Priscilla that she couldn't live the

way she had become used to without a hefty increase in the settlement. But there was also another reason for her demands. She was planning to go into business with Olivia to open the boutique.

She said she needed money not only to open the shop, but also to dress in a manner consistent with her occupation as a designer of women's clothes.

Bis & Beau, helped of course by the free publicity attracted by its glamorous co-owner, quickly became a shopping mecca for celebrities. Priscilla said that she and her partner sold items to Cher Bono Allman, Eva Gabor, Suzanne Pleshette, Barbara Parkins, Yvette Mimieux, Linda Blair, Twiggy, Natalie Wood, Barbara Eden, Joanne Woodward, Anna Karina, Lana Turner, and Cybill Shepherd, among others.

Many of Priscilla's famous customers had been friends and acquaintances before she became a businesswoman selling exclusive creations for sixty-five to one thousand dollars each.

For a time she cashed in on the "Gatsby Look," styling many of her fashions with inspiration from clothing of the 1930's. She added appeal to her fashions by modeling many of them herself.

Early in 1976 Priscilla sold her interest in the popular boutique, reportedly to concentrate on a youth-oriented syndicated television show.[1]

There have also been regular reports and rumors that Priscilla had entered or was going to enter college. One story had her about to sign up for classes at UCLA to study business administration. But it appears doubtful that now that she is over thirty she has the desire to become a college coed.

Priscilla kept in touch with the Graceland family after

her divorce and apparently still has a good relationship with Mr. Presley. Lisa is his only grandchild, and Priscilla is generous with visitation privileges.

She telephoned me at home a couple of times after the divorce. Once she asked me to send her the title to a horse trailer, but I told her that I would have to get permission from Mr. Presley. The title was eventually signed over to her with no fuss.

She was excited about the boutique when she talked with me, but she admitted that she was shocked at the expense of launching the new business. "It's costing more than I thought it would, Becky," she said. "I'm running short of money."

Priscilla returned to Graceland a couple of times after the divorce, both times while Elvis was away. She picked out her clothes, some glasses and dishes that she wanted, a few other wedding gifts, and had her bridal gown packed and sent to her mother in New Jersey. She also arranged to have her horses transported to the West Coast.

Many of her personal possessions, including several stuffed animals, were given to charity. She had won one of the animals at a carnival concession after spending about a hundred dollars.

The Presleys took the wedding pictures from the dining room and then seemed to put the divorce out of their minds.

I couldn't do that. I was still writing checks for bills Priscilla was running up. I was worried about it and asked Mr. Presley what I should do.

"Is she still charging things to Elvis?" he asked, surprised.

168

"Yes sir," I said, pointing to a stack of bills on my desk.

"Well, pay the bills and then cancel the accounts," he told me.

I wrote letters to the Shell Oil Company, The Broadway (a department store in Los Angeles), and others, telling them that Elvis would no longer pay for Priscilla's purchases. The bills stopped coming in.

Later I pointed out to Mr. Presley that Priscilla was still listed as beneficiary on several insurance policies. Those were also changed. Lisa replaced her mother as beneficiary.

1. Elvis, by Jerry Hopkins, Simon and Schuster, Inc., New York.
2. *Chicago Tribune*, April 26, 1976.

Chapter Nine

Lisa

On the preceding
page: Elvis and
Priscilla leave Baptist
Hospital in Memphis
with their baby, Lisa,
in February 1968.
(Beaverbrook News-
papers)

*M*onths before Lisa Marie Presley was born, her mother vowed that she wouldn't permit her to become spoiled.

"I don't care if it's a boy or a girl, Becky," Priscilla said one day. "But I'm not going to have my baby spoiled by being given everything it wants. If you want to build character you have to teach children that it takes effort to earn the good things."

Priscilla and I were driving to the nearby Howard Johnson's for lunch, and although it was only two or three months before Lisa's birth, her mother looked almost as slim, petite, and stylish as if she were not pregnant. Priscilla never wore maternity clothes. She didn't have to.

But it wasn't her shape that she was worrying about the day we lunched together. She was worried about the job ahead—being mother to the child of the most famous entertainer in the world.

173

"I know that people, fans, are going to love it because it's Elvis's baby," she said, momentarily turning her eyes from the road ahead as a stop light changed and she pulled Elvis's Cadillac into an intersection. "But I want the baby to have a normal childhood, and it's not going to be that way if presents and everything it wants are just heaped on it. I don't want him or her settling for living off Elvis's name."

Less than two months later, at 5:01 P. M. on February 1, 1968, Lisa Marie Presley was born. It was nine months to the day since Elvis and Priscilla had gotten married.

The infant's name was ready and waiting, picked from a baby book. If the baby had been a boy, he would have been named John Baron. "It's such a strong sounding name," Priscilla said. "It's perfect for a boy."

Elvis had remained in Memphis throughout January, the final month of Priscilla's pregnancy. And around eight-thirty on the morning of February 1, when Priscilla said it was time, he got into the back seat of a new Cadillac with her for the ride to Baptist Memorial Hospital. Four of Elvis's guys went along.

Charlie Hodge drove them, and another Cadillac, driven by Joe Esposito and carrying Richard Davis and Jerry Schilling, followed. It was the stand-by car, ordered to follow in case the first Cadillac broke down. Both luxury cars held up for the four- or five-mile trip.

Shown to the doctor's lounge to wait, Elvis also held up well. Joe, Charlie, Richard, and Jerry waited with him. Before long they were joined by Patsy and her husband, Gee Gee Gambill; Marty Lacker; Lamar Fike; George Klein; Jerry's wife; and, finally, Vernon and Dee.

On the maternity ward uniformed off-duty policemen

stood guard, one on each shift. They remained until Priscilla returned to Graceland with Lisa Marie four days later.

Within minutes of Priscilla's admittance, newspaper reporters began converging on the hospital. Fans took up the vigil soon after, and before Priscilla left there were scores of them milling about, vainly hoping for a chance to get into the hospital for a peek at Elvis, his wife, or his baby.

The commotion over the arrival of the six-pound, fifteen-ounce girl was just about what one would expect for the daughter of Elvis Presley. Hardly the low-key, quiet, private birth Priscilla had hoped for. And hardly the type of reception to indicate that Lisa would be allowed to grow up just as any other little girl.

Lisa was a healthy, happy baby, with shiny light brown hair and blue eyes. She had her father's square face, pouting mouth, high forehead and slightly spread tip of the nose.

She was as perfect as a baby could be, and Elvis and his father were equally pleased to point that out to anyone who might care to listen. There was always someone to listen.

Fans had been listening, of course, to radio and television reports of the birth, and in a few days cards, baby clothes, blankets, dolls, and other toys were arriving by mail.

A few presents made their way into the nursery, but most were eventually given away to Patsy or other relatives and employees with young children of their own.

A large ceramic rabbit, a gift from a fan, was kept in the office, and Mr. Presley amused himself almost every day by shooting rubber bands at the ears. The floor would be littered with them before Patsy or I picked them up.

Another fan (a man, of course) sent Lisa a pair of roller skates big enough for a ten-year-old. He may have thought they would be a welcome gift after the initial excitement was over and fans stopped mailing presents. But they didn't stop.

Every year on her birthday, and for Christmas, Easter, and other holidays, gifts poured in for the little girl in the big mansion.

Weeks before Lisa's birth, Priscilla had received gifts of baby clothes and nursery accoutrements at a shower given for her by two of her girlfriends. Guests brought gifts similar to those they would buy for any other mother-to-be. I gave her a sleeper outfit that snapped up the front.

The women employees were given half a day off work to go to the shower. It was at a private home in the Graceland subdivision, in the Whitehaven area of Memphis where I live, near the mansion.

A typical shower in every way except for the fame of the parents, it featured refreshments of cupcakes with tiny booties and babies on them, punch, nuts, mints, chips and dip.

With the baby's arrival, the attention at Graceland shifted from Elvis and Priscilla to Lisa Marie. And Priscilla quickly learned that there was more spoiling to fear from the loving indulgences of the proud father and grandfather than from fans.

Fans would have been happy to spoil Lisa, but Priscilla could keep them at a distance. Elvis and Mr. Presley were a more difficult problem.

Elvis himself shopped for statuettes, pictures, and knick-knacks to fill Lisa's new nursery, which had at one time been a little-used conference room.

Lisa wasn't old enough to toddle before Elvis had a gym set erected for her in the back yard. When she was big enough to play with it, Elvis often played with her. At other times we could look through the window or walk out the door and watch Elvis in a golf cart, with Lisa on his lap, driving slowly around the mansion grounds.

One time he thrilled fans and gave his security people goose bumps when he hoisted Lisa onto his broad shoulders and ambled down the driveway to greet the people standing in front of the Music Gate. It was one of the few times that Lisa was photographed at Graceland by persons other than family members.

Priscilla may have had something to say about the incident, because Elvis never did it again. Lisa's parents were understandably cautious about overexposing her and didn't usually invite picture taking. They never talked about kidnapers to others, but they must have been aware of the danger. Lisa is well protected.

As most children do, Lisa loves animals. She had at least three cats, including one that my husband and I gave her.

Some time after I had left Graceland, our cat had three kittens. When Sandy's son learned that we had them, he asked for one to give to his little sister, Laura, for her birthday. Sandy telephoned me the next day and said Laura and Lisa were fighting over the kitten, so we sent another one to the house. Lisa's kitten was white with black ears. She took it to California with her and sometimes took it riding in golf carts.

Lisa is fond of the cat, but it didn't take the place in

her heart of Snoopy, a Great Dane that is her almost constant shadow in California.

Earlier, before she was old enough to walk, Elvis bought her a pony. He carried her to the pony, helped her pet it, and held her in place on its back until she was big enough to ride by herself.

It was easier to shield Lisa from the loving indulgences of her father and grandfather while Priscilla was still living with Elvis. It was more difficult after the divorce, when Lisa would visit her daddy for long periods of time, either alone or with a nurse.

But Priscilla laughs about the time Lisa was visiting her father in Las Vegas and lost a baby tooth. The tooth fairy left her five dollars. "I told Elvis that the tooth fairy usually left fifty cents, that five dollars was a little steep," she said. "He knew I wasn't angry, and he laughed about it. After all, who would expect Elvis Presley to know the going rate for a tooth?"

Grandfathers are notorious for spoiling their grandchildren, and Mr. Presley was no exception. Snapshots of Lisa lined the walls of his home, outnumbering even the many photographs of Elvis.

Lisa got about all the candy and toys she wanted. She loved Barbie dolls and stuffed animals. And she was devoted to *Sesame Street,* the children's educational television program. For Christmas one year Paulette and I gave her a stuffed Big Bird doll fashioned after one of the Sesame Street animal characters.

Mr. Presley once brought a large doll into the office and had it walk along the floor for us. He confessed that he was a bit worried Priscilla might think it was too lavish a present for his granddaughter. "Priscilla doesn't want Lisa spoiled, you know," he told us.

178

Occasionally Colonel Parker mailed stuffed animals to Lisa and the other children of the Graceland clan. He once sent a stuffed camel used to promote Elvis's movie, *Harum Scarum,* and around Christmas time he mailed Santa Clauses and snow men. One year Mr. Presley distributed stuffed replicas of the RCA dog, Nipper, to those of us at Graceland who had young children.

Lisa is the darling of her grandparents and of all the aunts and uncles, cousins, and employees at Graceland. She has the run of the house and grounds, and she frequently wandered into the office to play.

She was about four years old when she started climbing onto my lap to punch the typewriter keys. She loved to pick out Elvis's name, her mother's, and her own.

She also used the telephones and would call the office to talk to us almost every day. From the office she would telephone her grandfather. Mr. Presley always had time to talk to her.

I once dialed the local "Smile" number, which plays short recordings of children's stories, and gave Lisa the telephone. After that she became a regular caller.

My son, Jerry, Jr., first met Lisa and Elvis one night when Patsy and I stopped at the mansion after taking our children to a local pizza restaurant.

Elvis was sitting on a sofa in the den, wearing sunglasses and playing with a fold-up nightstick while talking with George Klein.

After Jerry, Jr. shook hands with Elvis and George, the four children—my child, Patsy's two children, and Lisa—left to play in Lisa's room. In about five minutes they were all downstairs again, running through the house, screaming and roughhousing. Elvis continued talking as though he didn't notice the commotion.

I was worried that they would break something and yelled at Jerry to quiet down. But Lisa's nursemaid, Henrietta Gibson, said not to worry about it. "Mr. Presley doesn't mind," she said. "He's used to kids, honey. You just let them go ahead and play."

Henrietta was a maid whom Elvis and Priscilla hired in California. But they had hired special nursemaids from Japan and Germany when Lisa was a baby. The German woman was hospitalized after having an accident while riding one of Elvis's lawn vehicles.

The noise subsided after Henrietta took Lisa upstairs to get her ready for bed. Lisa toddled down in her pajamas later, holding her white cat Puff in her arms, and kissed her daddy goodnight.

Lisa hadn't been in bed long when Elvis called his cousin, Patsy, upstairs. As she was driving me home later she showed me a ring Elvis had given her. Elvis had gotten it in a swap with Welsh singer Tom Jones.

When we got hom that night I asked Jerry, Jr. what he thought of Elvis.

"Elvis? Oh, he's nice," Jerry said. "But gee, wait till I tell the other kids I met George Klein."

George was a popular radio disk jockey in Memphis and a hero to local kids who listened to him. Meeting him was a thrill. But to nine-year-old Jerry, Elvis was just his mother's boss. He had been hearing about Elvis all his life.

Later, Jerry got used to playing at Graceland, romping on the grounds, running through the house, and swimming in the pool. Priscilla taught Lisa to swim before she was three years old, and after that the kids spent much of their time at the pool.

In one of the more obvious gestures of Elvis's pride in

his daughter, he named his $1 million luxury jet aircraft after her. "Lisa Marie" is written in large bold script on the nose of the sleek converted Convair 880.

The giant blue-and-white jet was formerly flown by Delta Airlines and is the largest plane in a small fleet that Elvis began collecting in 1975. Although it is named after his daughter, it is also recognizable as Elvis's by the large "TCB" and the lightning bolt painted in gold under an American flag on the tail section.

Elvis sank an additional $750,000 into the pride of his air fleet to have it equipped and renovated in Fort Worth to his taste.

He bought two other airplanes and the Lisa Marie in a seven-month period in 1975 to use for his concert tours and his travels between Memphis, Las Vegas, and California.

The first jet he considered was owned by exiled millionaire financier Robert Vesco. But Elvis pulled out when legal complications developed.

Elvis had bid $1.5 million and had put up a $75,000 deposit in January for Vesco's luxury Boeing 707 jet. The offer was withdrawn a month later when Elvis's attorneys received a telegram from a South American company that claimed to own the jet. The firm said the airplane would be seized if it landed at an unprotected airport outside the United States.

The aircraft was eventually sold at auction for $650,000 to Pan American World Airways, and a suit to collect the $850,000 difference was filed against Elvis by the bankrupt firm formerly owned by Vesco. A Superior Court judge in New Jersey ruled that Elvis could withdraw his offer, but the decision was appealed to the New Jersey Supreme Court.

181

Elvis turned to Nigel Winfield, a Miami, Florida, entrepeneur, who located the Convair and two other aircraft for him after the Vesco deal collapsed. The Convair has a range of about three thousand miles, and Winfield has been quoted as saying it is better and more luxurious than the official presidential aircraft, Air Force One.

Requiring a crew of four, including a stewardess, the *Lisa Marie* has a galley with stove, refrigerator, and coffeemaker; a private bedroom with a queen-size bed where Elvis can relax and listen to piped-in stereo music; a dining room with eight chairs; a sitting room; a six-chair conference room with a lounge and four television sets; two bathrooms with gold-plated fixtures and a shower in one; and separate seats for twenty-nine passengers. There are seven telephones in the *Lisa Marie*.

The crew is well paid. In 1976 it was reported that the captain, Elwood David, was earning $43,000 a year, and copilot Ron Strauss and flight engineer James Manning were receiving $39,000 each.

Elvis already had a nine-seat Lockheed Jetstar and two other jets when he bought the *Lisa Marie*.

After buying the Convair, which he sometimes called his penthouse in the sky, Elvis sold one of his airplanes, a twin-engine jet Commander, to singer Wayne Newton for $300,000. Another, a Gulfstream twin-engine jet, was sold to a Mississippi construction company for $690,000, and the Jetstar was leased to a private airline.

Elvis kept a French-constructed Falcon DH-125, which be bought for $600,000, and there were stories that he was planning to buy another, possibly a giant jet like the *Lisa Marie*.

Although Elvis used to be leery of air travel and preferred driving between Memphis and California, he came to love flying.

During some of his tours he slept aboard the parked airplane instead of in hotels. It was a comfortable and convenient way to avoid harassment from fans.

In one respect I'm saddened when I think of Elvis naming the jet for his daughter. Elvis's expression of love naming his airplane after Lisa just reminds me that she will never again know the happiness of living with her mother and father.

Chapter Ten

The Holidays

On the preceding
page: Elvis during his
early days in Holly-
wood, with glamor-
ous Jane Russell and
Los Angeles Rams
star Elroy Hirsch.

*M*y first New Year's Eve party at Graceland is memorable because it was the first one Elvis attended with his future wife.

And the New Year's Eve party he gave four years later is memorable because it was the year Elvis didn't show up. He was so tired from riding horseback on December 31, 1967, that he left five hundred guests waiting all night for him at the Manhattan Club in Memphis.

Elvis hosted New Year's Eve parties alternately in the mansion and at rented nightclubs in Memphis during the years I was at Graceland. He sometimes stayed several hours with his wife or his date, and at other times he showed up for no longer than ten minutes.

If Elvis didn't feel like partying, he left and went to bed, regardless of the thousands of dollars invested in nightclub, food, drinks, and service.

In 1962 Elvis was in a party mood. A week earlier he had introduced his sixteen-year-old live-in girlfriend,

Priscilla, to friends at an intimate Christmas party at Graceland.

Hosting the party in the mansion for about 30 of his relatives, employees and closest friends, Elvis was resplendent in a new continental suit and flamenco boots. The boys wore similar outfits. Maids served turkey, ham, and other food buffet style in the dining room. It was as though a big family had gathered at the home of the head of the clan, and everyone enjoyed the warmth and fellowship. The only complaint I heard the entire evening was from Grandma Presley, who grumbled that there was too much rum in the rum balls.

The New Year's Eve party was more formal and lavish. Elvis rented the Manhattan Club and arranged for food, drinks, party favors, and entertainment. He arrived early with Priscilla, who was wearing a black dress with a black-and-gold jacket. She told me during the party that Elvis didn't like the original gown but bought it for her to get the jacket, which was then coordinated with another dress.

Elvis didn't dance at the party. At the infrequent parties when he did walk onto the dance floor, it was always with Priscilla. At those times other dancers either stopped or moved away, giving the host and hostess plenty of room—probably more than they wanted.

If the other dancers had been less intimidated, Elvis might have danced more. He seemed embarrassed, and when I stopped by his table to say hello he half-jokingly asked, "What's the matter with everyone? Nobody seems to want to dance when Priscilla and I get on the floor." Consequently, most of the time he sat at his table, sipping at a soft drink while watching others dance or listening to the entertainers.

Elvis always hired good entertainers for the night club parties, people like Ronnie Milsap, Willie Mitchell, and B. J. Thomas. Elvis allowed them to do all the singing. It was his night off and he stayed away from the microphone.

Milsap sang in 1970 when the party was at T. J.'s, a supper club managed by Alan Fortas. Several other musicians whom Elvis had previously worked with also did a turn on stage. It was one of the better parties.

During those years Elvis was generous with his party invitations, and several hundred people would crowd into the clubs. They were always full of beautiful girls, and some of the guys brought two or three each.

Most of the girls tried to get Elvis's attention, getting their dates to dance them by his table where they would talk loudly, suddenly laugh, wiggle their hips at him, or fake tripping.

A stunning brunette with shoulder-length hair and a beauty-pageant figure was the boldest of all at the 1963 party at the Manhattan Club. She was so desperate for Elvis's attention that she broke away from her boyfriend and started stripping her clothes off. Elvis turned away in his chair.

It was a moment or two before people realized what was happening. When her dress settled around her ankles and she stepped out wearing only shoes, hose and underwear, people just sat at their tables or stood, stunned, until someone yelled the obvious: "Hey! She's taking off her clothes."

A couple of the men then started stamping their feet and yelling, "Take it off!"

She was reaching for the clasp on her bra when one of the men rushed up to her and threw a coat over her

189

shoulders. A couple of Elvis's guys joined him and the three men hustled her out the door. Her boyfriend gathered up her clothes and followed. The girl was crying.

That was the high point of the party. People danced and drank the remainder of the evening until breakfast was served.

Elvis several times rented night clubs for New Year's Eve parties. The other secretaries and I were given guest lists to type for the guards on the door. But, like the more informal movie and fairground parties, the night clubs parties were surprisingly easy to enter, even without an invitation.

Invitations were always sent to the presidents of Elvis's larger fan clubs. But there was a catch: One of Elvis's guys always reminded us not to mail them until the day of the party.

I knew various fan club presidents and didn't approve of the deceit, so one year I mailed the invitations early. One of the fan club presidents surprised everyone by attending the party.

The boys were upset and asked me what had happened.

"I don't know," I told them, shaking my head and trying to look puzzled. "I mailed the invitations like I always do."

Elvis never said anything to me about it, and, in fact, I don't think he knew that his fans were being treated the way they were. He loved his fans and knew they were responsible for his success. He used to be hurt when others claimed that he didn't appreciate the people who attended his concerts, watched his movies, and bought his records.

"When I come back here to Graceland, it's not that

I'm trying to withdraw from my fans," he once told me. "I guess, if anything, I'm withdrawing into myself.

"I just don't always have that much left after working, and I have to come back home to think and relax. It's quiet here and I can get myself together and work things out."

The older Elvis got the more he valued his privacy, and the more conscious he became of his need for it.

That's why he arranged for the extravagant New Year's Eve party in 1966 and then let it proceed without him.

Elvis showed up for the 1973 New Year's Eve party— but barely.

This time he elected to host the party at Graceland, and only thirty of his closest friends were invited. There was champagne, and someone went out and bought chips and dip at Pancho's, a local Mexican restaurant. The only thing luxurious about the 1973 New Year's Eve party was the surroundings.

Elvis and his new girlfriend, Linda Thompson, didn't come downstairs until about eleven o'clock.

Elvis finally appeared wearing an all-black fringed Superfly outfit with a nearly knee-length coat and a wide-brimmed hat. Linda was beautifully made up and outfitted in a lacy silver pants suit with a see-through top.

Elvis and Linda walked around and greeted everyone. As they completed the circuit of the room they walked back out the door and returned upstairs. They were at the party less than ten minutes.

Joe Esposito had flown to Memphis from California to spend New Year's Eve with his friend. "Imagine," he grunted, as Elvis and Linda left, "I came eighteen hundred miles for this."

Lamar Fike, who was so huge that he could be twin to

a younger Jackie Gleason, slumped in a chair, blowing over and over on a party favor and muttering darkly, "This is the greatest party on earth. Fun! This is really great."

After Elvis left, most of the men moved into the dining room to play cards. At midnight the women gathered in front of Elvis's closed-circuit television and waved Happy New Year to him. It seemed to me that this was carrying technology a little too far.

The wives of Elvis's guys talked about their fur coats for a while, then watched one of the girls who had clearly had too much to drink. By two o'clock nearly all the guests had left for home or for all-night restaurants.

Elvis's friends never knew ahead of time if they would see Elvis at his parties, or how he would act if he did attend. He stayed at a club party one year for about an hour. After the band played "Auld Lang Syne," he shook hands with some of the men, hugged the girls, and had Joe Esposito drive him home.

Elvis dressed elegantly for the parties. The New Year's Eve after his wedding he wore a four-hundred-dollar black broadtail suede suit that Priscilla had ordered made for him as a Christmas present. By the mid-1970's he was dressing more casually and staying at the parties for shorter periods.

If some of the parties were disappointments because Elvis didn't appear or stayed only a few moments, the 1972 party was the most subdued, for a different reason. Elvis's and Priscilla's marital problems had already begun and the people close to them were aware of the tension. Everyone was worrying about the marriage.

Priscilla was stunning in a black-and-white leather-look gown with an ankle-length slit skirt and white boots. Elvis, as usual, was dressed completely in black.

The party was at the mansion, and Elvis and Priscilla were seldom in the same room. If Elvis walked into a room where Priscilla was, she acted as though she didn't notice he was there.

Jerry and I were seated on the sofa with her early in the evening, and she was telling us how proud she was of earning her green belt in karate.

Elvis walked over as she was talking, bent down and asked, "Anything you need, baby?"

"No, nothing. I'm fine," she said, without looking at him. She then turned her back to him and continued talking about karate. Elvis stood there for a moment, his eyes showing the hurt, before he turned and walked back across the room to his chair.

I left to get a couple of drinks, and when I returned my husband was still seated on the sofa, talking with Priscilla. Across the room Elvis was slumped in a chair by himself, glowering at him. It was an intense, cold stare.

That night Elvis had a few glasses of rum and cola. It was unusual. He seldom drank alcohol, and then usually no more than one drink that was almost all cola.

Elvis was quiet and morose. Priscilla, ebullient, was his exact opposite.

"Happy New Year," she beamed at one of the wives. "This has been the year I came out."

The next day Priscilla returned to California with Lisa. Elvis stayed behind.

The strain between Elvis and Priscilla wasn't the only problem at the New Year's Eve party that night. There were also two fires.

Elvis had installed a fountain and waterfall in the den off the kitchen, with lights to show it off and pumps to keep the water flowing. The water courses from a wall of sandstone and cascades into a planter. Early in the eve-

193

ning someone in the den noticed that smoke was wafting out of the sandstone wall. One of the men came into the front room and told Elvis. "Ah, don't worry about it," he mumbled, and turned away.

By the time someone had found Mr. Presley and told him, heavy gray smoke was billowing from the fountain and filling the den. People were beginning to move into other rooms. A few wiped at teary eyes with handkerchiefs.

Still no one appeared to be worried about the fire except Mr. Presley, Jerry, and Paul Shafer, the Malco Theatre executive who obtains the films for Elvis's private movie parties.

Jerry and Mr. Shafer began dismantling the fountain, disconnecting electrical fixtures and wiring. They didn't find the trouble, and the smoke was getting worse. They could hear sizzling noises inside the wall and were becoming genuinely worried that the mansion could burn.

By this time Sonny West had joined the other men. He broke a large hole in the base of the stucco wall with a sledgehammer. Jerry reached into the hole and felt the wiring. It was red hot. They clipped the wiring and the smoke soon cleared from the room.

Elvis's reaction was a measure of his mood that evening. "Funniest thing I've seen all night," he chuckled.

The other fire occurred while Elvis and the boys were outside having target practice with guns. But more about that fire in a later chapter.

Elvis and the boys looked forward to shooting guns on New Year's Eve, but they also played with fireworks after parties at the mansion, usually winding up their dangerous sport by dueling with roman candles.

The roman candle duels were more prevalent in the

194

1960's, but Elvis had planned for the 1971 New Year's Eve party by buying about a thousand dollars' worth of fireworks.

It was well past midnight on New Year's Day when Elvis pulled on a heavy jacket, gloves, and a football helmet before walking outside with about a dozen of his buddies.

Those chose sides, distributed roman candles, firecrackers, and cherry bombs to each participant, and began firing at each other.

No one was hurt that year, but when the men returned to the mansion, several of them had ugly scorched patches on their jackets and trousers. Smoke was still rising from some of the jackets.

The Christmas parties were predictably quieter.

Christmas meant presents. And at Graceland that meant excited anticipation of generous gifts from Elvis. It also meant facing the annual puzzle of finding a suitable present for a man who already has everything that appealed to him.

Elvis was generous with Christmas bonuses, and before I began working for him he distributed thousand-dollar checks to all of his employees.

The employees seriously sickened their own Christmas goose soon after Elvis returned from the army, when several of them cashed their checks, got drunk, and didn't return to work until the money ran out. The amount of the bonuses was drastically reduced the following Christmas.

The first year I worked for him he gave $250 bonuses to employees, but the next year he boosted the amount to $700. A year later the bonuses again dropped to $250 for everyone except the boys. They received more

195

generous gifts from Elvis at Christmas and throughout the year.

But even they could be surprised by Elvis's unpredictability. One Christmas he gave them gift certificates to McDonald restaurants.

Cash presents were given to many people who worked indirectly for Elvis. The women in his accountant's office, for example, received checks for one hundred dollars each. The postman who delivered mail to Graceland was given an annual fifty-dollar Christmas check.

Elvis's daddy bought a dozen or more country hams each year, which he sent to Colonel Parker, attorneys, the accountant, and others with whom he and Elvis had a professional relationship.

People who operated the concession stands at the theaters Elvis rented for his movie parties were given presents of small television sets, radios, watches, or clocks that reflected the time on the ceiling.

One of the television sets once disappeared from the mansion before it could be wrapped. When Elvis learned of it he raged around the house for a couple of hours. He was certain that someone had stolen it. Priscilla then told him that she had mailed it to her grandfather.

Elvis bought about thirty such gifts each Christmas. He sometimes shopped for them in stores that opened for him after hours. At other times he had Levitch or other jewelers bring jewelry to the house for him to inspect.

The first year Priscilla spent at Graceland, 1962, Elvis gave her a diamond ring for Christmas. Other Christmases he gave her more rings, watches, and a charm bracelet.

She mailed Christmas cards in 1966, the year before her marriage, showing Elvis and Priscilla standing in front of the outdoor Nativity scene. The cards were signed

196

"Elvis and Priscilla" and provided a broad, early hint of things to come.

On Christmas 1972, just before their separation, he told Priscilla he was going to buy her a new car. She said she didn't need another car, so he gave her ten thousand-dollar bills. Priscilla was already seeing Mike Stone.

The secretaries collected gifts mailed by fans, wrapped those that needed rewrapping, and carried them into the house each year to put under a tree Elvis had ordered cut, then helped to decorate.

The yard men were given responsibility for finding a tree large enough for the mansion. One year Elvis wasn't satisfied with the size of the tree and ordered them to find a bigger one. Other Christmas trees were set up in front of the mansion.

Priscilla collected the Christmas cards from fans and friends in the entertainment industry and took them inside the mansion, where she arranged them around the fireplace. After the holidays they were sent to Le Bonheur Children's Hospital to be used by patients making favors.

A story in a newspaper or magazine was printed one year saying that Elvis collected picture postcards. Mailbags full of them streamed into the mansion for months after that.

Dozens of shirts arrived for him every Christmas, usually the right size. He received piles of handkerchiefs, billfolds, key chains, cuff·links, neckties he never wore and gallons of shaving lotion. An affluent and more imaginative fan once sent him a gold toothpick.

Some fans fashioned their own presents for him, knitting sweaters, caps, and socks. Several, most of them from the Orient, mailed him gifts they made by folding paper, an

197

art the Japanese call origami. I tried to copy some of the charming little animals and other forms they created but was never successful.

The boys pooled their money and bought Elvis a gift each Christmas. Presents they selected include a Bible; a large statue of Jesus that was placed in the fountain near the swimming pool, and a modern clock so complex that Elvis had to show me how to operate it.

The other employees also collected money to buy Elvis gifts such as a Bible dictionary, pajamas, book ends, leather gloves, clothes hangers, pipes, and cologne.

Elvis always opened his presents on Christmas Eve with his closest friends and relatives.

Maids served hot Christmas drinks and snacks, records played Christmas music in the background, and the mansion and estate were decorated inside and out with lights, holly, and ornaments.

Elvis failed to open all his gifts on only one of the twelve Christmases that I was at Graceland. In 1973 there were still several wrapped packages under the tree when I returned to work after the holiday.

He loved Christmas so much that one year he telephoned from California and instructed the yard man to put lights all around the drive. They worked all day and half the night to get the job completed before Elvis arrived home at four o'clock the next morning. He was so pleased that he parked across Elvis Presley Boulevard and sat in the car, looking at the display for several minutes before driving onto the mansion grounds.

His enjoyment of Christmas lights resulted in post-holiday electric bills of about five hundred dollars. Graceland has been without an outdoor Christmas light display only once since Elvis moved in. That was in 1974, during the peak of the international energy crisis.

198

Easter Greeting

Elvis Presley

1967

Elvis's Easter 1967
greeting to his fans.

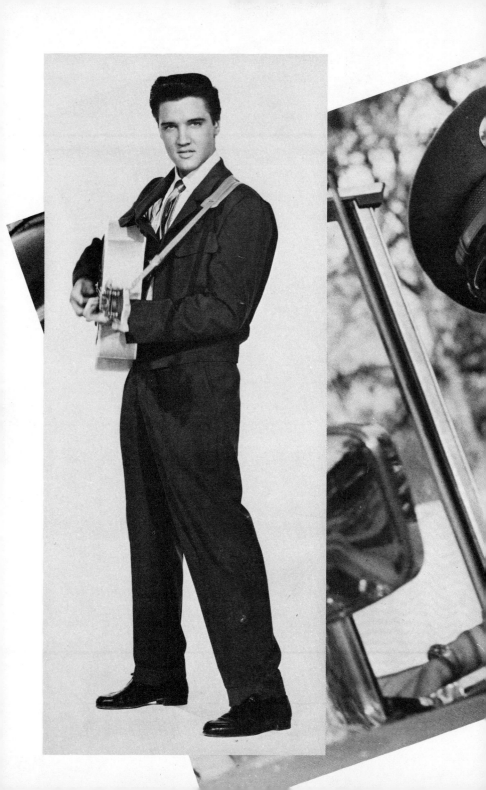

Elvis in uniform; many thought at the time that Army service would end his career.

202

Elvis on horseback, at his ranch in Mississippi. (Pictorial Parade)

Vernon and Dee Presley in front of the mansion at Graceland.

203

Elvis and co-star Carolyn Jones in *King Creole*. (Paramount Pictures)

Elvis in army days; left with the jeep he drove; right wearing his expert marksman medal.

207

208

Becky Yancey today.
(Beaverbrook Newspapers)

209

Elvis sings and plays in a scene from 1969's *Change of Habit*, co-starring Mary Tyler Moore. (Universal Pictures)

A souvenir for fans—
SP5 Presley playing
guitar.

Elvis during a tour
late in his career.

212

213

Elvis with old friend,
disc jockey George
Klein.

214

215

Elvis in performance, at his 1974 Memphis show. (Beaverbrook Newspapers)

216

218

Chapter Eleven

Graceland

On the preceding
page: Elvis disembarking
from a train, followed
by his ever-watchful
manager, Col. Tom
Parker (top)

*M*emphis, in the southwestern corner of Tennessee along the banks of the Mississippi River, has been called America's cleanest and quietest city.

It is the South's largest center of river, rail, and highway transportation. And it is the world's largest cotton market (where buyers can get immediate delivery) and producer of cottonseed products. It is the home of the Cotton Carnival.

Yet when visitors from other American cities and foreign lands come to the one-time tiny river settlement laid out in 1819 by General Andrew Jackson, John Overton, and James Winchester, they don't come to see the cotton, the rail center, or the clean streets.

Most of them climb into cars or tour buses and drive south on U. S. Highway 51 through the city of over 600,000 people until they arrive in what was the unincorporated town of Whitehaven before 1969, when Memphis annexed it. There a stately mansion sits on a small hill approached by a winding blacktop drive. Surrounded by trees and guarded by a ten-foot fence and a gate with two huge images of a man playing a guitar and music notes worked into its iron grill design, the mansion is Graceland—the home and hide-away of Elvis Presley. It is the pop-rock mecca of the world.

In honor of their most famous citizen, fellow Memphians renamed the ten-mile portion of the four-lane U.S. highway that extends through the city and past the mansion. Since January 18, 1972 it has been Elvis Presley Boulevard.

When Graceland was constructed during the last years of the Great Depression, Elvis Presley was a small boy living in a tiny clapboard house in Mississippi. The mansion was built by Doctor Thomas Moore who named it after Grace Toof, the aunt of his wife, Ruth Brown Moore. The Moores inherited the property from Mrs. Toof. Her name was to live on, but only because of the mansion's link to its later owner, who purchased the estate for himself and his parents in 1957 for almost $100,000. The $40,000 ranch style home on Audubon Drive in Memphis that the family had moved into earlier was used as the down payment. Elvis paid the remainder in cash.

It was early in Elvis's career, but the days when he could still find privacy living in a house in an average city neighborhood were already gone. Just as the meteoric rise of the young rock singer spelled the end to the Presley poverty, it also spelled the end to Elvis's privacy.

He was almost a deity to his fans, and their frenzied ob-

222

session forced him into a private life style that was both sad and fascinating. As the world's most popular singing star, Elvis learned he could find a measure of true privacy only at Graceland. Even at home he was surrounded by people, but they were his relatives and close personal friends and they could be called off. They could be told to leave him to himself whenever he wished.

After making his movies, playing Las Vegas, or performing on his tours, Graceland is where had always retreated with a select group of relatives and trusted friends to refresh and recreate himself. It was to Graceland that Elvis went to play touch football with his guys; to drive go-carts, golf carts or snowmobiles with the gas pedals pressed flush to the floor; to bicycle; or to circle model airplanes until he tired of the sport and permitted their engines to sputter out.

Later he could also relax surrounded by majestic cypresses at his half-million-dollar Truesdale Estates home in Beverly Hills or at one of his other homes in the West. To Elvis, however, Graceland, with its handsome oaks, manicured lawns, and imposing mansion, was where his roots were. "I never feel like I'm really home, Becky," he once told me, "until I get back to Graceland."

Maintaining Graceland as Elvis's home was a job that required the full-time attention of about a dozen employees.

Three men were employed to care for the grounds when I left Graceland in 1974: William Earl Pritchett, Albert Clark, Jr., and Mike McGregor. It was their job to keep the carpet of grass freshly mown, tend the few flowers, rake the leaves in the fall, shovel the light snow when Memphis had one of its rare snowfalls, and perform other outdoor maintenance. McGregor, who also

223

functioned as a handy man, performing minor repairs inside the mansion and caring for Elvis's horses, quit a couple of years later.

Peewee Jackson, a black man, worked as one of Elvis's yard men about that time. It was Peewee who was sick when the Presleys hired the temporary employee who tried to cause trouble between Dee, Mr. Presley, and me.

Peewee was cutting the grass behind the mansion one afternoon and paused to chat as I was walking to my car to leave for home. He was excited because Elvis was returning from the West Coast the next day; he said he wanted to get the lawn looking good. He stayed after quitting time to finish the job. The next morning I learned that Peewee had died overnight.

There was always a rush of activity before Elvis returned from one of his tours or trips west. The grounds keepers would sweep the drive, paint the curbs, cut the lawn, spruce up around the old wishing well if it needed the attention, and clean the swimming pool. Some of the boys usually helped with the washing and polishing of Elvis's fleet of cars. Food that Elvis especially liked was ordered from the market.

Elvis didn't use the swimming pool for swimming. He never took the time to learn to swim after he grew up. And his mama was so protective when he was little that she wouldn't allow him to play with other boys his age along the creeks near Tupelo. But he liked to lounge by the pool, lying flat on heavy towels along the edge or, more often, stretching out in one of the chairs while listening to music and reading or talking with a friend. He once had the pool covered, but the top was removed after a few weeks because it was too hot and humid inside.

224

In the early years, a juke box stood in a near-by pavilion. None of the songs Elvis had recorded were on it. There were songs he liked, some by relatively unknown singers and others by established stars like Jerry Lee Lewis, Sammy Davis, Jr., and Tom Jones. "Green, Green Grass of Home" was his favorite by Jones. He also liked "Autumn Leaves," "Gigi," and "What Now My Love," by other artists.

A chicken house, two or three mobile homes, a large barn, a garage, and the building housing our office and the wellhouse shared space on the estate. Some time after I left, Elvis constructed a tall masonry building behind the old patio to play racquetball in.

Two gates open into the complex: the Music Gate, and another that Elvis had installed several yards north of it. The Music Gate was sometimes so crowded with fans that it was inconvenient to use, and the second gate provided an alternate exit. A small gate also opened from the back yard of Mr. Presley's home onto the estate near the barn. When he used his private gate, however, it meant a long walk through the pasture, so Mr. Presley usually drove around to the Music Gate when coming to the house or office.

Most painted portions of the ocher Tennessee limestone-and-wood mansion and all the outbuildings are white, despite a story in a national magazine that reported it was painted luminous blue and gold and glowed in the dark.[1] The shutters are painted a non-luminous green. The confusion is understandable. Elvis has huge spotlights mounted in the yard that beam colored lights on the house at night.

When Elvis was away fans were often permitted to tour part of the grounds and take pictures. They walked away carrying little pebbles, leaves and—when their way of access had been picked clean of every other possible memento—blades of grass plucked from Elvis's lawn. Anything that has ever belonged to Elvis can become a fan's priceless treasure. Fans and their cameras were barred from the rear of the estate.

Many fans touring the estate asked to see the 1956 pink-and-white Cadillac Elvis reportedly bought for his mother. It was the first Cadillac he had ever purchased. Years after Mrs. Presley's death the car was still parked in front of our office and was regularly washed, polished, and cared for by employees. Patsy Gimball and I sometimes used it for trips to the post office and other errands.

Keys to the Cadillac and most of the other cars, including a Lincoln Continental Mark I, were kept in a box in Grandma's room, and whenever we needed something to drive we went inside and asked her for a key. Usually we asked for the Cadillac.

Did Elvis really buy the car for his mother? One of Elvis's musicians once came into the office and asked Mr. Presley. He shook his head. "Gladys didn't drive," he said. The car was purchased for the family—Elvis, his mother and father.

The mansion has been described variously in print as a seventeen-room colonial home, an eighteen-room old-style southern manor, and a twenty-three-room antebellum mansion. Twenty-three rooms, at least, is just about correct—although at the rate Elvis renovated, adding and enlarging rooms, it is easy enough for anyone, especially someone who is not a regular visitor to Graceland, to become mixed up.

One of the boys once suggested that a bowling alley

be built onto the house, but Elvis wasn't interested. He had tried bowling a few times and hadn't liked it.

There isn't another house like Graceland anywhere in the world. There can't be. Its physical features—the wooden pillars, the imposing size, and the grounds outside—are not what make it unique. It's what goes on inside. People are always moving about; the house fairly pulsates.

At one time there were twenty-seven telephones at Graceland (including two mobile phones in cars and a rarely used phone in the barn). The gate guards installed an additional telephone in the gatehouse and paid the bill themselves. I accidentally picked up an office phone once when Elvis was on the same line talking to one of the boys. "Goddammit!" Elvis yelled. "Whoever's on the phone, hang up." I quickly hung up, thankful he didn't know who had interrupted his conversation.

Graceland was constantly changing appearance. Elvis had it redecorated almost once a year after he became the owner. He probably spent at least twice the original purchase price on renovations—and more additional thousands for furnishings and decorating. Carpenters and decorators were always in the mansion, sawing wood and hammering nails or comparing drapery materials and experimenting with color combinations.

Immediately after Elvis purchased the mansion, he had flooring laid in the dirt basement, walls paneled throughout the house, and the walls of the living room, dining room, and sunporch painted heliotrope with gold trim. Heliotrope, pink, and black were almost "trademark" colors for Elvis at different times during his career. White corduroy drapes were hung, and a projector screen was installed for movies. It was beginning to look like home to him.

By 1965 he was firmly settled in the house and the decorating scheme was even more unmistakenly Elvis. His living room was dominated by ceiling-to-floor red velvet drapes hung on push-button electric rods, a twenty-foot long white couch, and white carpeting. White chairs and cushions of various colors were scattered about the room. A fireplace of smoky molded glass was on the wall facing the couch.

A guy at one of the first parties I attended at Graceland whispered to a buddy that Elvis must have had the same decorator who had done Pauline Tabor's houses in Bowling Green and Louisville. It was several years before I saw a book written by her and learned that she was a famous madam.

When Priscilla, Dee, and professional decorators from Goldsmith's Department Store in Memphis did the mansion or portions of it later, Graceland temporarily lost much of its garish look.

A realtor complained that he had a terrible time selling Elvis's house in Holmby Hills near Hollywood because the decorating was so bad.[2] He said that Elvis had practically ruined the place, having done the carpets and ceiling in a "moldy" green. The bedroom had a platform bed surrounded by mirrors and marble. "It looked like it belonged in a bordello," the realtor said. Elvis's tastes in decorating are like his tastes in cars, jewelry, and clothes: flashy and emphatic.

His tastes in decorating didn't significantly change from the time he lived on Audubon Drive where he bought a house for himself and his parents before purchasing Graceland. He bought rose rayon draperies and bright, shiny bedspreads and pillows for his bedroom there.

He was decorating again when I left Graceland. Not long after I left, Elvis carpeted some of the ceilings at the mansion. He selected massive African style furniture for the den off the kitchen, new carpeting, drapes, and blood-red couches with little mirrors all over them for the living room, and carpeting for the kitchen.

Elvis kept an expensive four-inch refracting telescope in the den. He became interested in astronomy when the astronauts were making their moon walks, and he and the guys often took the telescope out to look at the stars.

In the center of Elvis's dining room in the mid-1960's, a huge, star-shaped chandelier hung over a seldom-used walnut table. The chairs that ringed the table were covered with red velvet seat cushions.

Elvis always had half a dozen or so stuffed animal toys around the house when I first met him. Especially pandas and teddy bears. He never had a teddy bear as a child, but his song "Teddy Bear" spurted to the top of the charts in 1957, the same year that "All Shook Up," "Loving You" and "Jailhouse Rock" also became number-one song hits for Elvis.

In 1957 he began talking publicly about his infatuation with teddy bears and how he never traveled without them. The talk was undoubtedly generated at the urging of Colonel Parker. Fans loved it.

They sent dozens of the cuddly toys to Elvis. His stuffed animal menagerie included other teddys he collected primarily from his trips to the fairgrounds. He had a deadly aim with baseballs and won dozens of stuffed animals knocking down milk bottles or pitching the balls into tilted baskets. Most of the prizes were given away.

The first time I saw Elvis angry was also the first time I was at the mansion. He was raging because a girl had stolen one of his teddy bears. "If she would have asked me, I would have given it to her," he grumbled. He would have.

Elvis's trophy room, outfitted after he had tired of his slot-car track, is one of the most intriguing rooms at Graceland. There his entire career can be traced through scores of gold records, Grammys, and dozens of plaques and awards for nonmusical accomplishments. To make room for his continually growing collection of mementos and awards, the trophy room was expanded after I left from the original fifty by eighty feet. Included in the collection are trophies won by a policemen's softball team be sponsored at a cost of about three thousand dollars a year. His most important awards are locked in glass trophy cases. Too many people wander through the mansion for him to take chances with his valuables. A few years ago Elvis transferred all his albums and scrapbooks from the office to the trophy room. The scrapbooks were put on microfilm.

A hallway leading from the trophy room extends outside to a double men's and women's bathhouse beside the pool.

His music room is off the other end of the living room. There for his entertainment were a baby grand piano, white with gold trim, and a television set, also white. Elvis was a good piano player. There were times when I would walk inside the mansion in the early afternoon and hear Elvis singing to himself as he ran his hands over the keyboard.

He occasionally played and sang for pure pleasure with some of the boys or, if they were in Memphis, with some of the professional singers who backed him at concerts. Elvis said that Bill Baize, a young vocalist with J. D. Sumner and the Stamps, had one of the most splendid voices in the world.

But Elvis was especially fond of the gospels done by black bass singers. His own voice was, of course, a high baritone.

For years Elvis did his recording live in Las Vegas, New York, and Honolulu, and in studio sessions in Los Angeles, Nashville, Las Vegas, and—after leaving Sam Phillips and the Sun label, for which he had made his earlier recordings—at the Stax Recording Studios and the American Studios in Memphis. I sometimes typed Elvis's lyrics for him before he left for recording sessions in Nashville.

Occasionally Elvis would do a little rehearsing in one of his dens, familiarizing himself with a new song. Guitars and drums were kept there. But Elvis did not use Graceland for full-scale rehearsals or recording sessions while I was there. In fact, he always kept rehearsals at a minimum. And Elvis wanted Graceland to be his home, not his place of business. (A couple of years after I left Graceland, however, he began doing some recording there in RCA mobile studios brought from Nashville.)

The downstairs den is also where Elvis's famous soda fountain is installed. He also kept some of his favorite pipes there in an exquisite pipe rack on a table next to the couch. For years he favored a pipe shaped like a lion, with the bowl fashioned into the shape of the animal's head. He usually smoked pipes when he smoked at home but would occasionally clamp a cigar in his

231

mouth, chewing on it more than smoking. He rarely smoked cigarettes.

Elvis once had the basement decorated completely in brown and white while he was on the West Coast. He decided he didn't like it when he returned home and had it redone in two of his favorite colors at the time, blue and green. Like many people, Elvis's favorite colors changed through the years.

The second floor was occupied by Elvis's bedroom, his bath, office, dressing room, a former bedroom made into a clothes closet, Lisa's room, another bath, and a sun-porch over the den near the kitchen. There were enough clothes in his closet to stock a haberdashery.

Elvis's bed was larger than king-size, and sheets, bedspread, and blankets were made specially for it. His bedroom drapes had blackout lining to keep the light out. The bedroom was done Spanish style in red and black with red-and-gold shag carpeting. Massive black padded leather doors opened into his room.

A closed-circuit television system with the master controls in Elvis's bedroom was installed by Charles R. Church. Church is a Whitehaven businessman who operates an indoor shooting range and a police accessories store, where he sells guns, ammunition, and other law enforcement equipment. Elvis was a good customer of his.

Cameras for the closed-circuit TV were installed at the Music Gate, the front door to the mansion, in the hallway, in one of the dens, and in Lisa's room. Elvis sometimes sat in his rooms for hours, watching the fans at the gate. And I had a monitor that I could watch in my office.

232

The system's contribution to the security of Graceland is debatable. Elvis appeared to consider it primarily a toy. He had the boys and the Graceland guards for security. Both Uncle Vester and Uncle Travis, as well as another gate guard, Harold Loyd, sometimes carried guns, although they were not required to do so by Elvis or his daddy. Vester patrolled the grounds on Saturday nights.

A guard was hired later to patrol the grounds every night, and another was added for the side entrance to Graceland near the trailers. A security guard was hired briefly to patrol inside the mansion itself after evidence was found that someone had tried to force the door from the hallway to a storage closet just off the kitchen.

Elvis also had his homes in California patrolled. I made out regular checks for bills from private patrol services there.

Elvis apparently never seriously considered guard or attack dogs for Graceland, although many other celebrities have them. Professional guard and attack dog trainers reported that they couldn't supply animals fast enough for celebrities just after the Manson murders of Sharon Tate and others on the West Coast. Charles Bronson, Marlon Brando, and Rock Hudson have all used guard dogs, according to newspaper reports.[3] Although Elvis valued his privacy and security, he thought too much of the safety of his fans to take a chance on using attack-trained dogs to patrol Graceland. Fans are always hanging around the gate and sometimes slipping onto the grounds. It would seem too easy for a tragedy to occur. And after Lisa was born, there was always the danger that she could have been bitten.

Two television sets were mounted in the ceiling of Elvis's room. Television sets were in every room in the house except the closets and the utility room. Elvis paid nearly four thousand dollars for one set with a six-foot metal screen mounted into the wall and a smaller floor console. He liked it so well that he bought his daddy one like it.

Lisa's room was done in yellow and white. A round black-and-white raised bed, covered with fur, required three steps to mount. Elvis bought her the bed one Christmas, and it dominated the room. Mirrors were hung over the bed and dozens of stuffed toys, dolls, and doll houses were scattered about.

After Priscilla left, Elvis stored the furniture she had picked out for the mansion, and redecorated.

The redecorating craze at Graceland extended to our office a few times. When the noise, dirt, blowing sawdust, and general confusion became too great, we moved into the mansion to work or stayed home to wait it out.

One of the workmen advised Mr. Presley in 1973, when the office was enlarged, that a back door should be installed to comply with Memphis fire codes. Mr. Presley agreed. After the door was installed, he had a heavy file cabinet placed in front of it.

We were concerned, because we'd had a small fire years earlier that started when wiring in the office ceiling shorted. Paulette and I noticed smoke and I called the fire department. We were running for the mansion when Paulette turned and darted back into the office to get her Sears catalogue. By that time the office was filling with heavy gray smoke.

A television studio mobile unit followed the fire truck through the Music Gate, and I went out to tell the crew that they couldn't take pictures in back of the mansion.

They asked what the trouble was, and I told them. I didn't realize they were shooting film while we were talking. When they asked me to repeat our conversation so they could record it, I told them I thought it best that I didn't. That night I watched myself on the news. As I was being interviewed my lips were moving, but no sound was coming out.

Mr. Presley telephoned after the show and told me that I was all ready for Hollywood. But he advised me not to try the talkies.

1. *Newsweek,* August 11, 1969.
2. *National Enquirer,* November 25, 1975.
3. *National Enquirer,* June 22, 1976.

Chapter Twelve

The Menagerie

On the preceding
page: The main street
in front of Graceland
was renamed in
honor of the city's
leading citizen.

*E*lvis collected animals the way he collected everything else. When he saw something he liked he bought it. Or he had someone buy it for him.

Graceland has at various times been home for cats, dogs, chickens, ducks, horses, goldfish, peacocks, a parrot, and a hard-drinking, girl-chasing chimpanzee named Scatter.

Although uninvited, wild squirrels have also found shelter and handy snacks among Graceland's pecan trees, and a few nonpoisonous snakes made brief but (for them) tragic excursions onto the estate. They were killed on sight by the yardmen or any of the male employees who happened to be available when the snakes crawled into the open. The squirrels weren't killed, but they were peppered by bee-bee guns whenever they were spotted in the pecans. Domestic animals fared better.

Scatter was without doubt Elvis's most famous and most eccentric pet. My introduction to Scatter occurred at a party when I carelessly walked past his cage, unaware there was a lecherous animal inside. He reached out his long arm, grabbing my wrap-around skirt. I was spun half around by the sudden tug and almost knocked off my feet. He let go when I screamed, and I lurched away, my face red with embarrassment as the other young people in the room guffawed and giggled. Though my modesty was still intact, the waistband of my skirt had been twisted halfway around my hips so that the front was near my back.

I wasn't the first female to become Scatter's victim. The boys taught him to pinch girls and grab their skirts. Not everyone was as lucky as I, and the skirts weren't always Scatter-proof. Some were ripped or hoisted embarrassingly high, or strategic buttons were popped before the girl knew what was happening.

When Scatter wasn't harassing one of the dozen or so pretty girls always at Elvis's parties in Memphis or on the West Coast, he was boozing. The boys taught him to drink bourbon—neat. Someone bought him some little-boy clothes while he was in California, and the boys said he looked like a hairy dwarf seated in shirt and trousers, banging his glass on the bar top until someone filled it with good whiskey. He didn't dress at Graceland. And he didn't dump his drink on the floor when he'd had enough, as I heard he did at the parties in California.

He was taught to use the bathroom almost like a human. Lamar Fike had Scatter give a demonstration at one of the parties. He told Scatter to go to the bathroom, and the chimpanzee jumped up on the stool and perched there expectantly until Lamar ordered him to get down.

240

He was outside another time when he ran through the field at the back of the house and scrambled over the fence. Elvis and about five of the boys were right after him; they all piled over the fence at once. A couple of people were walking nearby and almost began running themselves when they saw the chimpanzee and gang of guys rushing at them.

Scatter was understandably more popular with the boys than with the girls. I wasn't too saddened when one of the maids found him dead. I never learned what Scatter died of but I've wondered if it could have been cirrhosis of the liver caused by his heavy drinking. Elvis and the boys missed him more. He had his own, unique personality and could be as grouchy and irascible as a nasty old man at times. But Elvis and the boys thought he was funny, and they treated him as if he were a small human, letting him party with them and eat at table.

I heard that Elvis had acquired Scatter from an artist who drew cartoons for one of the local Memphis television stations, but I was never able to learn whether this was true. He wasn't mourned long.

Although Elvis enjoyed Scatter, I once saw him show more emotion over one of his peacocks than he had ever shown for the chimpanzee. The emotion was anger.

For all their beauty, peacocks can be noisy, quarrelsome, dirty creatures. Elvis had a flock of them, and he let them run wild around the estate, screeching and filling the air with their shrill calls as they strutted about, fanning their brilliant tail feathers. At times they wandered onto neighboring property, and Elvis's Whitehaven neighbors telephoned for him to send someone after the exotic birds.

My son once gathered about fifty of the feathers the

birds lost while molting and brought them home. I threw them out. A few days later I was shopping and saw peacock feathers, not as nice as those from Graceland, on sale for thirty cents each.

A peacock almost lost more than his feathers when he picked a fight with his own reflection in the shine on Elvis's prize Rolls-Royce. The luxury car had about a dozen or more coats of paint and was polished to a fine sheen when one of the peacocks hopped onto the hood late one afternoon.

Elvis walked out of the mansion a few minutes later and saw the bird furiously prancing over the hood of his expensive vehicle, raking sharp talons over the shiny finish, pecking angrily with his beak, and battering the surface with his outspread wings. It was a vicious fight with a tough opponent whose luminescent image matched every move and attack.

Elvis bellowed and launched himself across the lawn toward his car, spitting out a blue stream of curses and threats. He was the image of approaching doom. Alarmed, the peacock forgot the fight with its reflection. It squawked and scurried off the car.

Elvis was fast, but the bird was faster. Running for its life, the frenzied peacock half flew, half leaped in its flight for safety. Its feet touched the ground only once every two or three yards, and its head jutted forward as if the bird were trying to outdistance the rest of its body, its open beak letting out one ear-rattling shriek after another. The bird quickly disappeared among the trees, its outstretched wings fanning the air in panic and its gorgeous tail trailing, fan down, straight out behind it.

Elvis abruptly stopped running.

He was empty-handed and out of breath. His face was

242

red as he marched tight-lipped to the Rolls Royce and inspected the long, deep scratches on the hood. The peacock escaped, but he must have told the tale to his relatives. I never saw a peacock on any of Elvis's cars after that.

The chase was one of the funniest things I'd ever heard of. But I didn't laugh right away. I would have been scared to laugh where Elvis might hear me; he was in a dark mood. I waited until I got home where it was safe. Then I told my husband and we both broke up, laughing until we had to stop because our stomach muscles hurt so much.

Elvis had a warmer relationship with his dogs—most of them. Muffin was the exception. Notwithstanding his name, Muffin was no softy.

A meticulously groomed Great Pyrenees with soft, long, white hair, he was as bad-tempered as he was beautiful. Elvis and Priscilla were returning home early one morning from Los Angeles when Muffin chased them across the yard, snarling and barking savagely. Elvis had just enough time to shove Priscilla inside the mansion ahead of him, squeeze in behind her, and slam the door. Muffin clattered against the door an instant later, snapping and growling ferociously.

Elvis didn't get rid of the dog. His daddy said he would never sell a dog because something in the Bible said it was wrong to sell dogs. I've read the Bible some and I never saw anything about selling dogs. But Mr. Presley said it was there, and he abided by it.

So Muffin was sent to obedience school. It didn't help. Muffin was simply a vicious dog; no one really knew why. He had never been abused since Elvis had him and was treated as much as possible like the other dogs. But

243

no one could trust him, and he wouldn't change his savage ways. After Muffin was accidentally hurt at the obedience school, Elvis had him sent to a veterinarian and put to sleep. He hated to do it, because he loved dogs.

Elvis must have spent more than a thousand dollars trying to save the life of another of his dogs. Getlo, a ten-month-old chow, became critically ill in 1975, alarming Elvis. Getlo had the best medical care available for man or beast. She was flown across country in Elvis's private Lear jet between Memphis and Boston with two pilots and an M.D. in attendance.

She was rushed to the East Coast metropolis in the wee hours of August 12, accompanied by Elvis's then-constant companion, Linda Thompson, and Dr. Tom Miller, of the acute kidney dialysis unit at Baptist Hospital in Memphis. At Boston it was determined that the dog was too ill to make the remaining fifty-mile trip to the New England Institute of Comparative Medicine in West Boylston, Massachusetts, and accommodations were arranged in the swank Copley Plaza Hotel for two days.

An emergency mobile unit was brought in and doctors worked from the van, treating Getlo until she was strong enough to travel again. "The dog had a serious kidney problem," said the doctor in charge, Dr. S. Lynn Kittleson, director of the Institute. "Its blood picture was very bad. We were even thinking about a kidney transplant or dialysis."[1]

Doctors decided to try a conservative approach first and administered fluid to the dog daily. She responded well enough so that a transplant and dialysis were avoided. She was transferred to Dr. Kittleson's home, where she had the healing companionship of a friendly Great Dane, and was given blood transfusions.

Getlo's health improved sufficiently after two months for her to make the return flight to Memphis. Dr. Kittleson said the dog would continue to require daily fluid injections to prevent dehydration.

The doctor would not disclose the cost of treatment. She said only that ". . . . this dog was treated very specially. I kept the dog home and kept it with me. He [she] really required intensive care." Dr. Kittleson and other central Massachusetts veterinarians collaborated with Memphis physicians and never had direct contact with Elvis.

Dr. Robert J. Tashjian, president of the Institute and a spokesman for the medical team, indicated that the dog's presence in West Boylston was kept secret until after its return to Memphis, partly because of kidnap fears.

"We didn't want to tell anyone because we were afraid the farm would be mobbed and the dog be stolen and ransomed," he said.

But Getlo died a few months after her return home.

There were always dogs around the estate. When I first began working for Elvis, he had a kennel full of poodles. But he preferred larger dogs, and it wasn't long before the poodles were given away and the kennel was torn down. After that he acquired an affectionate collie named Baba that was one of his favorites.

There were other dogs around the estate that were owned by relatives or employees, and Elvis was as fond of some of them as he was of his own.

Mike McGregor had a lovable old tramp dog that hung around sometimes, when he wasn't wandering off on his own. Aunt Delta had Stuff, a black poodle, and a little Maltese that Priscilla gave to her. Linda also kept her poodle at Graceland while she was staying there. And Sonny West sometimes brought his German shepherd with him when he flew in from Los Angeles.

If there was anyone at Graceland who loved dogs more than Elvis, it was Priscilla. She walked into the office one day, and it was immediately obvious that she was upset about something. It was about the time rumors had started about trouble between her and Elvis. I expected the worst. It wasn't that at all.

She said she had been driving through Whitehaven when she saw a dog crumpled at the side of the highway. It had been hit by a car and was trying desperately to get up, but its hindquarters had been damaged and it couldn't drag itself to its feet.

Everyone else was driving past, unconcerned, but Priscilla stopped. Oblivious to the danger of being bitten by the frightened, pain-wracked animal, she lifted it gently into her car and drove it to a veterinarian. Elvis paid the medical bills.

"I just don't understand how someone can treat a poor dumb animal that way, Becky," Priscilla said. "The poor thing was hurt so bad. It was so pathetic."

Priscilla took good care of her pets. Her first dog at Graceland was a poodle, but she was more attached to a pair of Great Danes that Elvis later bought for her— Snoopy and Brutus.

If Priscilla went to California with Elvis, the Great Danes were loaded in crates and flown to the West Coast. When Priscilla returned to Graceland, Snoopy and Brutus returned with her.

They were gentle dogs, as are most Great Danes I've

246

known. But they were so huge that I was terrified of them. They could knock you over if they jumped on you, and I didn't want to be in a clumsy demonstration of affection any more than I would have cared to be hurt through viciousness. When the dogs were loose in the yard, I stayed inside. And when Priscilla brought them into the office with her, I kept my desk between myself and the dogs. I liked them best at a distance.

Brutus died sometime after Elvis and Priscilla's divorce. Snoopy lived to become Lisa's companion and protector, as I've mentioned.

Grandma Presley didn't take kindly to Elvis's private zoo, and it wasn't uncommon to see her walking through the house grumbling and spraying the paths of the animals with a disinfectant. Although most of the animals were kept outside, many were also familiar with the inside of the mansion. Scatter, of course, was a regular in the den for a while. Elvis kept goldfish in the office off his bedroom. He was also fond of a parrot that he kept for a time, and people were always trying to get the bird to talk.

Both Delta and Dee loved cats. Aunt Delta took care of the strays that wandered onto the estate. She fed them until they decided, through whatever reasoning cats use, that it was time to move on.

The baby ducks credited to Ann-Margret grew up with the run of the Graceland yard, developing an easy association with the chickens that were left over from the days when Elvis's mother was alive. Mrs. Presley, like many rural women, felt most at home when she had a flock of chickens in the yard to feed and care for. Someone once recalled that Elvis and his daddy were standing on the front steps at Graceland looking out over the lawn shortly after Mrs. Presley's burial. "Look, Daddy," Elvis sadly observed, pointing to the chickens scratching and clucking in the yard. "Mama won't never feed them chickens no more."

Elvis didn't buy any more chickens after his mother's death. But I never heard that any of her chickens were slaughtered or dressed for table use. They probably were allowed to die of old age.

Elvis loved dogs and other animals, but he enjoyed horses most of all. When he was making movies like *Charro,* (released in 1969), *Flaming Star* (1960), and others that involved horses, Elvis never had to have a double for his riding scenes. Just as he did when he was making movies with motorcycles or dune buggies, Elvis did his own riding. He admired and loved horses, and he was a good horseman. He liked other people to enjoy them as well, and got several of his buddies and girlfriends interested in horseback riding. He once donated a pony and saddle to a Memphis charity.

Most of the time Elvis kept his horses in the barn behind the mansion at Graceland.

Elvis's trips to Las Vegas somehow seemed to be bad luck for his horses. Elvis was telephoned there twice and advised that horses of his had died at Graceland. One death occurred just after Priscilla told Elvis she was leaving. Elvis was already depressed, and losing one of his favorite horses didn't help his emotional condition. Despite all, he had to perform.

The few times that I saw Elvis awake in the morning, he was usually riding one of his horses. One of his favorites was a spirited and strikingly beautiful palomino, Rising Sun.

The palomino was one of my favorites also, and I

248

thought that of all the horses at the estate, he and Domino, a horse that Elvis gave to Priscilla, were the most beautiful. Priscilla took Domino with her to California after she and Elvis broke up, and kept it there with a horse owned by Mike Stone. She said that riding was one of the activities she and Mike most enjoyed together. A few short months earlier she and Elvis had been riding their horses together at Graceland.

There were always horses at Graceland, except for a few months just before and during Elvis's marriage to Priscilla. That was when Elvis was a gentleman rancher.

1. United Press International, *Miami Herald,* October 25, 1975.

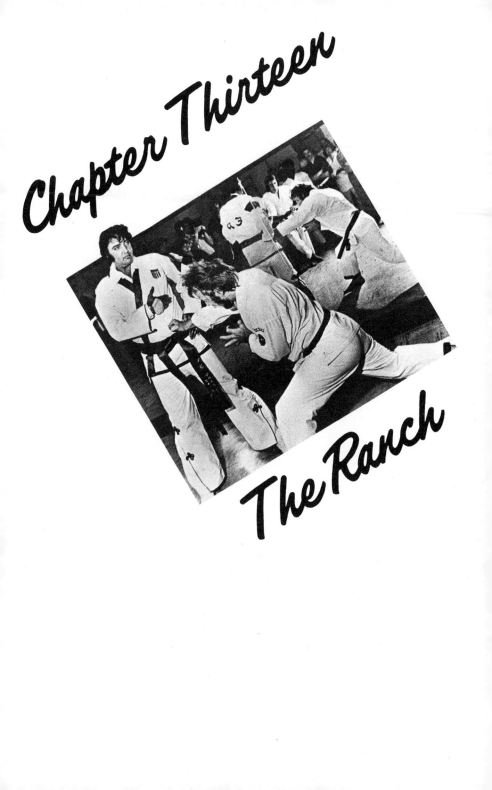

Chapter Thirteen

The Ranch

On the preceding
page: Elvis practicing
karate with body-
guard Red West, in
this picture taken in
1974. (Beaverbrook
Newspapers)

*I*n February 1967 Elvis bought a Mississippi ranch. Dubbed the Circle G—"G" for Graceland—it was one hundred and sixty-three acres of Mississippi pasture land in DeSoto county about ten miles south of Elvis's Memphis estate.

He paid just over $300,000 for a modest one-bedroom wood and brick home, furnishings, a few cattle barns, cattle, and the land. That was just the beginning of the expenses involved in turning Elvis Presley, singer, into Elvis Presley, Mississippi cowboy and gentleman rancher.

Elvis had barely planted his booted heels on the red dirt near Walls, Mississippi, just south of the Tennessee state line, when fans began showing up. The more timid stood with their faces pressed against the sturdy chain link fence surrounding the property. The more adventuresome clambered over.

The Circle G was at the corner of Horn Lake and

Goodman Roads, easily accessible public thoroughfares, and fans could sit in their cars or walk to the fence and watch Elvis as he moved between the house and the long horse stables.

Elvis ordered plywood panels hung at strategic locations along the eight-foot fence near the house. He instructed employees to keep the fans off the property and began contacting neighbors, attempting to buy more land. No one would sell.

His inability to acquire more land didn't dampen Elvis's enthusiasm for the ranch. It was his newest toy and he spared no expense renovating and outfitting it to conform to his likes and Priscilla's.

The house was obviously too small for Elvis and his coterie to live in, so they used it as a meeting place and headquarters during the day, returning to Graceland at night after the work and play were done. Alan Fortas stopped traveling with Elvis and moved to the Circle G to become ranch manager.

Priscilla took my husband and me on a tour of the house and the rest of the ranch one day.

She met us there and first showed us into the brightly pleasant bedroom. Elvis's unique touch was noticeably absent. It was smartly appointed and had paneled walls. The full length of the long front windows was louvered. The spread on the bed and almost everything else inside the house came with the property. Elvis, Priscilla said, bought it almost exactly as it had been when the previous occupants lived there. The furniture, the set of unusual black dishes, even the pots and pans in the modern kitchen, came with the ranch.

Priscilla led us from the back of the house to a new luxury mobile home that she and Elvis planned to live in.

254

Workmen were already busy arranging it to the owner's taste. New carpeting had been installed and the original furniture replaced. A king-size bed and an electric fireplace were installed. I've never seen another mobile home like it. The rooms were huge and there were enormous windows at the front. Priscilla was delighted with it.

We walked from the trailer outside, past a cattle crossing and a bridge on one of the roads, finally reaching the stables. A pond was stocked, and employees were permitted to fish there.

Elvis and his incipient-cowhand buddies were lounging in front of the stables, trying to look like experienced wranglers. Some of them wore horseshoe pins they had been given at a service station, and most of them looked lost in their shiny new bluejeans, chaps, cotton shirts, boots, and Stetson hats. A short time earlier they'd been strutting along the cement sidewalks of Hollywood and Los Angeles dressed in the latest California fashions. But if Elvis, who looked completely relaxed in his ranch outfit, was on a cowboy kick, they were on a cowboy kick. Whatever Elvis liked, they liked.

Jerry and I were impressed with the ranch. It would be good for Elvis, we decided. He had been cooped up too long at Graceland and at his heavily guarded estates in California. He now had miles of his own land that he could range over in privacy, riding his horses, accompanied only by his dogs, his buddies, or his girlfriends. Actually, there had been very few girlfriends besides Priscilla recently. But their romance had been an on-and-off affair ever since she came to live at Graceland a few years earlier. They would be solely devoted to each other for a while, and then Elvis would be seen somewhere with another girl on his arm. Although he was

255

spending more and more time with her and their relationship had obviously deepened, Priscilla had been increasingly ignored—or overlooked—by the gossip writers who made their living following and speculating on Elvis's romances.

In early 1967, when Elvis bought the ranch, he was taking a rare break in his recording sessions and movie making. He hadn't made a concert tour for about five years and was not to resume touring until 1970. He was tired, and he was refreshing himself, recharging his batteries. He had time only for Priscilla and for his new plaything, the ranch.

He went on a spending spree. The boys were given horses and pickup trucks. Elvis bought more mobile homes and had them hauled to the ranch for the boys and their wives or girlfriends. Incredibly, he financed the trailers through the Westinghouse Credit Corporation. It was the first and only time I knew Elvis to buy anything on time.

He didn't finance the twenty-five or thirty new Ford Rancheros he gave away. Elvis began giving Rancheros to the boys and to anyone else who happened to be present when he was in one of his giving moods. During the first few months at the ranch, he was in a giving mood most of the time.

A workman with one of the construction companies was so excited that for a week he stopped anyone who would listen to him tell about the new truck Elvis gave to him. Elvis presented another truck to an electrician. The Ford dealer in nearby Hernando, Mississippi, had a hard time keeping enough vehicles in stock. They were being purchased almost as fast as he could have them driven to the ranch.

256

If Elvis wasn't buying rolling stock or riding horses, he was bouncing over the pitted one-time cotton fields in a white Dodge crew cab truck, kicking up a cloud of red dust behind him. Elvis was a good ole boy driving a redneck limousine long before anyone ever heard of Billy Carter or redneck rock. He had "Circle G Ranch" painted on the doors of his truck, and on the white Dodge the painter had added "House of the Rising Sun." Rising Sun was Elvis's personal horse, and he bought an expensive trailer for him.

Elvis paid some $75,000 for new cars and trucks in a single month. Back in the office at Graceland I was having a difficult time keeping up with the transactions. I had to make sure that all of Elvis's vehicles were covered with insurance. Mr. Presley and I attempted to keep our records current with Elvis's impetuous gift giving, but it was impossible. Mr. Presley would look through the files, shake his head, pull out a set of insurance papers, point to them and ask, "Where's this truck at?"

Half the time, when we finally tracked it down it was a truck Elvis had already given away. And he was still paying the insurance.

Money was streaming out at the same time for riding equipment, blue jeans, and assorted Western clothing. The boys were putting so much on Elvis's account at Sears that we had to type a list of people authorized to charge items in his name. It was a long list.

Salaries and purchase and upkeep of livestock accounted for two of the more serious drains on Elvis's bank accounts during the ranch period.

Several new people were added to the payroll. Ralph Boucher, who had worked for the former owner, was retained by Elvis to care for the cattle. It was a full-time job. If Elvis was going to be a cattle rancher, he was going to have some of the best stock in the South. He bought good animals, and the telephones were busy for a while with calls from cattlemen conferring with Elvis or his employees. Many of the animals arrived with papers certifying their lineage and breeding, and that meant more work for me to do. I typed several letters Boucher dictated over the telephone.

Elvis's uncles Travis Smith and Earl Pritchett joined the staff at the ranch. Uncle Earl, who was married to Mr. Presley's sister, Nashval, came with his family from Missouri to work on the ranch. Uncle Travis already had been working as a gate guard at Graceland. Mike McGregor was hired then, and Elvis took on several other new employees. The time sheet was beginning to look like a roster for an army regiment.

Any ranch worthy of the name has three components: cattle, cowboys, and horses. Elvis had the cattle and the cowboys, but only a few horses. So he made the rounds of area saddle clubs, inspecting horses. As the word got around, people also began showing up at the ranch with horses to sell.

Elvis was a knowledgeable horse buyer, and his horses had to be the best. Most of the would-be sellers who approached him were turned away. But he looked at enough horses to put together an exciting stable of handsome animals, led by Rising Sun, that any horseman would be proud of. Elvis had a mare that he named for William B. Ingram, who at that time was mayor of Memphis. He called her "Mare Ingram." It was while he was at the ranch that he bought Domino for Priscilla.

Elvis visited the GLL Farms owned by George L. Lenox, Jr., at nearby Collierville, Tennessee, a few times

258

to look at Carbon Copy, a prize Tennessee Walking Horse, and other animals. Lenox had some three hundred horses on the fifty-acre breeding farm, and they were all said to be premium animals. Elvis talked a few times about how he would like to own Carbon Copy, who was earning thousands of dollars in stud fees for his owners. Carbon Copy must not have been for sale, because Elvis never acquired him.

The horse was finally sold to someone else for $100,000 in 1976—six years after Mr. Lenox was found murdered in his parked Cadillac on a Mississippi back road near his home. Long before that time Elvis had lost interest in the ranch.

After only a couple of months at the ranch and even without buying Carbon Copy, Elvis's total expenditures for the ranch were climbing near the half-million-dollar mark. His daddy and Colonel Parker were becoming worried. So much was going out and so little—by Elvis standards—was coming in. He hadn't cut a number-one record in about five years. And although his movies still packed in fans, the scripts were showing no signs of improvement.

I eavesdropped one afternoon as Mr. Presley was talking to Colonel Parker by telephone about Elvis's wild spending. Neither of them could get him to slow down. Mr. Presley asked me to compile some totals of monthly expenditures, and when he tried to show them to Elvis, Elvis said he didn't want to see them. Expenses for maintaining Graceland and Elvis's homes in California were, of course, adding to the drain on his finances. I wrote checks for bills totalling $100,000 a month while Elvis had the ranch.

As the situation became more threatening, Mr. Presley

ordered me to type letters to all employees, notifying them that there would be no more loans from Elvis. (The loans resumed a year or two later.)

Elvis seemed oblivious of his worsening financial state. He thought only of the ranch. He was infatuated with it, and he began talking of making it the new Graceland and moving everything to the Circle G. There was plenty of room, he said, to build a house for himself and another for his daddy and Dee.

Mr. Presley asked me if I would mind driving to work at the Circle G instead of at Graceland. Although I would have minded it, I didn't say so. I wanted to keep my job, but the extra miles between my home and the Circle G would make it inconvenient. I had a husband and a young son to cook and care for after leaving work at night, and the extra miles would add at least another hour, maybe two, to my work day.

Memphis was alive with talk of the new Graceland. Some of the guys closest to Elvis were already talking about relocating permanently in Mississippi. Letters began arriving from fans wanting to know if Elvis was going to leave Graceland. A few fans asked whether it was true that his twin was buried at the Circle G. I have no idea how the rumor got started.

I was certain that it was only a matter of weeks before I would either have to quit my job or begin driving almost to Walls, Mississippi, to work.

Suddenly, with no warning, the danger eased. Elvis went back to work. He had to, to support his profligate life style. He and Priscilla returned to California, where he was to begin work in June on *Speedway*, a movie with Nancy Sinatra. Life at the ranch settled down. Titles to new cars and trucks were no longer changing hands faster than I could keep up with the paper work; men with fancy horses to sell stopped showing up at the gate; and the fans drifted back to Memphis and resumed hanging around the Music Gate. The boys, except for Alan, were either with Elvis in California or back at Graceland.

Elvis had been in California only a few weeks when he and Priscilla were married. That marked the death knell for the ranch. A husband and, less than a year later, a father, Elvis's interests were refocused almost completely on the lovely girl he had married.

He and Priscilla visited the ranch a few times when they returned from California, but the old excitement was gone. Neither wished to live in the luxurious but comparatively cramped trailer in DeSoto County, Mississippi. When they came home they came to Graceland. Elvis packed away his chaps and spurs.

As ranch manager Alan took advantage of the decline in activity and traffic to put the Circle G in tiptop shape. The large Circle G painted on the side of the horse barn was the only thing that differentiated it from any other well-groomed country gentleman's farm. Mr. Boucher continued caring for the cattle, now virtually forgotten by Elvis.

I knew the end for the ranch was near when Mr. Presley told me they were going to auction some of the equipment, furnishings, and animals. Many items from Graceland were auctioned at the same time. Fewer fans attended that were anticipated; there hadn't been time for the news to appear in the fan magazines.

Not long after the auction the ranch was sold. It was bought by Lou McClellan, who planned to turn it into an

261

exclusive gun club with a swimming pool, clubhouse, and miniature golf course. McClellan purchased the ranch for $440,100 on a note carried by Elvis.

Elvis had already transferred his horses back to Graceland. The prize cattle were sold to the Winthrop Rockefeller family in Arkansas.

McClellan ran into troubles with neighbors who opposed his application for a permit for the gun club. Problems continued to mount until he had to abandon the project, and the ranch was put up for auction. Elvis bought it back. Eventually it was sold once more to the Boyle Investment Company in Memphis. This time it was gone for good.

A few years later I accompanied my husband on a sales trip into Mississippi, and we drove past the ranch. The grass had grown long. The hot Mississippi sun had begun to peel the white paint from the house, and the printed "Circle G" had all but disappeared from the side of the horse barn.

It was hard to believe that a few years earlier it had almost become the new Graceland, the shrine for thousands of Elvis's fans. The ranch shared the same fate of almost all of Elvis's hobbies except karate. He would come, spend, and lose interest, moving on to something else.

Elvis was too open and inquiring, and his opportunities were too great, for him to tie himself down for long to one or two major interests. There was too much to do and see. He was a Capricorn; and Capricorns are not only ambitious and hard workers, they are deep thinkers. That made him curious about a lot of things. Things like religion. Thing like self-realization.

Chapter Fourteen

Self-
Realization

"*C*alifornia," says author David St. Clair, "is America's most psychic, occult, and mystic state. California is the strangest state in the nation."[1]

Quoting mystics and some historians, St. Clair draws on history and legend to identify California as a remnant of the fabled continent of Lemuria, which students of such things believe existed before Atlantis. Certain wise men survived, they say, settled, and went underground in areas of California including Mount Shasta, and Santa Barbara, near Hollywood.

Whatever people may believe about ancient Lemuria and its wise men, there is something strange about California. Only California, it seems, could produce such "weirdos" as Charles Manson, members of the Symbionese Liberation Army, the Zodiac Killer, and the kidnappers of an entire busload of school children, all within a decade or less.

And it is in California that religions and philosophies like Scientology, Krishna Consciousness, the Divine Light Mission (the Guru Maharaj Ji), the Children of God, Meher Baba, Nichiren Shoshu, and Transcendental Meditation have found their firmest footholds and most fervent followers. They always seem to start or to work best in California.

So it shouldn't have been surprising when Elvis became involved in the teachings of the late Yogi Paramahansa Yogananda. It shouldn't have been surprising, but it was.

Patsy and I were busy answering letters from fans early one afternoon not long after Elvis returned from one of his trips to Hollywood, when he walked into the office, settled himself onto the edge of my desk, and began to talk. We weren't ready for what he talked abouut.

Elvis talked about religion. He talked about the meaning of life, life after death, good and evil, and realizing one's own life potential and place in the cosmos. I was raised as a Baptist and never spent much time worrying about the fine points of such questions. I always felt they could be answered simply and in understandable terms by the Bible or in the sermons of my minister. But Elvis was digging deeper.

"Did you ever hear of Yogi Paramahansa Yogananda?" Elvis asked.[2]

We hadn't.

Yogananda, Elvis told us, was a respected yogi who died in March 1952 in Los Angeles after founding the Self-Realization Fellowship (SRF) headquartered in the United States and the Yogoda Sat-Sanga Society (YSS) in India. When the yogi's body was buried twenty days after his death, it still showed no signs of physical disintegration or decay.

To his followers that was a demonstration in death of the knowledge he had imparted in life: the value of yoga as a technique for God-realization.

Elvis was impressed. He told us he had talked with people who belonged to the SRF and was reading their literature. He said it was helping him to develop a new perspective on religion and man's place in the universe.

Elvis was losing me, but I listened attentively.

There followed a pause in the one-sided conversation. Elvis was sitting quietly, pondering. Then he blurted out:

"Adam and Eve never really existed, you know. They are part of an allegory. It's a story you're told to help you understand the teachings of the Bible."

I was stunned. I couldn't believe that Elvis was sitting there telling me that part of the Bible was something someone just made up. That kind of talk didn't fit in with my Baptist background, and it didn't fit in with Elvis's religious upbringing. But people didn't argue with Elvis. Besides, he was talking about things I had never heard of before, things he was better prepared to discuss because he had been studying them. Most of all, I didn't want to chance provoking the Presley temper. Elvis was used to people agreeing with him. So I listened, nodding my head occasionally or muttering a soft, "Oh, I see."

Elvis told us how a yogi, or guru—a spiritual master— is able to lessen the sorrows of mankind by providing spiritual and intellectual counseling; and by performing healings, sometimes by transferring the illnesses into his own body.

Patsy and I didn't know what to say to each other

when Elvis left—about three hours later. We were both shaken. It wasn't the kind of talk that we were used to from Elvis. Elvis was raised as a Christian and lived as a Christian. But he didn't sound like a Christian talking to us that day. It was unsettling.

We didn't say anything to him about our discomfort, but either he sensed it or someone closer to him said what we were afraid to say. A couple of days later when he stopped in the office to talk about Self-Realization and the meditative discipline of Kriya Yoga that it teaches, he told us that it wasn't something that could ever replace his Christian beliefs. He said it made his Christian faith stronger.

Elvis told us that in the early 1930's Yogananda initiated a practice of day-long meditation on December 23 in honor of Jesus Christ. The meditation, Yogananda said, would cultivate awareness of Christ-consciousness through Christ's vibrations of wisdom and love. The yogi also drew parallels in the lives and teachings of Christ and of the Lord Krishna of the Hindu religion. He frequently talked of the divinity of Christ and of Christ's teachings. So the teachings of Yogananda were not inconsistent with Christian beliefs, Elvis explained.

Regardless of how consistent Elvis said Self-Realization was with Christianity, I worried about him. I didn't like the sound of what was happening. But I couldn't do anything about it, and didn't dare try. His daddy was also concerned, however, and he *could* try to do something about it.

After the death of Yogananda, leadership of the SRF and the YSS passed on to one of his disciples, James J. Lynn, and in 1955 to Yogananda's former secretary, Daya Mata, who is still president.

Elvis sometimes received letters from her or from

268

others belonging to the SRF and he told us always to send it direct to him in the mansion or to forward it to him in California. Books and copies of the SRF magazine, *Self-Realization,* also were mailed to him.

A couple of years after we were given those instructions, Mr. Presley told us to stop giving the SRF mail to Elvis. Elvis later had us looking all over the office for a letter from Daya Mata, which he said he knew had been mailed to him. We never found it. Elvis's life was manipulated by his relatives and his friends more than he realized.

Elvis gave a generous donation to the SRF about 1973, and that may have had Mr. Presley upset. He also worried that the organization might try to use Elvis to promote itself. A celebrity's name and reputation can be a powerful force for any group or society trying to attract converts.

The Beatles helped prove that several years earlier. They disclosed that they were students of the teachings of the Maharishi Mahesh Yogi, and the Transcendental Meditation movement exploded on world consciousness. When Cassius Clay converted to the Black Muslim faith and became Muhammad Ali, he focused national attention on the sect and helped attract thousands of converts.

It makes news when a celebrity embraces a lesser-known religion, and press coverage helps a faith to capitalize on the event to bring in new converts and financial donations. Promoters are not shy about pointing out that John Denver practices est; that Kareem Abdul Jabbar is a Hanafi Muslim; or that all four members of the soft rock duos England Dan (Seals) and John Ford Coley and Seals & Crofts embrace the Baha'i faith. The Seals are brothers.

If it isn't the leaders of the various religions, cults, or

269

movements who try to recruit celebrities like Elvis, it is the rank and file. I received several letters and telephone calls from a woman trying to involve me in the First Century Church headed by David Bubar, a Memphis psychic and minister. Presumably if I joined or became a convert, I could use my supposed influence to interest Elvis in the Reverand Bubar and his church. I never became involved with the First Century Church, nor did Elvis.

Several years later Bubar made national headlines when he was implicated in arson by investigators of the burning of a sponge rubber products factory in Shelton, Connecticut he had predicted would be razed by fire. Spokesmen for the FBI said destruction of the fourteen million dollar factory in 1975 was the costliest industrial arson case it ever investigated. The publicity wouldn't have helped Elvis if he had been publicly identified with Bubar or the First Century Church.

Mormons sent literature and books to Elvis, Jehovah's Witnesses mailed issues of the *Watchtower* to him, and he received copies of the *Living Bible* and dozens of other Bibles in the mail from people who asked that he read them. (When stories circulated that he was losing his eyesight, someone sent him a Bible in braille.)

Any struggle there may have been for Elvis's soul wasn't with the devil. Elvis received literature, pleas for donations, and invitations from dozens of religious sects and denominations, all anxious for him to make public commitments to their belief. Most of the literature was filed, thrown away, or passed on to someone else before Elvis saw it.

Writing to Elvis was not the way to introduce him to new ideas or interests. I never learned for sure how Elvis became involved in Self-Realization, but it may have been through his one-time hairdresser, Larry Geller.

If Larry didn't interest Elvis in the yogi's teachings, then Elvis may have sparked Larry's interest, because it was something they shared. Geller and his wife took easily to the southern California life style and bought a home in Bel Air, where I heard they went on to sample various movements popular in that part of the country.

Elvis's reading could also have introduced him to Self-Realization. He was deeply interested in religion and was curious about all kinds of unusual subjects. While he was filming the Hal Wallis picture, *Easy Come, Easy Go* for Paramount in 1966, he read several books that the boys bought at a nearby occult bookstore. Eventually he had collected dozens of books about parapsychology and the occult.

There was a segment in the movie about a group of artists practicing yoga, and one of Elvis's songs in the picture was "Yoga Is as Yoga Does."[3] There was ample opportunity in California for him to develop interests in the Eastern religions or things occult—things like yoga, and also things like numerology and palmistry.

Elvis said everyone has a life number that illustrates his character. There are different systems for arriving at the number, and Elvis talked about it so late one afternoon that it was long after quitting time before he finally walked out of the office and I could go home. I simply wasn't able to say to Elvis that I couldn't listen any longer because I had to go home to put on the bacon and the beans.

Elvis is a five. The number was determined by analyzing his name and converting the letters to their corres-

271

ponding numbers. The resulting number is believed by numerologists to reveal the character and destiny of the individual.

Five was found to be the number ruling Elvis's character and destiny by using the following conversion table:

1 2 3 4 5 6 7 8 9
A B C D E F G H I
J K L M N O P Q R
S T U V W X Y Z

To determine Elvis's number, yours, or anyone elses, begin by converting each letter in the name into the corresponding number. Then add the numbers.

Using the name Elvis Presley, as he and others most commonly write it, without the middle name or initial, the numbers add up to 59.

E L V I S   P R E S L E Y
5 3 4 9 1   7 9 5 1 3 5 7   = 59

Since most numerologists say that one's number must be a single digit, the five and nine are then added to get 14. Fourteen is still a two-digit number, so one and four are added to arrive at five—Elvis's mystical number.[4]

Richard Cavendish, an author who is a student of the occult, says of people whose names add up to the mystical number five:

"A five is a much brighter person altogether [than solid, practical fours]. He is restless and jumpy, clever, impatient. He lives on his nerves. The unusual and the bizarre fascinate him. He loves travel, new people, different surroundings. Fives are jacks of all trades and masters of none, attracted by everything but held by nothing. They enjoy gambling, speculation and risks. They make excellent salesmen. They are adventurous, attractive people, quick-tempered, sometimes conceited and sarcastic. They detest responsibility and avoid it. They hate to be tied down or in a rut. Often inconsiderate and self-indulgent, they are resourceful, resilient, many-sided people, hard to analyze or pin down. For reasons explained later, the key to 5 is the fact that it is the number of sex. (The word 'sex' adds to 5, incidentally.) Fives have interesting but highly unstable love lives and the dark side of their nature may show itself in excess, debauchery or perversion."[5, 6]

It isn't difficult to see many of Elvis's characteristics in those listed for people who are fives. (Numerologists agree that people do not necessarily have all the characteristics consistent with their mystical number, so there's no need to worry about the "debauchery or perversion.")

But there are enough characteristics that I can recognize as consistent with those I've seen in Elvis to warrant serious thought. Elvis certainly has the quick temper, and he can be self-indulgent. He is also attracted to everything; is attractive, sometimes conceited; is resilient and many sided. He is not difficult to analyze; he is *impossible* to analyze.

Most intriguing of all is the comment that five is the number of sex. Elaborating on five, Cavendish writes that it "is the number of male sexuality, because it is made of the first feminine number (2) added to the first masculine number (3) and in love woman is 'added' to man for his possession and pleasure. Where 3 is the number of sex for procreation, 5 stands for sexual enjoyment, sex for its own sake."

Certainly there can be no valid argument that the foundation of Elvis's career was not established on his sexuality as well as his talent. Early in his career he and his performances were denounced almost everywhere as obscene. The criticism came from all quarters, ranging *from the pulpits of churches to the "Ohio Penitentiary News,"* which carried a story blasting his version of "White Christmas" as "a song beloved until this creature recorded his barnyard version of it."

Bluenoses were so repelled and frightened by Elvis's conspicuously sexual movements that a juvenile court judge in Florida had a warrant prepared for him, charging him with impairing the morals of minors. (It was never served.) About the same time, the Los Angeles vice squad ordered Elvis to clean up his act because it was too sexy. Critics all over the country and in Europe were blaming Elvis for everything from unwed motherhood to the decline of Western civilization. But the kids understood him—and loved him.

Colonel Parker was quoted as defending Elvis's controversial body movements at that time by explaining, "If I'd thought he was doing it on purpose, I'd have been against it; but he honestly just gets overexcited when he sings."[7]

Elvis himself said of charges that his on-stage gyrations were vulgar: "No, I don't think they are vulgar. I know that I get carried away with the music and the beat sometimes. And I don't know quite what I'm doing. But it is all rhythm and the beat—it's full of life. I enjoy it."[8]

Elvis wants to understand himself, and he became in-

274

terested for awhile in the study of palmistry. He was especially interested in what he identified as a "Cross," two tiny, almost perfectly formed creases that formed a cross on the palm of one of his hands.

At that time palmistry and its unique terminology was so unfamiliar to me that I'd forgotten the exact placement of the mark and Elvis's explanation of its meaning before leaving the office that day. Consequently it's impossible to describe the significance of the cross, because its exact location on the palm is supremely important in evaluating its meaning.

But those who believe in palmistry and were aware of subsequent events in Elvis's life might guess that it was on the mount of Venus, the fleshy elevation at the base of the thumb near the wrist, where it would indicate an unhappy love affair. If the cross intersects a line on the mount, it means loss of the person represented by that line.

I've also wondered, since reading more about palmistry, if Elvis's cross is on the quadrangle. It seems possible. A cross on the quadrangle, the space between the head and the heart lines, indicates an aptitude or interest in occultism and the mystical.

Elvis enjoyed reading the palms of other people and predicting their future or matching the marks with their characteristics. He studied my palm and there were no crosses, but he pointed out major lines that were consistent with my life experiences. Some of the boys said Elvis explained the meaning of their life lines for them while they were in Las Vegas.

Elvis is intensely spiritual, and Natalie Wood, who dated him before he went in the army, has been quoted as saying that he had strong, almost mystical beliefs. She said he talked about a supernatural force that plucked him from nowhere and made him what he was.

He was intrigued with spiritual and psychic healing and said that the color green could be used to heal the sick. At other times he talked about spiritualists and psychics.

Psychic Lou Wright, then from Indiana and later of Westminster, Colorado, did psychic readings for Elvis. She didn't talk with him personally, but with Charlie Hodge. Charlie sometimes contacted her, and at other times she telephoned him when she had something especially pertinent or urgent that she thought Elvis should know.

Lou began reading for Elvis after she telephoned the office one day while he and Priscilla were going through their separation and divorce. She said she had a message from Elvis's mother in the spirit world with advice about his financial matters. We explained that she couldn't talk to Elvis, so she read for the other secretary at that time, Paulette. "My God," Paulette said, when she hung up the telephone, "that woman really hit me." Lou had described exactly the clothing she was wearing and the number (two) of children she had at that time.

About a week later Lou read for me, and eventually I mentioned the calls to Charlie Hodge. He asked for her number, and telephoned her. That's when Charlie began getting readings for himself and Elvis. Elvis never mentioned Lou to me and I didn't ask him about her. But for a couple of years she kept in touch with Charlie, who also became involved in Self Realization with Elvis.

Elvis, like many celebrities, believed in the power of

meditation, which is one of the more important aspects of yoga and Self-Realization.

Priscilla also was experimenting with meditation and other means of using the concentrated powers of the mind to accomplish things not normally assumed possible through the use of will and mind power alone. She and the wife of one of the guys once told me they were going to try to contact Elvis and the other woman's husband in California by mental telepathy. They meditated in the bedroom for awhile, but after some time they quit and called their men by telephone. Years later, after her divorce, she considered sending Lisa to a church in California called the Religion of Science.

Although raised as a Roman Catholic, Priscilla had said she thought she would feel more comfortable with some other religion or denomination. She didn't discuss religious philosophy as often as Elvis did, and she didn't have a similarly intense religious background.

Elvis's background showed up in his love and respect for the Bible. He sometimes quoted it or read from it to the guys and his girlfriends at home or while they were traveling in cars and airplanes.

His Bible quoting was especially noticeable just after his interest in Self-Realization appeared to have peaked. It could be that Yogi Yogananda's many references to Christ and the writings of the Bible helped rekindle Elvis's interest.

Bible reading and strong religious beliefs were two of the things Elvis and Linda Thompson had in common. Linda was laughed at by other contestants in the 1972 Miss U.S.A. beauty pageant, newspapers reported, because she insisted on reading her Bible every day. It's natural that Elvis would be attracted to someone who was not only beautiful but also knowledgeable about the Bible and thoughtful about religion.

Elvis was serious about his beliefs and was upset when he learned that one of his fans wrote a letter comparing him with Jesus Christ. Fans frequently wrote letters referring to him as if he were a religious figure—quite a change from the earlier days of his career.

Elvis's religiosity shouldn't have been at all surprising. His mother was a devoted Christian, the kind who gave much more than mere lip service to her faith. She and Mr. Presley raised Elvis to have an abiding faith and respect for God and Christianity.

The first music Elvis remembered hearing was at the First Assembly of God Church in East Tupelo. He learned to sing with his parents in the church and at camp meetings and revivals.

He was affected by the gospels he learned to sing, but he was equally impressed by the preachers. It was from the preachers, he said, with their animated delivery of the Gospel, their leaping about, hopping up and down, arm-waving and foot-stomping, that he developed his performing style.

While he was studying the music and the preachers, Elvis was also absorbing the unbending conservative Christianity of the Pentecostal type congregations. He learned as a little boy that religion was to be taken seriously.

People in the Deep South feel that way about their religion. American linguist H. L. Mencken called Memphis "the buckle on the Bible belt," and he was right. That's why it was so shocking when Elvis began talking about spiritual beliefs that at first sounded completely alien to Christianity.

When I heard stories about Elvis and the boys going up on a hill in California to meditate, I was certain that he was straying too far from his down-home brand of Christianity. But I later learned that some forms of meditation are not all that different from silent prayer, and in his way Elvis was demonstrating a good deal more spirituality than were most of the people who were worrying about him.

Neither I nor anyone else needed to have worried about Elvis. His faith had a solid foundation. It is true that Elvis didn't go to church. He can't. He wasn't able to go to church like other people for about twenty years. Every time he walked into a church door people turned around and stared—or they mobbed him. Years ago when he wanted to hear gospel groups who were playing the Memphis Auditorium, he had to sit behind the curtain. He had to sneak in like a criminal and stay hidden or the other entertainers couldn't have performed.

If Elvis had tried to attend a church he would draw a bigger crowd than the president. At first he was hurt by criticism of his lack of church attendance. It hurt more that he had to give up church, but he knew that he had to accept churchgoing as something impossible.

Critics were quick to toss darts at him and Priscilla because they didn't have Lisa baptized when she was a baby. That was a personal decision that the parents had a right to make. Elvis and Priscilla had been raised in different religions, and they decided that they would withhold baptism until Lisa was old enough to make her own choice.

Although Lisa wasn't baptized, religious instruction was made part of her life, and she knows the same Bible stories that most Christian and Jewish children know. She had the additional advantage of listening in when her father and Charlie Hodge or others gathered around the piano at home to sing gospels.

Elvis never neglected recording spiritual songs. Ignoring the vicious attacks that followed the release of his recording of "White Christmas" and other Christmas songs early in his career, he continued doing religious singles and albums. The album *Peace in the Valley,* which was recorded in 1957, is still selling after twenty years.

But *How Great Thou Art* was his most important religious album. He and Colonel Parker paid the stations so the songs could be played without commercials, and the album was honored a year later with a Grammy award for the best sacred performance. Elvis was as pleased with that as with any award he ever received.

"Crying In The Chapel" was for many the most memorable cut on the album, but Elvis's favorite was the title song. The day he received his first copy of the album, he called the other secretary and me into the house to listen to it with him. Elvis said he had heard that the song was written by a woman just after she had survived a tornado, and he was impressed with the depth of feeling in the lyrics. It was whispered that Elvis was wrong about how the song came to be composed, but no one disputed him to his face.

Elvis's religious background showed up constantly, but it was most obvious in the way he treated people. He remembered the Golden Rule and treated others as he hoped to be treated. Certainly, there were times when

280

his temper flared, but Elvis always tried to do what was right. The lessons his mother taught him were learned well.

Some fans got the idea that Elvis's aunt Nashval Pritchett had a lot to do with his strong sense of spirituality. The story probably got started because she is an Assembly of God Minister. But although Elvis respects and likes his daddy's sister, Nashval, he said his mother and no one else had been the great religious influence in his life.

Aunt Nash was easy to like. She was always smiling. Her religion made her happy, not dour and depressed as some preachers become. But that doesn't mean she can't deliver a fire and brimstone sermon that will scorch the shine off your shoes. She has the style and most of the movements in the pulpit of the preachers who so impressed Elvis when he was a little boy. Nash and her husband, William Earl Pritchett, now live in one of the mobile homes on the estate.

Elvis purchased the land to build her a church not long after she and her husband came to Memphis. Elvis also gave her his once-white piano for the church. He had painted it gold by that time.

Both Nash and Elvis's Aunt Delta were nicknamed Peggy, but family members called them "Nash" and "Delta." It could be confusing, though, when other people telephoned the office and asked for "Peggy." Both women picked the nickname after they grew up, and neither knew immediately that the other had chosen it.

They had the same nicknames, but Delta and Nash were worlds apart. Aunt Delta had the Presley temper, and she let it flare more than once while I was at Graceland. She got so upset at a wig that she couldn't style to suit her one morning that she ran into the yard and set it afire.

Some of Elvis's relatives took advantage of him, but they had been poor and most of them were good folks. Like Elvis, they were raised with the Golden Rule. They treated people as Elvis treated his fans. With respect.

1. *The Psychic World of California,* by David St. Clair, Doubleday, New York, 1972.
2. One of the most important books in Elvis's library at that time was *Autobiography of a Yogi,* by Paramahansa Yogananda, Self-Realization Fellowship, Los Angeles, 1946, revised by the author in 1951.
3. A 45 rpm extended-play RCA album, *Easy Come, Easy Go* was released in 1967 and contained the songs Elvis sang in the movie. In addition to the title song and "Yoga Is as Yoga Does," the songs were "The Love Machine," "You Gotta Stop," "Sing, You Children," and "I'll Take Love."
4. The so-called modern system, one of two main systems for determining a person's personal number in numerology, was used to analyze Elvis's name. The other popular system is the Hebrew system, which utilizes the Hebrew alphabet with assistance from the Greek. The figure 9 is not used in the Hebrew system, and the alphabet is not listed in the normal order.
5. *The Black Arts,* by Richard Cavendish, Capricorn, New York, 1967.
6. Strangely, as my editor pointed out, by apparent accident the footnote giving the source for determining Elvis's life number is five. Furthermore the number of the chapter is fourteen, which when converted to a single digit again is found to be Elvis's life number, five.
7. *Coronet,* December 1969.
8. *Elvis and the Colonel,* by May Mann, Drake, New York, 1975.

Chapter Fifteen

The Music Gate

On the preceding
page: The *lei* around
Elvis's neck indicates
he's singing songs
from his hit movie
Blue Hawaii.

*I*n a list in the yellow pages of the South Central Bell Telephone Company phone book that serves Memphis, "Graceland" appears between the "Chucalissa Indian Town" and "Historic Homes" as a special attraction. Elvis's estate also shares space on the list with features and events such as the Mississippi River and the Mid-South Fair and Exposition. It's something the tourists must see.

Most of them do! Graceland is the place that epitomizes Memphis to most nonresidents.

Every day and every night hundreds, sometimes thousands, of people park their cars or climb off tour buses along Elvis Presley Boulevard and muster at the celebrated Music Gate.

Elvis Presley Boulevard (U. S. 51) is a busy highway. Not infrequently, though, fans and the idly curious have parked their vehicles on it or lingered there blocking traffic and endangering themselves and others.

In 1976 Elvis donated to the city a 12,530-square-foot piece of land directly in front of his property to be developed that year as a turn-out lane and parking area for motorists. Two years earlier a Kentucky mother and her child had been struck and killed by a car while crossing Elvis Presley Boulevard after congregating with other tourists in front of the gate. Police said the victims had been returning to their car, parked across the street from the Music Gate, when they were killed.

As part of the project to make the area around Graceland safer for tourists, the city also widened the boulevard at a nearby point at Old Hickory Road near the mansion and also in front of the Graceland Christian Church next door.

Fans were always waiting at the gate when I arrived for work in the morning; and fans were there when I left for home at night. Sometimes the same people waited all day, taking pictures, chatting with the gate guards when they could, or sipping at soda in six-packs and nibbling cold sandwiches carried in brown paper sacks while they peered through the iron-grill gate hoping for a glimpse of Elvis. They waited in good weather and they waited in rain.

There were regulars at the gate whom the guards and I, other employees, and sometimes Elvis himself got to know because we saw them so often. They were frank about confessing their dream that Elvis would get so used to them he would offer them jobs or accept them into his circle of personal friends. I recalled my own early visits to the Music Gate on learning that Pamela Parker had been hired as a secretary a couple of years after I'd left Graceland. She was given my old job of answering fan mail. Pamela, who used to work for Evangelist Oral

286

Roberts in Oklahoma, was a girl I had seen hanging around the gate for a while.

Not everyone who congregated at the gate was waiting for a job. Some sincerely wished only for a chance to see and perhaps speak to Elvis. Others, well aware of his reputation for impetuous generosity, hoped to strike it rich—as Tommy Milham did.

Milham wasn't waiting at the gate, but instead whiled away twenty hours in a line for tickets to an Elvis concert in Mobile, Alabama. He was first in line, and that achievement earned him a write-up in the *Mobile Press Register*.

The thirty-three-year-old antique dealer was up front at the concert, and near the end of the show he stood in his seat and shoved a copy of the newspaper article at Elvis to autograph. Elvis handed the article to an aide and started to give Milham a scarf.

"I don't want a scarf," the fan shouted, pointing at Elvis's hand. "I want that ring." Elvis shrugged, and gave him the ring. Its value was appraised at two thousand dollars.

If it happened in Mobile, many fans reasoned, it could happen at the Music Gate. An individual didn't have to stand long in the crowd at the gate to hear people speculating on the chances of Elvis's showing up and passing out cars, horses, or jewelry.

There were "professional fans" who went wherever Elvis went. If he was home at Graceland they looked for part-time jobs so they could stay in Memphis, working just enough so they could afford food and a motel room. Some slept in their cars. A few would show up in campers and, more recently, in distinctively decorated and outfitted panel trucks. When Elvis would leave Graceland to fly to California or Las Vegas, the fans would climb into their cars and trucks and head west, arriving a few days afterwards.

Most, less fanatical in their devotion, came a few times a year when they knew Elvis was home.

Often they saved for years before they could accumulate enough money to finance their pilgrimage to the Music Gate. Mike Gantner, a handsome young man from West Germany, worked for more than three years in a fruit factory to earn enough for his five-hundred-dollar round-trip airfare and other expenses so that he could stand outside the Music Gate for several days and take his chances on seeing Elvis. Gantner paced in front of the gate days and slept in the gatehouse nights. He got an autograph, obtained for him by a sympathetic guard, and three or four quick glimpses of Elvis for his money and effort.

Many fans came to Graceland in tour groups or visited at the Gate while they were in Memphis for conventions of Elvis boosters. Elvis Presley conventions mean busy days at the gate as well as at other spots in Memphis that are linked with Elvis, such as Humes High School, the house on Audubon Drive, locations of his former homes when the family first arrived from Tupelo, the old Sun recording studios, places where Elvis performed early in his career, and the pawnshop where he is said to have bought his first guitar for $12.50.

During the July 1976 Elvis Presley Convention sponsored by the Graceland Fan Clubs, Elvis fans attended a ceremony at the Everett R. Cook Convention Center, where the mayor of Memphis presented Mr. Presley with a plaque honoring his son. That day many of the fans had watched a special screening of Elvis Presley movies from midnight to six in the morning.

Not all the conventioneers who gather at the Music

288

Gate or tour Elvis's former haunts are fan club members. Shrine conventions and almost all gatherings at the convention center can be counted on to mean more people at the Music Gate. Many people plan their vacation trips to include stops there.

Memphis residents put the Music Gate near the top of their list of things to do when they entertain out-of-town friends. When Mrs. Wayne Doster's friend Mrs. Sandy Billiard came from Hellertown, Pennsylvania, to visit, the two promptly drove to the Music Gate. There Mrs. Billiard found a piece of stone that had fallen from the rock fence. She picked it up, and a few weeks after she returned home, both she and her friend were wearing some of the most distinctive earrings in the world. Mrs. Billiard had taken the stone to a jeweler, who crafted pieces of it into earrings for herself and her hostess from Memphis.

Groups like The Elvis Presley Fan Club of Great Britain, which has some twelve-thousand registered members throughout Europe, make annual tours. They not only stop at Graceland, but also visit Elvis's birthplace in Mississippi and catch his act when he is performing in Las Vegas.

During the club's tour in 1976, Tupelo officials unlocked the doors and reconnected the electricity to show the European fans through Elvis's boyhood home. After the tour of the house, Tupelo policemen gallantly gave motorcycle rides to the girls in the group.

At Graceland the Elvis buffs were greeted with less fanfare but were taken on a walking tour of grounds by one of the guards. The tours, by jeep or by foot, go up the drive to the front door of the mansion and back to the gate.

Fans often followed employees home. After my hus-

289

band dropped me off at work one day, two girls from Iowa followed him. They asked him who he was, why he was permitted to drive into the grounds, whether he worked for Elvis, and whether he was in the movies. (Jerry was a parts analysis clerk for General Motors at the time. Later he became field parts and service manager for the Lilly Company, distributors for Yale Forklift.) Fans sometimes tried to jump into the car when we drove through the gate. We learned to keep the doors locked.

Driving through the gate wasn't always as safe as it sounds, and the danger wasn't all from unpredictable fans. Breakdowns were common, and the gate might suddenly slam shut, clenching any car unfortunate enough to be in the entranceway in a grinding, vise-like grip. The gate could be closed using controls in the kitchen, but I never trusted it and considered it as eccentric as some of the flesh-and-blood fixtures of Graceland.

I'd been working at Graceland less than a week when fans first stopped Bonya and me and asked for our autographs. Soon after that I began getting personal letters from fans. My name on the envelopes changed from Hartley to Yancey immediately after I was married.

Somehow fans obtained my unlisted home telephone number, and they phoned in the evening as late as ten or eleven o'clock, sometimes midnight, asking me to help them get through to Elvis. People invited the other secretaries and me to lunch so they could drive onto the estate when they brought us back to work. Neighbors offered to pick me up after work so they could see Graceland from the inside. Those who offered lunches were the more successful.

January 8, Elvis's birthday, has always been busy day

and night at the Music Gate. Fans come from all over, carrying signs or arriving with birthday greetings mounted on their cars. Many leave gifts for him at the gate and then camp there, talking with each other about Elvis and keeping their eyes on the sloping drive. Fans who bring gifts are thanked and the presents are collected at the gatehouse to be brought to the office. Food is disposed of because of the danger that it may have been doctored or treated with poison or some other injurious substance.

Elvis wasn't home for his forty-first birthday observance in 1976, but hundreds of fans spent the day partying outside the gate anyway.

Two cute Mississippi Delta Junior College coeds shipped themselves to him in a ribbon-decorated wooden box that supposedly contained a pair of Russian wolfhounds. Aided by a couple of co-conspirators, seventeen-year-old Areecia (Honeybee) Benson and nineteen-year-old Patsy Haynes climbed into the crate in January 1976 and were loaded onto a truck for the trip to Graceland. Driver Sam Delisi was turned back at the gate when the guard explained that Elvis didn't need any more dogs.

The girls panicked when Delisi started back to the loading dock. They began screaming for him to stop and kicked their way out of the crate. "I thought they were taking us to the dog pound," Patsy later said. They talked Delisi into returning to the gate, and with their two friends, who had joined them, waited several hours trying to wheedle the guard into letting them see Elvis. It didn't work, and all but Honeybee left before midnight. She had talked herself into a place to nap, the leather sofa in the guardhouse.

291

Honeybee later said that although she didn't collect Elvis's records or posters, she liked him because he was "a perfect Southern gentleman." She felt sorry for him, however, because of the way some Elvis zealots act. "A woman was out there at two o'clock in the morning," Honeybee said. "She was maybe thirty, but she looked older because she didn't have any teeth, and she was screaming 'Elvis, I love you. Don't leave me.' "

"I don't think that's right," Honeybee mused. "I would just like to say 'hi' to him. I don't want to tear his clothes off or anything like that."

Shortly after I began working for Elvis, a man from Toronto disguised himself as a priest and tried to get inside the gate. He was no more successful than the girls had been.

Besides stopping at the Music Gate, the Gray Line tour takes visitors to see Beale Street; the Mississippi River, where they can shoot pictures of the *Memphis Queen* riverboat; the Goldsmith Civic Garden Center; and the Lorraine Motel, where Martin Luther King, Jr., was slain.

A number of talented musicians live in Memphis. Charlie Rich, Marguerite Piazza, Al Green, Isaac Hayes, and others help Memphis maintain the reputation it carried as a music center during the days when Beale Street was the home of the blues. But tourists don't ask to see the homes of Rich, Hayes, or Piazza. They demand to be taken to the Music Gate.

One tour guide learned to make sure that only Gray Line tourists are aboard when the bus leaves the Music Gate. Lex Bonner said that one day his charges were safely loaded when a husky man on the bus approached him and politely inquired whether they were about to be taken through Elvis's mansion. He and three other fans had climbed aboard assuming the bus was going to tour Graceland.

The wrong-way Corrigans politely disembarked. But some fans won't take no for an answer when they are told that they can't tour the grounds or Elvis's house. They take matters into their own hands. Some simply boost each other over the ten-foot fence and run for the house. Fans have stolen baby toys, cigarette lighters, and sun-tan lotion from the pool. Anything that is loose or can be pried loose is a potential souvenir. Years ago Elvis chased a couple of fans all the way into Mississippi before he was able to stop their car and retrieve a stolen lawn chair.

Items consistently appear in the local newspapers about fans who have slipped onto the grounds and gotten into trouble.

In December 1976 a twenty-six-year-old man dressed in mod clothing and wearing a Santa Claus hat with Elvis's name on it bulled his way through the gate and ran to the pool, where police found him sitting on a lawn chair. He was singing "Hound Dog" as loudly as he could.

At about eight-thirty that morning the man had strolled through the gate and was stopped by guard Fred Stoll, who advised him he was on private property and had to leave. The gate is frequently left open in the mornings and the guard sits outside on a lawn chair, chatting with tourists.

"This is my house, I have a right to be on my own property," the intruder responded. When Stoll tried to lead him outside the gate, the man shouted: "You're fired!" He shoved Stoll and ran.

Police said that the gate crasher, who aimed several

karate kicks at them before he was subdued and hand-cuffed, warned them that he held a black belt in the martial art. The identification he carried included a driver's license, karate card, army discharge, and birth certificates—all with Elvis's name.

A man from Maryland later contacted Memphis authorities and identified the Elvis impersonator as his son. He said that his son, who had a red guitar with Elvis's name stamped on it and who somewhat resembled Elvis, was not a musician but idolized Elvis. The young man was referred to a hospital for psychiatric testing.

Another incident at the gate occurred about the same time, but it drew wider attention because it involved another famous rock-and-roller and a former buddy of Elvis's, Jerry Lee Lewis.

Lewis—who is called the Killer because of his energetic performing style and because he calls eveyone else that—showed up at the gate shortly after midnight driving a new Lincoln Continental Mark IV and demanding to see Elvis. Harold Loyd, Elvis's first cousin and the gate guard, turned him away.

At two-fifty the Killer was back. Harold said that when Lewis was told again he couldn't see Elvis, he began yelling and waving a two-shot 38-caliber derringer in the air.

Although Lewis didn't actually threaten him, Harold figured that now was a good time to get some help. So he called police after telling his agitated visitor that he was phoning Elvis. The first policeman was at the gate less than a minute after Harold hung up the telephone. Lewis, whom Harold said was glassy-eyed and slurring his speech, was arrested and charged with being drunk and with carrying a pistol. He was found not guilty of both charges at a Memphis City Court hearing the following May.

Elvis's cousin later said that he hadn't been surprised to see the rock star because Lewis had been at the gate about the same time the previous night. Lewis had driven up to the gate around four o'clock that morning in his Silver Shadow Rolls Royce, introduced himself, and politely asked to see Elvis. According to Harold, the visitor explained that he and Elvis had been trying to get together for some time. When Harold said that Elvis was sure to be asleep by then, Lewis drove away.

About five hours after his first effort to see Elvis, Lewis turned his Rolls Royce over trying to negotiate a corner near his home in nearby Collierville. A "breathalyzer" test at Collierville was negative, but he was arrested anyway and charged with driving while intoxicated, reckless driving, and failure to carry a driver's license.

It was a distressing period for Lewis, whose troubles had started in 1958 when he married his thirteen-year-old cousin and was effectively blackballed in the music business for years.

Two months before his troubles at the Music Gate, Lewis accidentally shot and wounded his bass player, Norman (Butch) Owens, and was consequently charged with shooting a firearm within the city limits of Collierville. A few days later, on October 12, he was charged with disorderly conduct after his neighbors complained that he was shouting obscenities at them. And only a couple of hours before the Killer's arrest at the Music Gate, his seventy-eight-year-old father, Elmo Lewis, had been bailed out of the Tunica County Jail in Mississippi after an arrest for speeding and driving while under the influence of an intoxicant.

295

In January 1977, after all his problems with the police, Lewis had his gall bladder removed. His physician said that while Lewis was hospitalized it was discovered that he had injured his back and neck when he wrecked the Rolls Royce. He had previously had a collapsed lung and other medical problems.

Lewis blamed Elvis, or at least his employees, for the troubles at the Music Gate. In an article by Bill Morrison in *Country Rambler* magazine, Lewis claimed he had been the victim of some kind of "setup."[1]

He said he had received two invitations from Elvis to visit him at Graceland. "I'd like to know what other reason I would have been doing up there for if it weren't to see an old friend," he said.

"When you have an invitation to go somewhere, and you get there, and you're waiting in your car for the guard to call the house, and six squad cars surround your car in less than three minutes, and there's a guy taking pictures from a TV station, something's going on somewhere," he complained. "It sounds like a setup to me."

Elvis didn't make a public statement about the incident, but he had said years earlier that Lewis was one of the most original of all the great performers of rock and roll. Lewis's "Whole Lotta Shakin' Goin' On," a huge hit in 1957, had a respected spot in Elvis's record collection.

Other people have occasionally appeared at the Music Gate with guns, and a few years ago a fan rammed the iron grillwork with his car.

More recently a truck driver from Berwyn, Illinois, slammed the edge of his hand three times into the massive rock fence surrounding the estate and knocked off a piece of stone. Jerry Dye, who had been showing his karate card to other fans a few moments before and talking about how he would like to work out with Elvis, scooped up the broken chunks of stone and kept them as souvenirs.

Chewing on the stub of a cold cigar, Uncle Vester ambled out of the brick gatehouse and looked at the damage. "They're getting as bad as they were twenty years ago," he muttered, shaking his head. "People weren't coming by so much when he was making his movies. But now he's making his tours again, and it's just like before."

Mr. Presley's brother Vester has been around the gate long enough to see many strange sights. One incident embarrassed him. "This girl just streaked on me one day," he marveled. "I don't know why she did it."

Uncle Vester, who is now in his sixties, told me he taught Elvis to chord a guitar and coached his singing when Elvis was a little boy. Elvis didn't take special interest in singing until he was fourteen or fifteen, Uncle Vester said. "But I could tell he had a wonderful voice. Wonderful, but different."

Uncle Vester chats easily with fans and maintains a friendly relationship with them, even when he has to reject firmly their pleas to be taken to Elvis. It gets wild sometimes! Fans get nervous when they think Elvis is about to appear. Uncle Vester is a good psychologist. He tries to calm them by making them laugh or giving them a picture of Elvis. It usually helps.

When Elvis was home and Uncle Vester couldn't drive fans around the grounds to take pictures, he borrowed their cameras and snapped the photographs for them.

He has seen fans at the gate as young as three and as old as eighty-seven. At three and one-half, Deral Davidson had already made more than one pilgrimage to the Music Gate. His parents, Richey and Brenda Davidson, of Garland, Texas, are fans, and his mother was president of the "Raised on Elvis Fan Club." Deral, his parents boasted, had learned to stand on the fireplace, use the poker for a microphone, and strum his guitar while wriggling his hips 'just like Elvis.'

The eighty-seven-year-old was a woman who was nearly blind and from out of state, but she managed to visit the mansion annually for several years. When she appeared she always asked the same thing: "How's my boy doing today?"

Uncle Vester has coped with hysterical girls, sullen and disappointed young men and, when necessary, has administered first aid to fans.

A girl passed out one hot July day when he told her that Elvis was coming after she had waited hours in the blistering summer sun. Her legs collapsed and she tumbled into his arms. He held her up until she regained consciousness. Then he washed her face. His clothes were smeared with lipstick when she left. Much worse, by the time she had come to, Elvis had gone.

The most difficult times for Uncle Vester were those when Elvis made one of his increasingly rare appearances at the gate to sign autographs, or when he would ride a golf cart or his palomino to the gate to chat with fans. People would materialize from everywhere. Tires squealed and cars pulled off the highway, parking willy-nilly as passengers would leap out and run toward Elvis. Memphis police were dispatched to Graceland on those occasions to direct traffic on Elvis Presley Boulevard.

Elvis was signing authographs at the gate one day

298

when without realizing it he and a crowd of people edged out into the middle of the highway. Cars were stopped in both lanes. Uncle Vester stepped in and led Elvis and the crowd back to the safety of the gate.

Young girls play up to Uncle Vester and the other guards, promising anything for a chance to see Elvis. It doesn't do them any good, although one of the guards got in trouble several years ago for sneaking fans up to the pool for midnight dips.

Fred Stoll and Sterling Pepper were the only guards working at the Music Gate while I was at Graceland who were not related to Elvis.

The gate guards, whoever they are, rely on diplomacy, tact, and a conscientious but friendly attitude when dealing with fans. They will do what they can to help them, but they are always aware that their first duty is to protect Elvis and his privacy. Fans can't get to Elvis by giving presents or money to the guards or by promising them favors of any kind.

The only people who get to come through the gate to see Elvis are his family, some business associates and friends, the boys, and his girlfriends.

---

1. *Country Rambler,* February 10, 1977. Author Morrison interviewed Lewis by telephone in Lewis's room in a Memphis hospital, where he was admitted for treatment of ulcers shortly after his arrest at the Music Gate.

Chapter Sixteen

Linda and the Girls

*I*t all started with Dixie Locke. Dixie, a vivacious little brunette Elvis began dating during his last year of high school, was his first girlfriend of any real consequence.

But Dixie missed most of the action.

Elvis was on the road driving trucks too much after he got out of high school and they broke up. She was the first girl Elvis ever told anyone he wanted to marry.

In the following quarter-century, there were dozens of others whom people speculated Elvis wanted to marry.

Pound for pound of newspaper clippings and magazine articles, more speculation has centered around shapely Linda Thompson than around any other girl who has dated Elvis—including Priscilla. Linda, the five-nine, one hundred twenty-three-pound, 36-23-36 Miss Tennessee of 1972 in the Miss Universe contest, was Elvis's closest companion for almost four years. They began seeing each other soon after Elvis and Priscilla had separated. Except for Priscilla, his relationship with Linda was his longest-running romance.

Elvis dated other girls during their love affair. Sometimes Linda appeared with Elvis as one of two companions. Diana Goodman, a fresh-faced beauty with cornhusk yellow hair who was Miss Georgia in the 1975 Miss U.S.A. Pageant, dated Elvis for a while and said that Linda often went along.[1]

Diana was in Memphis in June of that year checking out a possible modeling job when she visited the Music Gate. One of the guys saw her there and invited her inside to meet Elvis. Elvis was sleeping, but she met him that night and he asked her to go to the movies with him. She went with Elvis, Linda, and a bunch of the guys.

Diana flew back to Los Angeles after the six-hour movie date. A few hours after her arrival there, Elvis telephoned and asked her whether she would like to go on tour with him. He sent his private jet to pick her up, and she met him in Connecticut.

She spent several weeks with Elvis, often with Linda present and almost always with several of the boys around.

Linda and Elvis had a "buddy relationship," according to Diana. "She is always there when he needs her, and vice-versa. If there were anything more they would be married by now. When the three of us were together, I was his date. Linda was his friend."

She was a good friend. It was Linda who stood by Elvis and provided emotional support while he was going through the anxiety of his separation and divorce from Priscilla.

He tried to be cheerful during those days and occasionally stopped in the office to talk. Now and then he warned us to watch out, because he was a swinging bachelor again. But he didn't fool us. He was terribly hurt by the divorce.

Linda and Elvis didn't start dating until after Priscilla had moved out. She wasn't at the mansion even as a member of one of Elvis's party groups while Priscilla was still living there.

Linda is a local Memphis girl, but I've been told that Elvis didn't meet her until she and a group of girlfriends went to Las Vegas to see one of his shows. I've also heard that they met at a party at Graceland.

Regardless of where and when they met, Linda became a regular part of the scenery at the mansion. If she wasn't hanging onto Elvis's arm while he was boarding or disembarking from his private jet, she was sunbathing on the sun porch, applying lotion to her perfectly proportioned slender legs, or wheeling through the Music Gate in a new Lincoln Continental Elvis had bought for her.

Linda took easily to the good life and enjoyed the cars, the clothes, the jewelry and the giddy distinction of being Elvis's special girlfriend.

She is bolder than Priscilla. After the eleven judges had selected other girls for the queen and court at the 1972 Miss Universe beauty pageant in Puerto Rico, she strolled over to one of them and demanded: "Tell me the truth. What was wrong with me?" Linda isn't timid.

Tall, with long, shimmering, dark brown hair, she wore clothes that were far more revealing than Priscilla ever wore. Linda chose daring styles that would appeal to Cher Bono Allman. Priscilla often wore blue jeans around Graceland; Linda didn't. She liked spangles, see-through blouses, furs, and exclusively fashioned pants suits that showed off her willowy figure.

Linda showed none of Priscilla's old reluctance to take advantage of Elvis's name when it could help her. Before her marriage, Priscilla never made a point of telling business people who she was or whom she dated.

By contrast, Jeanne LeMay, a former Miss Rhode Island and a friend of Linda's, told me that they used Elvis's name when they made reservations at a restaurant. They made sure that the people at the restaurant knew the table was for Elvis Presley's girlfriend.

Linda signaled a change in Elvis's taste in women. Priscilla is petite, as most of Elvis's girlfriends before her had been. Linda and almost all the girls Elvis had dated since meeting Linda are showgirl tall.

Linda is utterly outgoing and spontaneously enthusiastic. Some of the wives of the guys said she was friendlier than Priscilla, but I disagreed. I like them both, but their personalities are different. True friendliness isn't a matter of style.

Many members of Elvis's circle of intimates, especially the females, disliked anyone he dated—or almost anyone. They seemed to like Linda. She was with Elvis at a time when he needed her, and most of Elvis's family and friends were concerned only that he be happy. If a girlfriend made Elvis happy, they were happy.

Yet when Linda was away she was almost never mentioned by members of Elvis's family. They still talked about Priscilla. Incredibly, they talked as though there had never been a divorce. It was no secret that she would have been welcomed genuinely if she had decided to come back.

The older Elvis got, the moodier he became. He had

periods of depression. But Linda was on hand to talk with him and be his friend through his dark moods. She, better than anyone else, could elevate Elvis's spirits when he was depressed.

She talked baby talk to him when he was dejected. It was so lightheartedly inane that sometimes it snapped him out of his dark mood. At other times they used baby talk with each other for no special reason. They just liked it, and they had special words and absurd phrases that they tossed back and forth. They were Elvis's and Linda's secret words and no one else tried to decipher their meaning—if there was any.

Linda used the same words when she talked to Foxhugh, her poodle. A mailgram she sent from Graceland to Elvis in Beverly Hills would take a master cryptographer to decode; I couldn't resist copying it down:

> Baby gullion you are just a little fella. Little fellas need lots of butch, ducklin, and iddytream sure. Sure I said it. Iddytream. Iddytream? Grit. Chock. Chock. Shake. Rattle. Roll. Hmmmm. . . . Grit. Roll again. Hit. Hit. Pinch. Bite. Bite. Bite. Hurt. Grit. Whew.
> My baby don't care for rings, da, da, etc. etc. Pablam lullion (in or out of the hospital) P. S. Foxhugh will bite sooties if you say iddytream again. Grit. Grit. Ariadne Pennington (3 years old)

Linda used baby talk, but she is intelligent. She was an English major at Memphis State University with three and one-half years of credits before she met Elvis and dropped out of school. In Linda Elvis found a girl he could talk to about his inner feelings; about life, books, almost anything. And she is as cheerful as a morning glory.

Shopping sprees apparently helped keep her spirits high. I realized that Elvis had a serious new girlfriend when I began receiving bills at the office for her shopping excursions.

Mr. Presley instructed me to hold a twelve-thousand-dollar bill that arrived after a three-day foray by Linda at Georgio's, an exclusive shop in Beverly Hills. He called her on the telephone and asked her to come to the office to discuss it with him because the bill was so high. Patsy and I were told we could go to the house and have a cup of coffee when Linda arrived to talk. When I returned, Mr. Presley told me to pay the bill.

Priscilla later told me during a telephone call that she had heard Elvis's new girlfriend was buying clothes at Georgio's. "I never bought my clothes there," she said. "They're too high." Priscilla looked at price tags before she bought clothes. I'm not sure that Linda did. She was much more extravagant than Priscilla.

Many of Linda's purchases were mailed to Graceland. Aunt Delta opened the packages when Linda wasn't there and told us or showed us what was inside.

Elvis gave Linda her own American Express card. The total of charges on the card one month was six thousand dollars. Mr. Presley asked me to itemize the charges, and when I showed him the result of my work, he stared, shook his head, grabbed the sheet from my hand, and walked away. She had a paid membership to a health spa, and Elvis had obviously put no limit on her spending. In return, Linda turn Elvis on to "Whammies." As if by magic, the boxes of the ice cream confection suddenly appeared all over the house.

As Gladys Presley, Dee, Priscilla, and Elvis had done before her, Linda took a hand in decorating Graceland.

Although her efforts were a good deal less extensive than her predecessors', she charged some four hundred dollars to a credit card from a Memphis department store for a new set of dishes. She bought new curtains, placemats, napkins, glasses, and wall decorations for the kitchen.

She selected plants and ordered them placed all around the drive to the Music Gate. She was quietly asserting herself as the new mistress of Graceland. But she was considerate and did not walk around giving orders to people. She occasionally left letters or packages in the mansion for Patsy or me to mail.

The Christmas after the divorce of Elvis and Priscilla, there were again three stockings hung on the staircase. The names on them were Elvis, Lisa, and Linda. Elvis gave Linda a mink coat that year. She gave him a cross on a chain. Linda and Lisa had a close relationship. Linda took Lisa places with her when the little girl was visiting at Graceland. Lisa showed Patsy and me her Christmas gift from Linda before returning to Los Angeles: It was a pretty locket with Linda's and Elvis's pictures in it. Linda gave the same gift to some of Elvis's relatives.

She was with Elvis in Las Vegas once when Aunt Delta took Patsy and me upstairs to show us where rats had found their way into Priscilla's former bathroom. The bathroom then belonged to Linda. While we were there we went into Elvis's office, between Linda's bath and his bedroom. The trophies and crowns she had won in beauty contests were there, and Patsy and I tried them on to see whether we would make good beauty queens. They looked good. And they fit.

Aunt Delta sneaked me upstairs a second time to show me some of Linda's jackets, which were hanging in Elvis's closet. Some still had the price tags on them. They had cost nearly a thousand dollars each.

Elvis purchased or helped to purchase houses in Whitehaven for Linda, her parents, and her brother. Elvis paid notes on her parents' house, and her brother paid the notes on his own. At one time, at least, the homes of her parents and her brother were in Elvis's name. The value of each of the houses was more than $30,000. Linda's, which was in her own name, cost $52,000. I learned after I left Graceland that she'd had shag carpeting installed in the kitchen. Her bedroom was done in white and gold, with an old brass bed.

I was told by friends of Graceland that when Linda's grandmother died a few years ago, Elvis paid for her funeral.

A year or more after I left, Elvis's and Linda's romance apparently began to cool to the "buddy relationship" Diana Goodman talked about. If so, he treated her even better than his other buddies and continued paying for shopping excursions and buying her expensive presents. Linda sported a number of exquisite rings on her fingers, and she continued to dress flamboyantly in fashions from Las Vegas and Hollywood.

As Elvis increasingly dated other girls and Linda was seen with him less often, stories circulated that he was secretly helping her break into Hollywood. In early 1976 Linda made the gossip columns with news that she had landed a role in one segment of the television series *Starsky & Hutch*. Her career hasn't been exactly meteoric since then, but Linda is still trying.

During Elvis's separation from Priscilla and after he first dated Linda, he also began taking out Sandra Zancan, a leggy Las Vegas showgirl, and Cybill Shepherd, a

310

model and budding movie actress whose first big film was *The Last Picture Show*. I became familiar with Sandra's name as one of those of several girls whose aire fare Elvis was paying periodically when they would fly to Graceland, Las Vegas, Vail, Colorado, or to cities on his show tours.

The two beauties were the favorites of the gossip columnists for a while. Newspapers across the country carried the item when Hollywood columnist James Bacon reported that Cybill Shepherd took four days off from filming *The Last Picture Show* to spend with Elvis in Las Vegas. The day Cybill left, Bacon wrote, Sandra flew in on a week-long vacation from *No, No, Nanette*. And the day Sandra left, Linda was back with Elvis.

One of the most titillating of Elvis's recent romances was with Sheila Ryan. A big-city model from Chicago, she was not a show business name. But she had the knack of attracting virile male celebrities. In 1975 she began visiting Elvis at Graceland and accompanying him on tours.

When she wasn't with Elvis, actor James Caan was escorting her to parties. During one three-month period columnists traced the twenty-two-year-old beauty to Elvis on his show tour, to Caan at a party in Beverly Hills for the Rolling Stones, to Elvis in Nassau, New York, and to Caan again in Hollywood. Sheila was obviously much like Elvis. She liked to play the field.

Sheila once parked cars at a posh restaurant in Chicago, and her picture is on the October 1973 cover of *Playboy* magazine.[2] She moved for a time in the social circle of *Playboy* founder and owner Hugh Hefner. Hefner at one time dated another beauty, Connie Kreski, who appeared in the pages of his magazine. Caan broke

311

up with Connie when he met Sheila. Such are the goings-on of the Beautiful People.

Beholding the tableau from the perspective of Memphis, I knew Elvis well enough not to be too impressed about the stories predicting that he had finally found the girl to replace Priscilla as his wife. My suspicions were confirmed in January 1976 when Sheila, then twenty-three, became Mrs. James Caan.

Elvis dated dozens of beautiful girls after his divorce from Priscilla. Brunette Malessa Blackwood was the twenty-year-old reigning Miss Memphis Southmen, representing the city's former professional football team, when she first met Elvis. And as he'd done the first time he took me out, he took Malessa to the movies on their first date.

Not long after that Elvis invited her to Graceland for breakfast, and while she was drinking orange juice with him some of the boys drove up in a sparkling white Grand Prix. Elvis handed her the keys and told Malessa it was hers.

If Elvis ever dated girls after he became famous and failed to shower them with expensive gifts, it was probably some of the movie stars he was romantically linked with. Many of those relationships were studio romances fostered by press agents anxious to generate publicity for young actresses. He was genuinely interested in some of the young women, however.

Natalie Wood was one of the actresses he liked well enough to invite to his home on Audubon Drive not long before his army hitch. For a few days she and Elvis scooted around the streets and roads of Whitehaven on one of his Harley Davidsons. She said that every time they ventured out on Elvis's motorcycle, there was an in-

312

stant motorcade behind them. The lines were so long, she recalled, that she felt as though she were leading the Rose Bowl Parade. On one of the jaunts Natalie tumbled off the motorcycle but wasn't hurt. Both she and Elvis were teen-age idols then, and a photographer stalked them long enough to get a picture that soon appeared in newspapers around the world.

Elvis was no Lothario, Natalie said. She described him as more like a high school date. They had fun together.

At about the same time Elvis was also dating Anita Wood, a Southern girl and Memphis television hostess. She was his frequent companion in the months before he was drafted and sent overseas. He gave her a friendship ring, and after he got to Germany he shipped her a toy poodle for Christmas.[3]

In Germany he met Priscilla. He also dined with Vera Tschechowa, a young Berlin actress, and dated Margit Buergin, a sixteen-year-old Frankfurt beauty.

After Elvis was discharged, the friendship with Anita Wood failed to pick up where it had left off. He once remarked that he didn't know why. She must have just tired of waiting for him, he said.

Years later the girl who hadn't waited, by that time Mrs. Johnny Brewer, with her former professional football player husband, filed a $2 million libel suit against *The Commercial Appeal*. They took issue with a September 8, 1972, article written by copy editor Hope Pectol that stated Mrs. Brewer was divorced from her husband and had what was apparently a reunion in Las Vegas with an old friend, Elvis Presley. The couple claimed her reputation had been damaged by the article.

At subsequent trials the Brewers and other witnesses testified that at the time she was reputed to be meeting with Elvis, she was instead on a camping trip to the Smoky Mountains with her parents and three children. The Brewers were awarded $800,000 damages in the first of two trials, but the award was reduced to $150,000. The newspaper appealed the decision and a second trial was ordered. At the conclusion of that trial the Brewers were awarded $210,000.

During his Hollywood years and later, Elvis dated at various times or was reportedly romantically involved with Juliet Prowse, Deborah Walley, Mary Ann Mobley, Rita Moreno, Kim Novak, Yvonne Lime, Yvonne Craig, Peggy Lipton, Bobbie Gentry and half a dozen or more other actresses or show business people. And, of course, there was the reputed romance with Ann-Margret.

It was reported in one of the Memphis newspapers one day that Ann-Margret was there and was seen riding one of Elvis's motorcycles. The story apparently started when Elvis's Army buddy, Joe Esposito, went riding with a red wig on. Ann-Margret and Joe Esposito hardly resemble each other, but it was a good example of how crazy the rumors could become when Elvis's love-life was supposedly involved. To my knowledge Ann-Margret never visited Graceland until Elvis's funeral.

There are several other Hollywood ladies whom Elvis considers expecially good friends, but as with his relationship with Shelley Fabares, that's all it has ever been—good friendship. Mary Tyler Moore, who played the nun in *Change of Habit,* was one of the actresses he sometimes mentioned as someone he especially enjoyed working with and considered a friend.

The feelings were obviously reciprocated. "I was an Elvis fan before I ever met him. . . .[3] He's gorgeous," Mary said, adding that she had never worked with a more gentlemanly, kinder man.

314

Nancy Sinatra is also one of Elvis's very special but reputedly platonic friends. Her former husband, vocalist Tommy Sands, was another of Colonel Parker's discoveries, and she and Elvis have been friends for years.

"Basically, Elvis is a shy sweet guy who built a wall around himself to survive," she said after co-starring with him in *Speedway*.[4] "His life is work and home, nothing in between. He lives in a shell but he's comfortable."

Living in a shell wasn't enough to protect Elvis from the Pat Parker paternity suit, or a much earlier suit by another girl who charged she was similarly mistreated by Elvis. The first suit died with little fanfare. The later suit, filed in Los Angeles Superior Court on August 21, 1970, by a twenty-one-year-old North Hollywood waitress, drew world-wide attention.

Although paternity suits are considered almost normal vocational hazards by top male stars in Hollywood, Elvis was deeply hurt. He couldn't believe that one of his fans, whom he'd posed with for a photograph in his Las Vegas hotel, would do such a thing to him.

The young woman asked for medical expenses and monthly child support of a thousand dollars for her son, Jason, who was born in October 1970. She also wanted Elvis to be declared the father. Fans wrote to Graceland to assure Elvis they didn't believe the charges. Some added that although they trusted him completely, they would like to adopt the baby.

Understandably, Elvis didn't talk much at Graceland about the suit, and no one else brought it up. No one told me or anyone else not to talk about it; we just didn't.

Priscilla and others who were a regular part of Elvis's family and circle of companions were at the hotel the night the girl said she'd been with him, and it seemed

315

improbable he could have fathered the child. Furthermore, Pat Parker was a rather ordinary-looking girl. Elvis has always had his pick of beauties.

Mr. Presley mentioned the suit to me just once, when he remarked that he saw the baby's picture in a movie magazine. "He's a cute little fellow," he said.

By the time Elvis's engagement to a forty-two-year-old Athens, Alabama, widow and mother of four grown children was announced in her local weekly newspaper, *The Limestone Reporter,* in early 1976, the paternity suit had been all but forgotten. The announcement, published under a picture of Mrs. Iladean Tribble, said she would wed "E. A. Presley, son of Mr. Vernon Presley and the late Gladys Smith Presley."

I'd already left Graceland and thought the news was unbelievable when I read about it after a larger paper had picked up the story. Mrs. Homer McLemore, mother of the bride-to-be, had confirmed in a telephone interview that the story was true.

I was right. The story was unbelievable. Mrs. Tribble and her mother were the victims of a cruel hoax. Elvis didn't show up for the wedding at the First Baptist Church of Athens, although about one hundred and fifty other people did, hoping to catch a glimpse of him. Mrs. Tribble, who had quit her job as secretary to get married, became unavailable for comment.

One of her sons explained that she met the man she thought to be Elvis in a Memphis hospital in 1974. The impostor had visited her at her home and had telephoned her several times before the marriage plans were announced.

Hardly had Elvis's friends relaxed when a telephone call was made to the Kirk of the Heather Chapel in Las

316

Vegas advising that they should prepare for the wedding of Elvis Presley and twenty-four-year-old Alexis Skylar on Monday (the following afternoon).

Shortly before, both United Press International and the Associated Press were carrying stories about Elvis's impending wedding. UPI credited Allan Wexler, vice president of RCA Records, with announcing Sunday night in New York City that the couple would be married in a civil ceremony.

AP identified Miss Skylar as a "94-pound petite brunette" who had been Elvis's secretary since 1973, when she quit her job with RCA. Wexler was quoted as saying Elvis and Miss Skylar were expected to fly from New York to Las Vegas for the ceremony. Elvis, it was said, had been in Connecticut on personal business. When he was contacted by the press, Mr. Presley said Elvis was in Palm Springs and had been there for several days since completing an eleven-day tour. Linda was vacationing with him.

An RCA executive informed callers there was no vice president of the firm named Allan Wexler. Both news agencies withdrew their stories within a few hours of their original release.

It was too late. Contacted by telephone in Las Vegas, Mrs. Geraldine Mulholland, wedding director and manager of the chapel, was first quoted as saying it was true that Elvis was to be married there. Then she was quoted as denying she said he definitely would be married there. She had said, Mrs. Mulholland explained, that "as far as I know" Elvis would be married in the chapel the next day.

Unsurprisingly, Elvis had no ninety-four-pound secretary he planned to marry. Nevertheless there was a large crowd in front of the chapel the day of the anticipated wedding, and chapel employees received calls from all over the United States as well as from England and Germany. A Las Vegas newspaper had run a front-page story about the supposed marriage.

There were no hoaxes involved in Elvis's romance with twenty-year-old Ginger Alden, first runner-up in the 1976 contest for the Miss Tennessee Universe beauty crown that Linda once wore. Elvis likes home-grown southern girls, and Ginger—like Linda—was from Memphis. He began dating his new beauty queen near the end of the year, buying her jewelry and lavishing other gifts on her as he did on all his serious and most of his not-so-serious girlfriends.

In December he ordered out his private jet to fly his girlfriend's parents, two sisters, and brother to Nevada to see his show at the Las Vegas Hilton Hotel.

Their relationship did not progress as smoothly as news of the friendly family gathering in Las Vegas might have indicated. Ginger showed more independence than Elvis was used to encountering and wouldn't always do everything she was told to do. They'd been dating only a few weeks when events in Nashville and at Graceland began to indicate that all was not well between her and Elvis.

Elvis had camped three days at the Sheraton South Motor Inn in Nashville, where he'd gone to record. But he left without recording and flew back to Graceland. The trouble, it was said, was that Ginger didn't like Nashville and had refused to go there. They had argued and Elvis had gone alone. His presence in the city and refusal to work, although other musicians were waiting and drawing pay, made news in the Nashville press.

318

He made more news after returning to Memphis when newspapers reported that he had fired a gun into the air during a quarrel with Ginger. She had threatened to leave Graceland and was on her way out when Elvis appeared at the door, the newspapers said, and fired the shot. Ginger returned to the house.

Elvis changed in the months after I left Graceland. The disparity between his age and the age of his girlfriends became greater than ever. He was beginning to act like a middle-aged man who was becoming unsure of his sex appeal.

1. *National Tattler,* November 2, 1975. Miss Goodman was interviewed when she telephoned to "set the record straight" after a published picture of her mistakenly identified her as another girlfriend of Elvis's.
2. Maggie Daley column, *The Chicago Tribune,* January 23, 1976.
3. *Coronet,* December 1969.
4. *Cosmopolitan,* November 1968.

Chapter Seventeen

Cops 'n' Robbers

On the preceding page: Elvis and Priscilla leaving a chartered plane in Memphis in 1971. (Beaverbrook Newspapers)

*I*t was late afternoon and Paulette and I were straightening our desks, getting ready to go home. I'd just finished putting the cover on my typewriter when Charlie Hodge walked in.

"You can't go out there now," he told us.

Paulette and I looked at each other, puzzled.

I knew my husband would soon be waiting with the car in front of the old wellhouse attached to the office, and I wasn't in the mood for games. I had worked all day and I was tired. And I had supper to cook and the dishes to do.

"I'm gonna leave," I whispered to Paulette. "I'm not working for Charlie."

Paulette opened her mouth to reply but the words never were spoken. There was a series of sharp, short explosions and I watched in disbelief as chunks of wood were torn from the heavy door of the wellhouse in the

323

next room. Ragged chips—some as large as dollar bills, others the size of needles and equally sharp—showered the room like so much wooden confetti. At the same time a series of powerful, invisible blows slammed into the back wall.

Paulette and I screamed and scrambled for cover under our desks.

Elvis and the boys were playing with their guns. They had attached a man-shaped target to the other side of the wellhouse door and were blasting away at it with powerful .357 magnums.

"Oh my God," I cried. My hands shook as I realized that Paulette or I could have been in the bathroom, only a few feet from the wellhouse door.

As Paulette and I were cowering under our desks and Elvis and four or five of the guys were tearing the door to pieces with their guns, my husband, Jerry, drove up outside.

"I had just stopped the car when one of those magnums went off," he told me later. "It like to knock my ears off and it scared the hell out of me when I saw what was going on.

"If you or Paulette had been hit by one of those bullets your heads would have exploded like ripe watermelons. Those guys had to be crazy to be doing that with two women in there."

Paulette and I cowered twice more while Elvis and the boys practiced their target shooting on the wellhouse door, before I finally approached Mr. Presley.

"We're just scared to death to be in there when Elvis and the guys are shooting," I told him. "What if someone was in the bathroom, or there was a ricochet?"

Mr. Presley must have talked to Elvis about it, because

324

they didn't shoot at the wellhouse again until after we'd left work at night. But I know they were still shooting because several mornings when I came to work I saw new holes in the door.

And they continued to shoot the wellhouse up on New Year's Eve.

The same night the wiring in Elvis's indoor fountain overheated, he and his buddies shot so many rounds so rapidly into the wellhouse door that they set it on fire.

Shortly before midnight Elvis sent one of the boys upstairs to get some guns so they could go outside and welcome the new year in style. A few minutes later the guy walked downstairs with so many guns in his arms that he had to bend backwards to hold them.

I never saw anything like two of those guns. They looked like something people would use in war. One of the guys said they *were* used in war. "They're BAR's, Browning Automatic Rifles," he said. "They're the next thing to machine guns."

Elvis's cousin Billie Smith went to the office and got the key to the wellhouse out of my desk so that he could turn the lights on and set targets up. One target was shaped like a man, and others were clay discs lined in a row. The discs were for the BAR's.

Mr. Presley and others who had parked cars near the wellhouse, moved them.

When he was told everything was ready, Elvis, carrying two guns, led his small platoon outside. At twelve o'clock they started firing. Elvis, of course, was the first to shoot.

Elvis and the others warmed up with the handguns and rifles, then started in with the BAR's. Elvis, his body bucking and jerking as he held the BAR under one arm,

325

fired twenty-five or thirty rounds into the wellhouse in less than a minute. Chunks of the clay targets flew in every direction. And the wellhouse door started to burn.

I was watching from one of the windows in the mansion and I screamed, "Stop! Don't burn the office down. I need my job."

No one outside could hear me over the roar of the gunfire, and no one inside paid any attention.

However, Mr. Presley also worked in the office next to the wellhouse. He was as anxious as I was not to have it burned. He yelled at Elvis and the boys to stop shooting and ran to the wellhouse, where he started beating out the flames with a jacket and stomping on pieces of burning wood that had fallen to the ground.

The boys watched Elvis, to see what he was going to do, before offering to help Mr. Presley. "Oh hell, Daddy," Elvis finally yelled. "Let it burn. It's only money."

Mr. Presley ignored him and put out the fire. Elvis told the boys to pick the guns up and take them inside the mansion. Someone set up the BAR's on the dining room table, and Jerry and another man moved them into the den.

Guns always held a fascination for Elvis. There were guns of all descriptions, from B.B. guns to BAR's, all over Graceland. His daddy also collected guns.

At one of Elvis's parties my husband happened to glance into a wastebasket next to the sofa he was sitting on. His eyes widened when he saw a fully loaded .38 caliber automatic inside.

"Uh, I found this in the wastebasket," Jerry said, handing the gun to one of Elvis's guys. "I guess somebody forgot it there."

The guy didn't say anything. He just took the gun and put it away somewhere.

One of Elvis's buddies was once stopped at the Los Angeles airport when a metal detector showed he was carrying a gun. Another time Elvis was stopped when the scanner at the airport made warning noises, but he was waved through when he pointed to his heavy metal belt buckle. He had a small gun under the buckle.

Elvis bought guns from a company in Memphis, called Law Enforcement, that had installed the closed-circuit TV in the mansion for him. He also bought guns and police equipment from a firm in California.

The guys sometimes carried guns and police night sticks around the estate. Elvis had at least two flashing blue lights. One was installed on one of his cars and the other was kept in our office for months.

Ownership of some of the guns—the automatic rifles, for instance—is supposedly against federal law. I never asked Elvis about it, but perhaps he was allowed to own them because he was a deputy sheriff. Elvis, as I previously mentioned, his daddy, and some of the boys are sheriff's deputies.

Elvis was enchanted with law enforcement. A frequent visitor to the Shelby County Sheriff's office, he gave gifts of expensive new cars to any number of policemen. He told me that as a teen-ager he wanted to be a policeman, and planned to apply to some law enforcement agency when he reached twenty-one. By that time, however, he had already become the world's most famous rock star.

The ability to arm themselves legally has probably made the boys' job of guarding Elvis an easier one. But still the job can be harrowing. As the world's best-known celebrity, Elvis's life was constantly in danger. He was vulnerable to sudden attack by any kook who might take it into his twisted brain to achieve instant fame and notoriety by killing him.

His life was threatened many times. There were numerous bomb scares and Elvis and his daughter were faced with kidnaping threats.

He was doing a New Year's Eve concert before more than sixty thousand people at Pontiac, Michigan, in 1975 when police arrested a nineteen-year-old youth who threatened to kill him. Another concert at Phoenix Coliseum had to be postponed while police searched for a bomb reportedly hidden inside.

But ironically enough, most of the danger to Elvis is from the people who love him the most. His fans.

At a concert in 1970, Elvis was severely bitten on the neck by a female fan who approached him as he was leaving the stage. Thereafter, whenever the boys spotted the girl at concerts they made sure they kept her far away from him.

Have you ever noticed those huge sunglasses Elvis wears? One of the reasons he wears them is to protect his eyes from overly enthusiastic fans.

"Elvis has been caught more than once by an accidental punch in the eye or by a long fingernail raking across his cheek," Red West once said at a party. "His fans don't mean to hurt him, but they do. They would pull him to pieces if he didn't have protection.

"They just don't think. It's all emotion. They go crazy, grabbing for him, trying to love him to death. It's a very hairy job sometimes, trying to protect him," Red mused, shaking his head.

"You'd think he'd be safe with the police lines holding

328

back all those fans, but it's like walking along a weak ocean dike. When somebody breaks through a police line, everybody goes. They can be out of control in less than a minute." Elvis's security is carefully arranged to try to avoid incidents like that.

In late 1976, when Elvis spent three days in Huntsville, Alabama, to give a series of concerts, Colonel Parker and some of the boys arrived in the city two days ahead of time to arrange accommodations and security. An entire wing of the top floor of the Hilton Motel was reserved for Elvis and his crowd across the street from the Von Braun Civic Center, where he was booked for five performances that had been sold out weeks in advance.

A table was set up by the motel security staff just outside the elevators, and it was manned around the clock while Elvis was there to intercept any intruders. A couple of the boys maintained a second line of defense, sitting in rooms flanking Elvis's. Their doors to the corridor were left open. Outside, off-duty policemen screened every car entering the motel parking lot to insure that the occupants were guests or diners at the restaurant there.

Only Elvis's group was permitted on a certain elevator while he was using it to go to or from the civic center. Colonel Parker personally selected the lone maid authorized to clean his room, and she was permitted inside only when Elvis was away performing. Security was equally tight at the civic center.

The tight security net loosened after the colonel left town for Mobile, Alabama, to make arrangements for the next series of concerts. Elvis actually stopped in the motel kitchen, talked, and shook hands with employees, giving friendly pats on the back to a couple of waitresses.

329

Press cards are ignored by the boys, and most reporters gave up years ago trying to get through Elvis's security screen.

When I left, Joe Esposito was the highest paid and was receiving $500 a week. The other guys were getting about $225, but their weekly pay checks represented only a fraction of their true income from Elvis.

All their expenses were paid when they were with him. Elvis wound up with a $6,000 hotel bill after a two-day stay in Charleston, West Virginia, during one of his tours. Although he ate only sandwiches and short-order meals, the guys lived it up with steaks and drinks from the bar.

Elvis provided or paid for their housing and much of their clothing. He gave them expensive cars, gifts of cash sometimes as large as $10,000, jewelry, furniture, and countless other lavish presents. In Las Vegas the boys were given money to gamble with. Their wives and girlfriends shared in the largesse. Importantly, many of the gifts and services Elvis provided for them were not taxable.

There was more than one complaint that some of the boys were too fast with their karate-toughened fists when it came to protecting Elvis.

A number of lawsuits were filed in recent years by people who claim they were injured or roughed up by the boys.

Suits were filed against Elvis by two men who said they had been beaten by the boys in separate incidents during parties at Elvis's suites in Las Vegas, according to news reports.[1] Red was reportedly named in one of the suits as the guy who did most of the beating.

A man named K. Peter Pajarinen claimed he was at a party in Elvis's suite in the Hilton Hotel when he was

330

told to leave. He said he started to go, but before he could get to the door, Red and a couple of other guys jumped him. He was thrown out with a broken nose and other injuries. Pajarinen said in the suit that Red is a naturally vicious person, and that Elvis knows it.

Edward Ashley, of Grass Valley, California, filed a $5 million lawsuit against Elvis after what he described as a fracas occurred at another party. It was reported that Ashley charged he was trying to get into Elvis's suite at the Sahara Tahoe Hotel when he was beaten.

Whether the guys are vicious, I don't know. Certainly there's no denying that Red, his cousin Sonny West, and some of the other boys are pretty tough. They're a lot like Elvis. They love physical contact. They rough-and-tumble among themselves at the slightest challenge.

And don't forget that the strain of protecting Elvis could be wearing after a while. Some think it's better to hit first and ask questions later. After all, a lawsuit couldn't have been as bad as having Elvis injured or perhaps even killed.

Elvis and the boys were under heavy pressure all the time he was on tour or performing, and they had their own way of letting off steam.

For years there was talk at Graceland that Elvis carried his guns with him. Then I heard stories that he was shooting out his hotel room lights during his cross-country tours.

But to my knowledge the only time anything was said publicly about it was when Columnist Jack Martin discussed the subject in the *National Enquirer*.[2] Martin quoted a "confidante" of Elvis's as saying that Elvis took pot shots at the lighting fixtures to help himself wind down after performances.

331

Elvis likes badges and other accoutrements of law enforcement almost as well as he likes guns and was a regular customer of Charlie Church, who operated Law Enforcement.

Charlie walked into the office one day and said to Paulette and me, "I have something for you girls." He handed each of us a little box. Inside were sets of earrings shaped like tiny handcuffs.

Elvis distributed mace to all girls for protection.

He had a huge collection of police badges. Most of the boys carried badges, which they had to turn in to me when they left. I kept them in a desk drawer.

Elvis's craze for badges led to one of the most bizarre happenings to occur while I was at Graceland.

It was 1971 when he flew to Washington and got President Nixon to present him personally with a federal narcotics officer's badge. Elvis returned to Memphis with the badge to prove it. We later paid annual membership fees to a narcotics enforcement association, and Elvis received a monthly magazine.

We didn't know anything unusual was going on until one day the boys suddenly realized that Elvis wasn't at Graceland and no one knew where he was. There was near panic as everyone spread out to look for him.

His car was finally discovered parked at the airport. But no amount of questioning could get the airlines reservation people to tell where he had gone. Elvis had left instructions not to tell anyone his destination, they said, ignoring the hard stares of the guys.

That evening while everyone was sitting around at Graceland pulling at his or her hair, trying to figure out what was happening, Elvis telephoned. He said he was in Washington, D. C., and that he was going to see President Nixon.

332

Elvis had slipped into Washington, using one of his favorite aliases, John Burrows, to see John Finlater, deputy director of the Federal Narcotics Bureau. Finlater, we later learned, had been mostly responsible for the secrecy. It hardly availed him.[3]

Carrying a white walking stick, Elvis swept into the White House wearing a purple velvet suit, a cape, a gold belt buckle, and amber-lensed sunglasses.

And when he slipped into the narcotics enforcement executive's office, he left a wake of bedazzled secretaries and jumbled business letters in the typewriters behind him. He was about as unobtrusive as King Kong climbing the Empire State Building with Fay Wray clutched in his massive paw.

It was said that Elvis had more bodyguards with him that day than the President. That isn't true. Elvis slipped out of Graceland by himself and no one knew where he was going.

We were told that Finlater had high hopes of getting Elvis to endorse the agency's nation-wide fight against drug abuse. Additional details were subsequently filled in by Elvis and others.

Finlater balked at the request for a badge. There was no way he could give a federal narcotics officer's badge to Elvis or to any other civilian, he said. He suggested an FBI shield instead. But Elvis insisted on a narcotics badge.

The exasperated Finlater finally told Elvis that he absolutely couldn't let him have a badge.

Elvis asked whether Finlater would mind if he asked President Nixon for a Narcotics Bureau badge.

That was the only way, Finlater reportedly told him, that he would ever get one.

Not long after that Elvis was sitting in the Oval Office

333

with President Nixon. He brought up the badge business.

Nixon told an aide, Egil (Bud) Krogh, to see that Elvis got the badge. Krogh immediately telephoned Finlater and instructed him to bring the badge to the White House, where the President presented it to Elvis.

1. *Modern People,* September 21, 1975.
2. *National Enquirer,* September 2, 1975.
3. "The Washington Merry-go-round," by Jack Anderson, *Chicago Daily News,* January 27, 1972.

334

Chapter Eighteen

A Matter of Health

On the preceding
page: Elvis during
one of his last con-
cert tours, in March
1977. His problems
with overweight are
apparent. (Globe
Photos)

*A*bout the time Elvis observed his fortieth birthday, newspaper and magazine stories began talking of his "bulging waistline," "lackluster performances," and "mysterious trips to hospitals."

The consensus was that Elvis was sick. He was!

The question is, how sick? Elvis, his doctors, and possibly one or two of his intimates were the only people who knew the real answer.

Elvis's health was beginning to deteriorate during my last years at Graceland. His moods became more unpredictable. His weight ballooned, then suddenly dropped as he went from uncontrollable binges, eating mounds of junk food, to a succession of fad, starvation, and doctor-controlled diets.

Increasingly he arranged to have a physician travel with him or stay nearby when he was performing in Las

Vegas or on tour. And he once became so ill that an emergency squad was rushed to Graceland to administer oxygen to him. There was frightened whispering that day among his friends and employees.

I was working paying bills when a truck speeded up the drive and skidded to a stop in front of the office. Two men jumped out and ran inside the mansion, carrying a bottle of oxygen and a mask. Moments later Mr. Presley and Dee ran past the office and into the house.

"What's going on?" I yelled at one of Elvis's guys.

"Elvis is sick," he yelled back.

"What's the oxygen for?

"They said he stopped breathing," the guy shouted, before he turned and ran into the mansion behind Elvis's daddy and stepmother. "Oh my God," I said to myself. "Elvis is dead." I stumbled back into the office. After all the good Elvis had done for people, I couldn't conceive of him being dead. My legs were numb and I could feel a chill tracing a path up my back. I had to sit down.

It seemed like an hour, but I'm sure it was only minutes before Elvis was carried out of the mansion on a stretcher. Patsy and I had left the office and gone into the mansion. We stood by helplessly as he was loaded into a waiting ambulance. Blanketed, with only his head showing, he looked small, sick, and pathetic. But he was alive.

Elvis was taken to Baptist Hospital, and the next day newspapers all over the country carried the stories that he was ill. There had been rumors that Elvis was dying or dead ever since he became a star in the 1950's. It didn't take much to start a story that he was sick or badly injured. He once cut his finger playing football, and a couple of days later fans were telephoning me at Grace-

338

land to ask how Elvis had broken his arm. This time, however it was true. Elvis was sick.

It was the beginning for him of a long series of sudden trips to the hospital that was to have his family, friends, fans, and the journalists puzzled and apprehensive about his health and future.

Soon there were more trips to hospitals. On January 29, 1975, he entered Baptist Hospital for a stay of more than two weeks for what spokesmen said were tests and treatment of an intestinal obstruction.

In June he was in another Mid-South hospital for two days for what doctors said was "an extensive eye examination."

In August 1975 he was back in Baptist Hospital after abruptly breaking off a two-week engagement at the Las Vegas Hilton and rushing to Memphis with his personal physician, Dr. Nichopoulos, by private jet. One night Elvis was on stage looking good despite the presence of an extra forty pounds he hadn't been able to trim from his expanding shape. The next night his performance was spiritless; he was white-faced and bloated. When he dragged himself offstage he said he felt terrible and was going home to Memphis. He left so suddenly, Hollywood columnist Marilyn Beck reported, that not even members of his backup band knew immediately that he had left and that the remainder of their engagement was canceled.[1]

At Baptist Hospital a spokesman tied Elvis's fatigue to an old problem with an enlarged colon. His troubled colon has been blamed for contributing to his weight problem, and one of the boys said that at times it even interfered with his breathing. Dr. Nichopoulos later enlarged on the diagnosis and in a written statement said the fatigue was due partly to dental work performed shortly before leaving for Las Vegas, and partly to frequent tours. Elvis had not been able to perform his usual exercise program prior to his tour and Las Vegas shows, and that lapse had also contributed to the performer's exhaustion, the doctor said. He added that there was a possibility that Elvis might also have "a mild liver disease."

Fans and the world press deluged the hospital switchboard with anxious inquiries about Elvis's health. Letters and cards were delivered by the hundreds, sometimes at the rate of more than one thousand a day. He received so many flowers that he had them sent to the rooms of other patients. One woman sent two hundred red roses. We bought five thousand "thank you" cards after one of his hospital stays to mail to fans.

The day after his release from Baptist Hospital he walked into the office smiling, wearing a black jump suit with metal studs. He looked wonderfully trim, rested, and healthy. It was temporary.

Elvis's illness triggered dozens of rumors of additional secret trips to hospitals, before he cut short another performance schedule on March 21, 1977, and flew back to Memphis with what Dr. Nichopoulos said was fatigue and intestinal flu with gastroenteritis.

Elvis was in Baton Rouge, Louisiana, and some fifteen thousand fans in the Louisiana State University Assembly Center had already watched the warm-up groups complete their acts when it was announced that the show was canceled. Governor Edward W. Edwards and several members of the Louisiana State Legislature were in the crowd.

Elvis had already played concert dates in Tempe,

Arizona; Amarillo, Texas; Norman, Oklahoma; Abilene, Texas; Austin, Texas; and Alexandria, Louisiana, before becoming ill. His physician said other members of the tour group had also gotten the flu.

Two events made the hospital stay memorable. One incident, not really that surprising, occurred when Elvis gave a new car to nursing supervisor Mrs. Marian Cocke. Mrs. Cocke, who had driven to work in her four-year-old Ford, said Elvis called her to his room about noon and told her he had bought a car for her. "I looked out the window," she said, "and there it was." Another patient might have given his nurse candy or flowers. Elvis showed his appreciation with a Pontiac Grand Prix.

The other event was more unusual. Former President Nixon telephoned Elvis during the Labor Day weekend to ask how he was feeling. Elvis had telephoned the president during Mr. Nixon's earlier hospitalization with blood poisoning.

Every time Elvis was hospitalized, various rumors warned that he was fighting a killer cancer; heart trouble; painful withdrawal from addiction to weight-reducing drugs; a stomach condition that required treatment with drugs that made the body retain fluid; or glaucoma that would permanently rob him of his sight.

Dr. Nichopoulas confirmed that Elvis had a history of glaucoma. He added that no surgery was required, however, and the ailment cleared up on its own.

Elvis's fondness for sunglasses and his insistence on darkened rooms in hospitals and motels indicated that his eyes still troubled him. When he entered Baptist Hospital, members of the housekeeping staff prepared his room by hanging large sheets of aluminum foil over the windows. The foil was not to frustrate window peeping

341

fans in helicopters, as one Memphis journalist claimed.

Although some accounts related that Elvis paid for an entire floor of the eighteen-story Baptist Hospital when he was a patient, he actually took only a suite of two rooms. But those rooms were closely guarded, and his security men were provided with a list of fifteen to twenty people normally authorized as visitors.

In 1977 *Press Scimitar* columnist Bill E. Burk wrote that Elvis's trip to a southern hospital in June 1975 was made not for eye surgery, as had been announced, but for a super-secret face lift by one of Memphis's best known plastic surgeons.[2]

Burk's allegation came at a time when Elvis was very obviously fighting the signs of aging, primarily his nagging weight problem. Rumors began circulating that Elvis had undergone operations to remove fat. Newspapers in cities where he was performing on tour were printing headlines like:

"Elvis Battles Middle Age," "Elvis's Waist Thicker, But Fans Still Loyal," "Fat and Forty, But Also Sold Out," and "Time Makes Listless Mechanic of Elvis." A national magazine captioned a picture, "Rock 'n' Roly-Poly Elvis In Florida."

They were unnecessarily cruel, but journalists and magazine writers have persisted in taking dubiously literary potshots at him since he had first risen to national prominence. They are perhaps angered by his unavailability for interviews.

Dale Rice, a reporter for the Syracuse (New York) *Post-Standard*, wrote that Elvis was "fat" and "musically his performance was mediocre." Other reviewers have called Elvis's performances "sloppy, and hurriedly rehearsed," "uneven," "occasionally monotonous," and "often silly."

342

Rice had said enough to enrage dedicated Elvis fans. The *Post-Standard* offices were bombarded with hundreds of angry telephone calls, and Rice said he received "one call after another" at his home from fans who shouted and swore.

Elvis's next performance in Syracuse was sold out, just as was the performance Rice reviewed.

Regardless of what the motives were for the sometimes sadistic taunting of the press, it wasn't necessary to tell Elvis that he was tired and overweight. Elvis, better than anyone, was aware of the difficulty of keeping his energy up and his weight down.

In his forties, Elvis still had to depend on his image as a sex symbol as much as on his music for his appeal.

He knew he wasn't the only entertainer with a weight problem. Elizabeth Taylor's classic beauty has been blurred at times by excessive weight. Actress Sally Struthers and singers Peggy Lee and Tony Orlando have all had their battles with bulging waistlines. But knowing that he had company in the battle against increasing weight was no help to Elvis, because he was aware that not many middle-aged men with burgeoning midriffs, hanging jowls, and double chins qualify as sex symbols. Furthermore, his weight problem was as bad for his self-image as it is for his public image.

Elvis always wore tight pants when he performed, and even in his youth occasional accidents occurred. Inevitably there were times when he would be startled by the unsettling sound of ripping cloth during performances. The cloth began ripping more frequently when his age reached the forties and his weight climbed into the 220's and 230's.

He had to leave the stage when his tight white trousers split up the middle at a New Year's Eve show in Pontiac,

343

Michigan. But he was back in new togs in time to sing "Auld Lang Syne" and to welcome in 1976 with sixty thousand people, the biggest live crowd of his career.

On another night, Elvis was playing before a Memphis crowd when he bent to kiss one of the girls in front of the stage and lost the seat of his pants. "Is it bad?" he asked, turning his head to look at Charlie. It was. "Of all the places in the world to split my pants," Elvis groaned to his audience, "it would have to be in my home town."

He popped a few buttons and belt buckles too, but a more foreboding incident occurred in 1975 when he interrupted his show during a concert in Norfolk, Virginia, to tell an audience of eleven thousand, "You stink!" He told them they reeked of "green peppers and onions." It wasn't a healthy Elvis talking.

At another performance he tossed a glass of water at some members of the audience he was peeved at, and forgot the words to "America the Beautiful."

Yet, at still other times Elvis gave performances reminiscent of the days when he used to shed ten pounds easily just rehearsing for a week prior to his Las Vegas shows. Using a program of strict diet and exercise, he sometimes slimmed down in recent years nearly to his former proportions, so that he showed only a slight midriff roll. His fans responded deliriously to the performances he gave on those occasions.

Unfortunately, the moments of renewed magic were mixed with other times when he was overweight, moody, and unwell.

As his health problems magnified, Elvis for the first time began looking as sick as he obviously felt. I had seen him run-down before. Although for years he depended on karate and other strenuous exercises to

344

build up his resistance, he caught colds easily and had pneumonia a couple of times while I was at Graceland. But even after his worst bouts with colds and viruses, he bounced back quickly, and I was used to seeing him trim and neatly groomed when he was around other people. Although he lounged downstairs in his pajamas and robe in the early afternoons, he was always clean shaven, his hair was combed, and he looked fresh and alert.

He wasn't fresh and alert when he walked into the office one morning a few days before he was rushed from the mansion to Baptist Hospital. He hadn't shaved. His flesh was puffy and had an unhealthy, damp look to it when he shuffled through the door and flopped down on the edge of his daddy's desk. He was wearing pajama bottoms with a karate shirt loosely hanging over them. There was no robe. He wore shoes but no socks.

He was about forty pounds over the 175 to 180 pounds he normally carried on his once-trim six-foot frame. His stomach, face, and hands were swollen, and he was lethargic.

He hung around for a few minutes and picked up a blue sash mailed to him by a fan. He put it over his shoulders, smiling slightly as he played with it.

"Hey, that looks real sharp on you, Elvis," I said. He grinned and picked up a pair of sunglasses, trying them on. They were round and too big. They slipped down off his cheekbones and slid a fraction of an inch forward on his nose. "Those look pretty bad, Elvis," I told him, shaking my head. Elvis slipped the glasses off and tossed them back on the desk. Then he walked out carrying the sash. He looked pitiful.

Elvis's visit was unusual. When he felt and looked as bad as he did that day, he usually holed up in his rooms upstairs. He sometimes stayed there for days, dieting or

345

just brooding and soaking up the solitude. He tele-phoned downstairs for his food, and it was left outside the door for him. His upstairs quarters were the perfect retreat. There was no practical reason he had to come down; he had everything he needed there.

Elvis's withdrawals to the second floor almost always coincided with his dieting, or at least came during periods when he was depressed about his weight and health. Dur-ing those periods Elvis might eat organically grown spinach and potatoes, or restrict himself to juices, cottage cheese, or yogurt until the pounds begin to melt away.

It could sometimes be more distressing at Graceland when Elvis didn't retreat to his rooms. During his worst periods of depression he would become uncharac-teristically ill tempered and would break up furniture, kick out the screens of TV sets, and toss a coffeepot through the kitchen window. Once the gates weren't opened quickly enough to suit him when he was return-ing home, and he ordered his driver to crash his limousine into the metal grating. The gates popped open.

Such outbursts by other people have been known to coincide with the heavy use of diet pills. I never saw Elvis take a diet pill, but I wrote checks to doctors in Las Vegas for nightly medication for him that amounted to thousands of dollars a month.

During one of his Las Vegas appearances we received a bill nightly from a doctor there listing treatment costs and "medication." The medication costs alone for an approximate four-week stay amounted to about three thousand dollars. The bills showed that Elvis received medicine twice nightly.

Mr. Presley once questioned the costs in a bill from a doctor who was giving Elvis vitamin B_{12} in Palm Springs. He told me to write to the doctor and ask why the bill

346

was so high. The doctor replied that Elvis had been given other medicine besides the vitamins and that Elvis had told him not to disclose what the additional injections were for. He told Mr. Presley to ask his son what the shots were for if he wanted to know. Mr. Presley told me to pay the bill.

Elvis seemed to have a doctor with him almost constantly for a while, and the rumors flew. There were stories that he was faking illness and injuries to get morphine, and that his buttocks looked like pin cushions from so many shots.

Fan magazines and Elvis watchers began speculating that he had taken so much medication over the years to keep slim that his system had rebelled and he could no longer use it. That, they suggested, was causing his weight problems.

Others blamed his trouble on conflicting treatment. They said Elvis had so many doctors working on him that one didn't know what the other was prescribing for him and it was messing up his system.

The stories infuriated Elvis. He always hated drugs and said he couldn't understand why people used such things as heroin, cocaine, and marijuana. Elvis didn't even abuse alcohol or tobacco.

Some of the boys came back from Las Vegas once and said that Elvis had told an audience he had never been "strung out" on drugs in his life and would smack the first person who said he had been.

Elvis put in more than two decades as the world's premier rock-and-roller. He put in twice that time as a premier human being.

And for Elvis, this was no time to change.

1. *Chicago Tribune,* August 27, 1975.
2. *Memphis Press-Scimitar,* February 17, 1977.

Epilogue

I wasn't surprised that it ended the way it did. Elvis's death had to be sudden and dramatic. Like his career.

But even though Elvis's death wasn't totally unexpected, it came as a shock to me.

I was at work at my new job at Howard Johnson's on Elvis Presley Boulevard less than a mile from Graceland mansion when the manager walked up to the desk and said that a man had just told her Elvis was dead. I didn't believe it. I had heard rumors like that before, so I telephoned the house to ask what was going on.

Elvis's daughter Lisa answered the phone. I asked her if I could speak to Patsy.

"Patsy, is it true about Elvis?" I asked. There was a pause. "Yes, its true," she said, and started to cry.

I told Patsy that I would remember Elvis and the rest of them—all the people he loved, and the people who loved him—in my prayers, and hung up the telephone.

351

"My God," I thought, "its finally over." Elvis was gone. He had been a part of my life since I was a kid. The exciting young rock and roll superstar I had worshipped as a teenager, grown up and dated and then worked for as a secretary for thirteen years, was dead.

Early reports indicated that Joe Esposito discovered Elvis lying on the floor of his combination bathroom and dressing room at about 2:30 p. m., Tuesday August 16. Later Ginger Alden, whom Elvis planned to marry, disclosed that it was she who discovered his unconscious body. She said she became concerned when she realized he had been absent from her for a lengthy time and called to him. When he failed to answer she opened the bathroom door and saw him lying on the floor.

Ginger summoned help from Esposito and Dr. Nichopoulos. "When Joe turned his head over I think he knew he was dead," Ginger said of Elvis. Dr. Nichopoulos tried repeatedly to revive him, first by performing heart-lung resuscitation as Elvis lay face up on the floor in blue pajama tops and yellow bottoms, and later on the way to Baptist hospital in an ambulance. "Come on Presley, breathe for me," he pleaded.

A special cardiac arrest team worked on Elvis for about 25 minutes in the hospital emergency room before he was pronounced dead at 3:30 p. m. Elvis was to have left that night for an eleven-day concert tour beginning the next day in Portland, Maine. The tour would have closed at the Mid-South Coliseum in Memphis.

Minutes after the first reports that Elvis was dead appeared on radio and television, crowds of people began assembling at the Music Gate. The atmosphere at the gate became surrealistic as the crowd swelled and people wailed, dropped to their knees and clutched at each other for comfort in their grief.

352

Fans stood limply as rag dolls, staring blankly at the house or stumbled aimlessly, moaning. Young girls and middle-aged women slumped on the asphalt parking area or sat in cars, weeping softly. Tears trickled down the cheeks of men in work clothes, their lunch buckets hanging slackly from their arms. Other men were in business suits and ties.

By 5 p. m., there were 1,000 fans at the gate. At 6 p. m., there were at least 3,000. A half-hour later there were tens of thousands. They were the same fans who loved Elvis so much that they forced him to become a recluse, an exile in his own home.

At Graceland Elvis was a prisoner of his own success. I thought of Elvis, the prisoner, as I stood in the crowd and watched his fans grieve for him.

Elvis could hire an entire theatre, a roller-rink, or an amusement park, or buy a Cadillac for someone whose smile he liked. But he could not take his daughter for a walk in a public park. He could not stroll with a friend along the street to see the lights at the Cotton Carnival. He could not even attend church like other people, even though he had deep religious feelings and enjoyed church services as a boy.

So he found satisfaction and release in other ways; living a sybaritic lifestyle surrounded by a coterie of trusted companions who enjoyed the same things he did.

Elvis was criticized for buying friends. It may have been partly true, but the criticism was also misleading and unfair. Elvis was a genuinely friendly person and could make friends easily, whether or not he was still a truck driver, or if he had been a factory worker or a businessman.

But he was Elvis, a super celebrity, and he was forced to live by himself or make it possible for his friends to

353

live with him. His seclusion and fame made it difficult to make friends as other people did. Other people had trouble relating to him as anyone but Elvis the superstar.

I had that problem even though I worked closely with him for nearly thirteen years. And most of the people around him, even many who loved him most, had the same difficulty to some degree. The fact was that Elvis was just not an average human being.

Although I never heard him say so, he must have wished at times however that he were an average person. Before I left Graceland to spend full time caring for my husband, son and my home I saw and came to know the human side of Elvis. He had millions of fans and was surrounded by people who loved him, but there were times when he was lonely. The rewards of his fame and popularity were great. But they demanded a high price.

The crowd's behavior had changed by the day after Elvis's death. Fans who had been stunned and stood in glassy-eyed shock only a few hours earlier, by then were hysterical.

Some fans said they borrowed money to fly to Memphis when they heard he had died. Teenagers arrived with backpacks and station wagons. Married couples drove to Memphis in campers and in vans. Young mothers held babies in their arms, some standing throughout the night. An Illinois woman was charged with child neglect when she returned home, after leaving her two, four and five-year-old children with a twelve-year-old babysitter so she could join the mourners at Graceland.

Restless lines of people stretched, 15 and 20 deep, as far as a mile from the gate on the second day, waiting for hours for a two or three second glimpse of Elvis in the expensive seamless copper coffin that had been hurriedly shipped to a Memphis funeral home from a manufacturer in Oklahoma.

Dressed in a white suit, light blue shirt and white tie, only the upper half of Elvis's body could be seen as he was laid out in a mirrored foyer at the front of the mansion. I didn't attend the viewing or the funeral. I preferred to remember Elvis in life.

Thousands filed past his body in the four hours before the wrought-iron Music Gate was finally forced shut at about 7:15 p. m., by a sweating squad of uniformed policemen, straining against screaming fans who had been driven frantic by the realization that they would not be given an opportunity to see Elvis.

Two hundred policemen were on hand to control the crowd, and a medical crew of 120 people was available to treat fans who became ill or fainted from the heat and emotional stress. Scores of men and women collapsed after staggering on wobbly legs past the casket and were loaded into waiting ambulances to be rushed to hospitals. My husband Jerry and I at one time counted 30 bodies stretched on the ground in front of the mansion.

I was reminded of a battle scene from a war movie I had once watched with Elvis, as policemen rushed down the driveway to waiting ambulances, carrying limp bodies of women and children over their shoulders and in their arms. Three or four policemen teamed up to carry some of the heavier men.

By Thursday morning, only hours before Elvis's private funeral, the mood of the crowd had changed again. At 4 a. m., they were stunned and then outraged by a second tragedy when a car swerved into the crowd of 2,000 standing an all-night vigil at the gate, killing two young

355

women from Monroe, Louisiana. Juanita Joan Johnson and Marie Alice Hovarter died. Tammy Baiter, 17, of St. Clair, Missouri was critically injured.

Treatise Wheeler, an 18-year-old Memphis youth, was named by police as driver of the car and he was charged with drunk driving, leaving the scene of an accident, reckless driving, public drunkenness and two counts of second degree murder. Two juvenile girls in the car with him were charged with being accessories to murder.

Police said Wheeler was chased about a block by a patrol car before he was stopped after leaving the scene of the accident. Maddened fans sprinted after the car shouting "Lynch 'em, hang him up." Police said cans of beer, two of them empty, were found in the car.

By mid-morning the angry mood at the Music Gate had changed into a near carnival atmosphere. Peddlers were hawking Elvis tee-shirts for $10, postcards of the mansion and soft drinks for $1.50 each. Others were selling pennants, ice cream and Elvis posters at inflated prices. And fans, dry-eyed, seemed more concerned with impressing each other with the long distances they had traveled or with the size of their Elvis record and memorabilia collections than they were in mourning. The mind compensates for shock and tragedy.

Emergency medical facilities were more sophisticated by that time. Tents had been pitched on the estate grounds and were manned by medical teams. But only a few fans required treatment. The only fans stretched out on the asphalt or gravel near the gate were sleeping or resting. Hundreds of them had stayed up all night because there were no hotel or motel rooms. A convention of some 70,000 Shriners combined with an estimated 130,000 Presley mourners who jammed into Memphis had made empty hotel rooms non-existent.

356

Some of the last available rooms in motels and private homes were taken by celebrities and other personal friends of Elvis who had come to Memphis for the funeral. Ann-Margret and her husband Roger Smith; Hollywood actors John Wayne, Burt Reynolds, and George Hamilton; country guitar picker Chet Atkins; Caroline Kennedy; and Tennessee Governor Ray Blanton were among guests at a private viewing and at the brief services in the mansion.

Other celebrity friends and admirers of Elvis had reacted with shock. Frank Sinatra told an audience at a performance in East Troy, Wisconsin, "We lost a good friend today."

Country singer Hank Snow described Elvis as a "genuine superstar," and remarked that he wished to remember him "as I knew him . . . . a perfect gentleman and a great example for American youth."

Disc jockey Wolf Man Jack declared in Toronto that "two thousand years from now they'll still be hearing about Elvis Presley."

President Jimmy Carter remarked that "Elvis Presley's death deprives our country of a part of itself. He was a symbol to the people of the world over of the vitality, rebelliousness and good humor of this country."

C. W. Bradley, minister of the Woodland Church of Christ in Memphis, officiated at the brief service at Graceland. Although Elvis could not attend Reverend Bradley's church, the minister was an old family friend. The Reverend Rex Humbard, who heads the Cathedral of Tomorrow in Akron, Ohio, had met Elvis in 1976 and also spoke briefly at the services.

After the service Elvis was carried from his home for the last time at the head of a cavalcade of sixteen cream-colored Cadillac limousines which inched slowly through the gate and four miles along Elvis Presley Boulevard carrying Mr. Presley, Priscilla, other family members, friends and celebrities to Forest Hills Cemetery where Elvis was laid to rest in a mausoleum. The somber stone structure was half-hidden by more than 3,100 floral arrangements, some in the shape of guitars or teddy bears and hound dogs in silent acknowledgment of two of Elvis's gold records from the 1950's. The mausoleum is near the grave of Elvis's mother and is fronted by wrought-iron door with glass inside through which his crypt can be viewed.

The day after the funeral, fans were given single flowers from the floral arrangements as they paid their respects at Elvis's final resting place. When the supply of flowers was exhausted they left clutching greenery or thorns from the sprays. Some fans slept all night on the sidewalk outside the cemetery gates so they could be among the first in line for flowers.

As Elvis's funeral approached its exhausting conclusion I began to more fully understand some of the occurrences that had puzzled me when I worked for him. I recalled the high bills for medication while he was on tour or performing in Las Vegas, which I had written checks for. They were so expensive and came into the office so frequently that even his Daddy questioned them. Ugly rumors began developing about Elvis abusing drugs.

Elvis wasn't a drug addict. He hated drug abuse. His doctors explained about Elvis's medication. He had been receiving medication for years for an eye problem and a twisted colon, they said after his death. He was also under a doctor's care for obesity and frequent exhaustion. His Mama had been overweight and perhaps the problem ran in the family.

Strangely, Elvis died just two days after the August 14, 1958 nineteenth anniversary of Gladys Presley's death.

Considering all the medication Elvis had to take, his sometimes sudden changes of mood, his depression and seemingly inexplicable bursts of temper were understandable.

A three-hour autopsy was performed on Elvis, and Dr. Jerry Francisco, Shelby County Medical Examiner, said the cause of death was "cardiac arrythmia," an irregular heart beat. "Just another name for a heart attack," he said.

There was on indication of drug abuse, despite earlier reports that police had been investigating that possibility, he said. George Klein, Elvis's friend since high school, responded angrily during a radio interview when he was asked about stories that Elvis was abusing narcotics. Kline said he didn't want to listen to that kind of talk and insisted that during a friendship of more than twenty years he never knew Elvis to abuse drugs.

Perhaps now the ugly rumors about narcotics addiction can be laid to rest. With Elvis.

Elvis deserves to hang onto his good name. He did so many good things for so many people. It was not only the charities and the impulsive gift-giving to friends and strangers that showed Elvis's generosity, but more importantly it was the way he treated people around him. He treated people; his friends and his fans with consideration and respect. He deserves at least as much in return.

In recent years Elvis didn't always receive the love and support he was entitled to. He never forgot the death of his mother, and when Priscilla left he had lost two of the three women who meant most to him in his life. Only his daughter Lisa remained. And more recently he was hurt by old friends, some of his most trusted companions, who turned against him.

But I've decided not to dwell on Elvis's disappointments or on his illnesses. Elvis wouldn't want that from me or from any of the millions of fans who loved him. I prefer other memories of Elvis. Like the time he took me on the Pipin with him, and the time he gave me the TLC necklace and kissed me.

Most of all I'll always remember Elvis The King, the super performer, and the super human being. There will never be another. He was unique.